WITHDRAWN

Reminiscences

of

Peace and War

BY

MRS. ROGER A. PRYOR

AUTHOR OF " THE MOTHER OF WASHINGTON AND HER TIMES "

Sarah Agnes (Rice) Pryor

New York

THE MACMILLAN COMPANY

LONDON: MACMILLAN & CO., LTD.

1904

Reminiscences

of

Peace and War

BY

MRS. ROGER A. PRYOR

AUTHOR OF "THE MOTHER OF WASHINGTON AND HER TIMES"

Sarah Agnes (Rice) Pryor

New York

THE MACMILLAN COMPANY

LONDON: MACMILLAN & CO., LTD.

1904

WITHDRAWN

I DEDICATE THIS BOOK TO THE MEMORY OF

My Son

WILLIAM RICE PRYOR, M.D.

WHO GAVE TO SUFFERING HUMANITY ALL THAT
GOD HAD GIVEN HIM

Preface

IT will be obvious to the reader that this book affects neither the " dignity of history " nor the authority of political instruction. The causes which precipitated the conflict between the sections and the momentous events which attended the struggle have been recounted by writers competent to the task. But descriptions of battles and civil convulsions do not exhibit the full condition of the South in the crisis. To complete the picture, social characteristics and incidents of private life are indispensable lineaments. It occurs to the author that a plain and unambitious narrative of her recollections of Washington society during the calm which preceded the storm, and of Virginia under the afflictions and sorrows of the fratricidal strife, will not be without interest in the retrospect of that memorable era. The present volume recalls that era in the aspect in which it appeared to a woman rather than as it appeared to a statesman or a philosopher.

ROGER A. PRYOR.

Contents

ix

Contents

Illustrations

PEACE AND WAR

Reminiscences of Peace and War

CHAPTER I

WASHINGTON IN THE FIFTIES

THE Washington that I knew in the fifties
was not the Washington of Dickens, Mrs.
Trollope, and Laurence Oliphant. When I
knew the capital of our country, it was not "a howl-
ing wilderness of deserted streets running out into
the country and ending nowhere, its population con-
sisting chiefly of politicians and negroes" ;[1] nor were
the streets overrun with pigs and infested with goats.
I never saw these animals in the streets of Washington; but a story, told to illustrate the best way
of disposing of the horns of a dilemma proves one
goat at least to have had the freedom of the city.
It seems that Henry Clay, overdue at the Senate
Chamber, was once hurrying along Pennsylvania
Avenue when he was attacked by a large goat. Mr.
Clay seized his adversary by the horns. So far so
good, but how about the next step? A crowd
of sympathetic bootblacks and newsboys gathered

---

[1] "Life of Oliphant," Vol. I. p. 109.

3

around offering advice. " Let go, Mr. Clay, and run like blazes," shouted one; and Mr. Clay did let go and did run, his senatorial coat-tails flying like pennons behind him.

But this was before my day. I remember Washington only as a garden of delights, over which the spring trailed an early robe of green, thickly embroidered with gems of amethyst and ruby, pearl and sapphire. The crocuses, hyacinths, tulips, and snowdrops made haste to bloom before the snows had fairly melted. The trees donned their diaphanous veils of green earlier in the White House grounds, the lawn of the Smithsonian Institution, and the gentle slopes around the Capitol, than anywhere in less distinguished localities. To walk through these incense-laden grounds, to traverse the avenue of blossoming crab-apples, was pure pleasure. The shaded avenues were delightful long lanes, where one was sure to meet friends, and where no law of etiquette forbade a pause in the public street for a few words of kindly inquiry, or a bit of gossip, or the development of some plan for future meetings. If one's steps tended to the neighborhood of 7th and D streets, nothing was more probable than a meeting with one of Washington's most noted citizens, — the superb mastiff of Mr. Gales, the veteran editor of the *National Intelligencer*, as the dog gravely bore in a large basket the mail for the office. No attendant was needed by this fine animal. He was fully competent to protect his master's private and official correspondence.

He had been taught to express stern disapproba-

tion of Democrats; so if a pleasant walk with him
was desired, it was expedient for members of that
party to perjure themselves and at once announce:
"I am an 'Old-Line Whig,' old man," and the dog's
tail would wag a cordial welcome.

Omnibuses ran along Pennsylvania Avenue, for
the convenience of Senators, Congressmen, and others
on their way to the Capitol, — but the saunter along
the avenue was so charming that I always preferred
it to the People's Line. There were few shops. But
such shops! There was Galt's, where the silver,
gems, and marbles were less attractive than the cultivated gentleman who sold them; Gautier's, the pal-
ace of sweets, with Mrs. Gautier in an arm-chair
before her counter to tell you the precise social
status of every one of her customers, and what is
more, to put you in your own; Harper's, where the
dainty, leisurely salesman treated his laces with respect, drawing up his cuffs lest they touch the ethe-
real beauties; and the little corner shop of stern
Madame Delarue, who imported as many (and no
more) hats and gloves as she was willing to sell as a
favor to the ladies of the diplomatic and official
circles, and whose dark-eyed daughter Léonide
(named for her godmother, a Greek lady of rank)
was susceptible of unreasoning friendships and could
be coaxed to preserve certain treasures for humbler
folk.

Léonide once awoke me in the middle of the
night with a note bidding me "come *tout de suite*,"
for "Maman" was asleep, the boxes had arrived;
and she and I could peep at the bonnets and choose

the best one for myself. Thus it was that I once bore away a " divine creation " of point lace, crêpe, and shaded asters before Madame had seen it. Otherwise it would have been reserved for Miss Harriet Lane or Mrs. Douglas. Madame had to know later; and Léonide was not much in evidence the rest of that season. At Madame Delarue's, if one was very *gentil*, very *convenable*, one might have the services of François, the one and only hair-dresser of note, who had adjusted coronets on noble heads, and who could (if he so minded) talk of them agreeably in Parisian French.

All these were little things; but do not pleasant trifles make the sum of pleasant hours? Washington was like a great village in those days of President Pierce and President Buchanan. To obtain the best of the few articles to be purchased was an achievement.

My own pride in the Federal City was such that my heart would swell within me at every glimpse of the Capitol: from the moment it rose like a white cloud above the smoke and mists, as I stood on the deck of the steamboat (having run up from my dinner to salute Mount Vernon), to the time when I was wont to watch from my window for the sunset, that I might catch the moment when a point on the unfinished dome glowed like a great blazing star after the sun had really gone down. No matter whether suns rose or set, there was the star of our country, — the star of our hearts and hopes.

I acknowledge that Wisdom is much to be desired of her children, but nowhere is it promised that they will be the happier for gaining her.   When my lot was cast in Washington, Wisdom had not taught me that the White House was less beautiful than a classic temple.   To be sure, Dickens had called it " like an English club-house," — that was bad enough, — but Mark Twain had not yet dubbed it " a fine, large, white barn with wide handsome grounds around it."   " The President lives there," says Washington Hawkins.   " It is ugly enough outside, but that is nothing to what it is inside." To my uneducated eye the East Room with its ornate chandeliers, fluted pillars, and floriated carpet was an audience chamber fit for a king.   A triumph of artistic perfection was the equestrian statue of the hero of New Orleans, now known to be out of all proportion, and condemned as " bad " and " very bad " by Wisdom's instructed children.   Raising his hat, indeed !   Why, any man in that position would be holding on to the mane with both hands to keep from sliding off.   And as for the Capitol — the sacred Capitol !   From foundation to turret it was to my eye all that genius and patriotism could achieve.   The splendid marbles at the entrance, the paintings, the bas-reliefs within the rotunda, — these were things to boast of, to dream of.   Not yet had arisen our irreverent humorist to warn us never to enter the dome of the Capitol, " because to get there you must pass through the great rotunda, and to do that you would have to see the marvellous historical paintings that hang there and the bas-reliefs, — and what have you done that you should suffer this ? "

When our friends came up from Virginia to make us visits, it was delightful to take a carriage and give up days to sight-seeing; to visit the White House and Capitol, the Patent Office with its miscellaneous treasures; to point with pride to the rich gifts from crowned heads which our adored first President was too conscientious to accept; to walk among the stones lying around the base of the unfinished monument and read the inscriptions from the states presenting them; to spend a day at the Smithsonian Institution, and to introduce our friends to its president, Mr. Henry; and to Mr. Spencer Baird and Mr. Gerard, eminent naturalists, who were giving their lives to the study of birds, beasts, and fishes, — finding them, Mr. Gerard said, "so much more interesting than men," adding hastily, "we do not say ladies," and blushing after the manner of cloistered scholars; to tell them interesting things about Mr. Gerard who was a melancholy young man, and who had confided to me that he had sustained a great sorrow. Had he lost his fortune, or been crossed in love, was he homesick for his native Switzerland? Worse than any one or all of these! He had been sent once to Nantucket in the interests of his profession. There he had found a strange fish, hitherto unknown to science. He had classified its bones and laid them out on his table to count them. In a moment's absence the housemaid had entered and dusted his table.

Then the visits to the galleries of the House and Senate Chamber, and the honor of pointing out the great men to our friends from rural districts; the

long listening to interminable speeches, not clearly
understood, but heard with a reverent conviction
that all was coming out right in the end, that everybody was really working for the good of his country,
and that we belonged to it all and were parts of
it all.

This was the thought behind all other thoughts
which glorified everything around us, enhanced every
fortunate circumstance, and caused us to ignore the
real discomforts of life in Washington: the cold,
the ice-laden streets in winter; the whirlwinds of
dust and driving rains of spring; the swift-coming
fierceness of summer heat; the rapid atmospheric
changes which would give us all these extremes
in one week, or even one day, until it became
the part of prudence never to sally forth on any
expedition without "a fan, an overcoat, and an
umbrella."

The social life in Washington was almost as vari-
able as the climate. At the end of every four
years the kaleidoscope turned, and lo! — a new
central jewel and new colors and combinations in
the setting.

But behind this "floating population," as the political circles were termed, there was a fine society in
the fifties of "old residents" who never bent the knee
to Baal. This society was sufficient to itself, never
seeking the new, while accepting it occasionally with
discretion, reservations, and much discriminating care.
The sisters, Mrs. Gales and Mrs. Seaton, wives of
the editors of the *National Intelligencer*, led this
society. Mrs. Gales's home was outside the city,

and thence every day Mr. Gales was driven in his
barouche to his office.   His paper was the exponent
of the Old-Line Whigs (the Republican party was
formed later) and in stern opposition to the Democrats.   It was, therefore, a special and unexpected
honor for a Democrat to be permitted to drive out
to "the cottage" for a glass of wine and a bit of
fruit-cake with Mrs. Gales and Mrs. Seaton.   Never
have I seen these gentlewomen excelled in genial
hospitality.   Mrs. Gales was a superb old lady and
a fine conversationalist.   She had the courteous repose born of dignity and intelligence.   She was literally her husband's right hand,—he had lost his own,
—and was the only person who could decipher his
left-hand writing.   So that when anything appeared
from his pen it had been copied by his wife before
it reached the type-setter.   A fine education this for
an intelligent woman ; the very best schooling for a
social life including diplomats from foreign countries, politicians of diverse opinions, artists, authors,
musicians, women of fashion, to entertain whom
required infinite tact, cleverness, and an intimate
acquaintance with the absorbing questions of the
day.

Of course the levees and state receptions, which
were accessible to all, required none of these things.
The rôle of hostess on state occasions could be
filled creditably by any woman of ordinary physical
strength, patience, and self-control, who knew when
to be silent.

Washington society, at the time of which I write,
was comparatively free from non-official men of

wealth from other cities who, weary with the monotonous round of travel,—to the Riviera, to Egypt, to Monte Carlo,—are attracted by the unique atmosphere of a city holding many foreigners, and devoted not to commercial but to social and political interests. The doors of the White House and Cabinet offices being open on occasions to all, they have opportunities denied them in their own homes. Society in Washington in the fifties was peculiarly interesting in that it was composed exclusively of men whose presence argued them to have been of importance at home. They had been elected by the people, or chosen by the President, or selected among the very best in foreign countries; or they belonged to the United States Army or Navy service, or to the descendants of the select society which had gathered in the city early in its history.

During the Fillmore administration there were peculiar elements in Washington society. The President was born of poor English parents. At the age of fifteen he was apprentice to a wool-carder in Livingston County, New York, representing in his father's mind no higher hope than gradual advancement until he should attain the proud place of woollen-draper. But at nineteen he had entered a lawyer's office, working all day, teaching and studying at night. When he became President his tastes had been sufficiently ripened to enable him to gather around him men of literary taste and attainment. John P. Kennedy, an author and a man of elegant accomplishments, was Secretary of the Navy. Washington Irving was Kennedy's friend, and often

his guest.   Lesser lights in the world of letters found
Washington an agreeable residence.   We knew many
of these men, and among them none was brighter,
wittier, or more genial than G. P. R. James, the
English novelist whose star rose and set before 1860.
He was the most prolific of writers, " Like an end-
less chain of buckets in a well," said one; " as fast
as one is emptied up comes another."

We were very fond of Mr. James.   One day he
dashed in, much excited : —

" Have you seen the *Intelligencer?*   By George,
it's all true!   Six times has my hero, a 'solitary
horseman,' emerged from a wood!   My word!
I was totally unconscious of it!   Fancy it!   Six
times!   Well, it's all up with that fellow.   He has
got to dismount and enter on foot : a beggar, or
burglar, or pedler, or at best a mendicant friar."

" But," suggested one, " he might drive, mightn't
he ? "

" Impossible ! " said Mr. James.   " Imagine a
hero in a gig or a curricle ! "

" Perhaps," said one, " the word ' solitary ' has
given offence.   Americans dislike exclusiveness.
They are sensitive, you see, and look out for
snobs."

He made himself very merry over it; but the solitary horseman appeared no more in the few novels
he was yet to write.

One day, after a pleasant visit from Mr. James
and his wife, I accompanied them at parting to the
front door, and found some difficulty in turning the
bolt.   He offered to assist, but I said no — he was

not supposed to understand the mystery of an American front door.

Having occasion a few minutes afterward to open the door for another departing guest, there on his knees outside was Mr. James, who laughingly explained that he had left his wife at the corner, and had come back to investigate that mystery. "Perhaps you will tell me," he added, and was much amused to learn that the American door opened of itself to an incoming guest, but positively refused without coaxing to let him out. "By George, that's fine!" he said, "that'll please the critics in my next." I never knew whether it was admitted, for I must confess that, even with the stimulus of his presence, his books were dreary reading to my uninstructed taste.

A very lovely and charming actress was prominent in Washington society at this time, — the daughter of an old New York family, Anna Cora (Ogden) Mowatt. She was especially interesting to Virginians, for she had captivated Foushee Ritchie, soon afterward my husband's partner on the editorship of the *Richmond Enquirer*. Mr. Ritchie, a confirmed old bachelor, had been fascinated by Mrs. Mowatt's Parthenia (in "Ingomar") and was now engaged to her. He proudly brought to me a pair of velvet slippers she had embroidered for him, working around them as a border a quotation from "Ingomar" : —

"Two souls with but a single thought,
Two hearts that beat as one."

And oh, *how* angry he was when an irreverent voice whispered one word, "Soles!"

"Cora must never hear of this," he declared indignantly; "she is, beyond all women, incapable of *double entendre,* of coarse allusion."

Alas! I cannot conclude my little story, "And they were married and lived happily ever after." They were married — and lived miserably — and were separated ever after. The single thought was how they could best escape each other — and the two hearts beat as one in the desire for freedom.

"The shadow of the coming war was even then beginning to darken the land and confuse legislation with bitter partisanship and continuous attempts at an impossible compromise," but, alas! our eyes were holden so we could not see.

CHAPTER II

ON the 4th of March, 1853, Franklin Pierce was inaugurated President of the United States. This was an exciting day for me. My husband had written articles for a Virginia paper which had won for him a place on the editorial staff of the *Washington Union*, and was now in a position to break a lance with my friends, Messrs. Gales and Seaton. Mr. Pierce had liked his articles in the *Union*, and sought his acquaintance. A friendship rapidly followed which was a happiness to us both. So when some member of the staff of the Democratic organ must be consulted about the inaugural address, the President had sent for my young husband and had taken counsel with him.

I was delighted when I received an invitation from my good friends of the Smithsonian Institution to join them in a pleasant room opening on a balcony and overlooking Pennsylvania Avenue, where we were to have a collation and witness the parade. My husband's sixteen-year-old sister, Fanny, was with me, and she was literally wild with delight. The rest of the party were Mr. and Mrs. Spencer Baird, little Lucy Baird, Mr. Gerard, and Mr. Turner. Little eight-year-old Lucy was the belle of the occasion; so wise in scientific matters, knowing so much about "specimens" and "extinct species" that we felt ourselves heavy and ignorant beside her. "Come now, Lucy," said Mr. Turner, "I expect you to take care of me on this occasion. These are painful scenes for an Englishman. When you see the Continental troops coming, give me the wink, and I'll slip away and stir the punch. Those are the fellows who whipped the British!"

The elements frowned upon the change of administration. The sun was blanketed with dark clouds, from which the snow fell thickly — not a soft, enfolding snow, but snow driven by an angry wind. The crowd in the avenue was immense; swelled by the presence of the largest number of strangers ever before gathered at an Inauguration, the majority of whom were members of the mighty army of office-seekers from the party recently come into power. From the White House to the Capitol, windows, balconies, and roofs were thronged; and the sidewalks of the avenue were filled with a motley crowd of men, women, and children, foreigners, government clerks, and negroes.

About twelve o'clock the boom of a great gun announced the moving of the procession. The throng in the streets surged toward the gates of the Capitol, and "lined up" on either side awaiting the arrival of the cortège. Carriages filled with women and children, some of them with the emblazoned panels of foreign ministers, passed rapidly in advance of the cavalcade — the police actively engaged the while in keeping the waiting crowd within bounds.   Presently distant music was heard, and a mighty cheer announced the near approach of the escort.   Six marshals in gay scarfs led the procession.   Then came the "flying artillery," drawn by fifty or more horses.   An interval, and then platoons of soldiers of diverse battalions filled square after square, and band after band of martial music mingled with the cheers of the crowd.

We were all out now on the balcony, little Lucy keenly alert.   Presently she touched Mr. Turner on his arm and he fled!   The Continentals were passing.

Following these, in an open carriage drawn by four fine horses, came our President: the youngest, handsomest President we had ever elected.   As he neared our balcony we stood up, waved and cheered, and threw him flowers, and so winning in their enthusiasm were little Lucy (her mind being now quite at rest about Mr. Turner) and my own young sister, that the President rose and bared his head to us.

A platform had been erected over the steps of the east wing, and on it was a table holding a Bible. The distinguished officials of the time were seated around this table, and beneath it the crowd pushed and scrambled and struggled for place within hearing.   Instantly there was silence.   The slender, almost boyish figure of our President approached the table, and with bared head under the falling snow stood for a moment surveying the crowd.

His face was pale, and his countenance wore an expression of weary sadness.   When he took the

c

oath he did not, as is the custom, use the word
"swear." Placing his left hand on the Bible without raising the book, he raised his right and, looking upward, "affirmed" that, God helping him, he
would be faithful to his trust.

There were tears in his voice, but it was musical,
and his enunciation was clear and distinct.

Only two months before, his only child, a beautiful boy of thirteen, had been killed in a railroad
collision — killed before his parents' eyes! His
address began, "My countrymen! It is a relief to
feel that no heart but my own can know the personal regret and bitter sorrow over which I have
been borne to a position so suitable for others
rather than desirable for myself."

The public does not tolerate the intrusion of a
man's personal joys and griefs into his official life.
However willing the world may be to sympathize,
it considers this indicative of a mind lacking fine-
ness and delicacy. To keep one's inner self in the
background should be the instinct, and is surely
the policy, of every man and woman who aspires to
popularity.

There were many who quickly criticised this unfortunate sentence of the President. The Whig
journals sneered at it as "a trick of the orator to
awaken personal interest before proceeding to unfold
his public policy." But he had the sympathetic
tears of many of his audience.

His address went on to discuss the annexation of
Cuba — a dream which lasted through many subse-
quent years. The Pearl of the Antilles was ardently

coveted as a pendant to our chain of states, but she will never belong to us, unless as the result of more misfortune. The President then pledged himself to the never dying Monroe Doctrine, prayed appealingly for the preservation of our Union, and touched upon the troubled questions which, despite all our wars and sufferings, are not yet fully settled. And then, amid cheers and shouts and salvos of artillery, he was driven to his new home, and it was all over.

Three days after the inauguration the Cabinet nominations were sent to the Senate. Mr. Marcy was to be Secretary of State; Mr. Guthrie, Secretary of the Treasury; Jefferson Davis, of War; James Dobbin, of the Navy: Robert McClellan, of the Interior; James Campbell, Postmaster-General; Caleb Cushing, Attorney-General — four men from the North, three from the South. These, then, with their families, were to lead the social life of Washington for four years. The Executive Mansion, shrouded in gloom, could never become a social centre.

We had the honor of knowing well the three most distinguished of these men, Mr. Marcy, Mr. Davis, and Mr. Cushing.

Mr. Marcy, the best-known member of the Cabinet, strong, honest, and an adroit politician, was a man of rugged and abrupt manners, yet a great favorite with the ladies. We at once became keenly interested in his initial proceedings. He was sternly democratic in his ideas. Absorbing as were the cares of his department, exciting and menacing as

were the questions of the hour, he inaugurated his
official life by settling matters of dress and etiquette
— so far as they related to the presence of American envoys at foreign courts. President Jackson
had been supposed to be democratic, but he was a
bloated aristocrat beside Mr. Marcy. Jackson had
rejected the prescribed court dress, — embroidered
cuffs and cape, white breeches, gold knee-buckles,
white silk stockings, gold shoe-buckles, chapeau-
bras, cockade, eagle, white feather, and sword.
Alackaday, that we should have lost all this
bravery! Jackson decreed no cape at all (such a
friendly fashion to laden shoulders), no embroidery except a gold star on the coat-collar, — but
breeches and modest buckles, a sword, a chapeau-
bras with eagle and cockade.

Now why should Mr. Marcy make trouble by
meddling with the cut of the garments of our representatives abroad — at a time, too, when such a
number of serious questions were about to come
before him; when filibusters were at work, a war
with Spain imminent, treaties to be made with
Mexico, and fishery questions to be settled with
England? Simply, I suppose, because great men
all over the world have condescended to prescribe
in trifling matters — matters belonging to the chef,
the milliner, the arbiter of fleeting fashions. It
would seem that the greater the man the greater
his appreciation of trifles. Everything to him is
important — from the signing of a treaty to the
tying of a shoestring.

The consequences of Mr. Marcy's meddling were

far-reaching.   On June 1, 1853, he issued a circu-
lar recommending that our representatives abroad
should, in order to show their devotion to republican institutions, appear whenever practicable in the
simple dress of an American citizen.

Our Minister at Berne found the court of Switzerland quite willing to receive him in his citizen's
dress.   The Ministers at Turin and Brussels reported
they would have no difficulty in carrying out the instructions of the State Department.   The representative at Berlin was at once informed that such action
would be considered disrespectful.   The king of
Sweden insisted on court dress at social functions.
Mr. August Belmont, at The Hague, received a cold
permission from the king to dress as he pleased —
and it is recorded (as matter for gratitude on the
part of the American Minister) that after all, and
notwithstanding, the queen actually danced with
him in his citizen's dress, and the king condescended to shake him by the hand and to talk with
him !

Mr. Mason, at the French court, could not face
the music !   He consulted his wife, and together
they agreed upon a compromise.   He appeared in
an embroidered coat, sword, and cocked hat, and
had the misfortune to receive from Mr. Marcy a
severe rebuke.

Mr. Buchanan, at the court of St. James, having
no wife to consult, thought long and anxiously on
the subject.   The question was still unsettled at the
opening of Parliament in February, 1854.   Our
Minister did not attend, — he had " nothing to

wear," — whereupon "there was quite a sensation in the House of Lords." "Indeed," he wrote to Mr. Marcy, "I have found difficulty in preventing this incident from becoming a subject of inquiry and remark in the House of Commons." Think of that! At a time when England was on the eve of a war with Russia, all the newspapers, court officials, House of Commons, exercised about the dress of the American Minister! The *London Times* stated that on a diplomatic occasion "the American Minister sate unpleasantly conscious of his singularity." The *London Chronicle* blamed General Pierce's republican ill manners, and the "American puppyism," and continued: "There is not the least reason why her Majesty should be troubled to receive the 'gentleman in the black coat' from Yankee-land! He can say his say at the Foreign Office, dine at a chop-house in King Street, sleep at the old Hummums, and be off as he came, per liner, when his business is done."

Poor Mr. Buchanan, sorely pressed, conceived the idea of costuming himself like General Washington, and to that end examined Stuart's portrait. He may even have gone so far as to indulge in a private rehearsal — *queue*, powdered wig, and all; but he seems to have perceived he would only make himself ridiculous; so he took his life in his hands and — brave gentleman as he was — appeared at the queen's levee in the dress of an American citizen; and she, true lady as she was, settled the matter, for her court at least, by receiving him as she did all others. Mr. Buchanan wrote to his niece, Miss Harriet Lane, "I wore a sword to gratify those who yielded so much, and to distinguish me from the upper court servants."

Mr. Soulé, at the court of Madrid, adopted the costume of Benjamin Franklin at the court of Louis XVI — sword, chapeau, black velvet, and much embroidery, looking, "with his black eyes, black looks, and pale complexion, less like the philosopher whose costume he imitated than the master of Ravenswood." There had been a lively discussion among the Austrian and Mexican Ministers and the Countess of Montijo, the mother of the Empress Eugénie and of the Duchess of Alba, whether or no he should be rejected; but Mr. Soulé did not know this. The queen received him, he wrote to Mr. Marcy, "with marked attention and courtesy."

There is no telling whether this simple deviation from the prescribed court dress was not the real cause of Mr. Soulé's serious troubles at court. It was the Duke of Alba who provided the spark which fired the train of Spanish indignation against him and occasioned a quarrel which resulted in two duels and strained relations which were never reconciled.

It is always dangerous to infringe upon accepted rules of etiquette, even in association with those who are themselves defiant of these rules. I discovered that Mr. Marcy was very jealous of respect due to himself, as well as to his government.

He was a prime favorite, as I have said, with the ladies — and with none more than the charming family of "Father Ritchie," as we called one of Washington's most esteemed citizens. Mr. Ritchie had been editor for forty years of the *Richmond Enquirer*, which he had founded under the auspices of Thomas Jefferson, and made one of the most influential Democratic papers of the country. His home in Washington was noted for elegant hospitality. He lived next door to Mr. Corcoran on Lafayette Square, near St. John's Church. He had lovely daughters, and whenever Mr. Marcy appeared in the salons of the town, one or more of these ladies was sure to be with him.

It so happened that some of us were much interested in a poor, worthy young man, who desired a position in the State Department. His application had long ago been filed in the office and we were afraid he had been forgotten. We longed to ask Mr. Marcy about it, but did not know how we could manage to bring the subject to his notice.

"Let's make Ann Eliza ask him," suggested one. Now, Ann Eliza Ritchie was a beauty, as fascinating a young creature as the Lord ever made, irresistible alike to man and woman. She hesitated, — everybody was afraid of Mr. Marcy — but goaded on by us, she ventured : —

"Oh, Mr. Marcy" (Virginia girls always begin with "Oh"), "Oh, Mr. Marcy! They all want to know if you are going to appoint Mr. Randolph in your department."

The lion turned. He did not growl, he simply roared : "*What* do you mean, madame? How

dare you take the bull by the horns in this un-
seemly manner?"

And so no more of Ann Eliza Ritchie. And so
no more of the rest of us. We learned a lesson
we never forgot; namely, not to meddle in Cabinet affairs, but to content ourselves with the honor
of amusing great men, — in short, to know our
place and keep it.

Mr. Jefferson Davis had been an eminent public
man long before the presidency of Mr. Pierce. He
was a graduate of West Point. He had been an
officer in the Indian wars. He was in the
House of Representatives at the age of thirty-
seven. John Quincy Adams heard his maiden
speech and said: "That young man is no ordinary man. He will make his mark yet, mind
me." His devotion to reading and study amounted
to a passion. He had served as a colonel in the
Mexican War. It was said of him that "his brilliant movement at Buena Vista carried the day, and
that his tactical conception was worthy of a Cæsar
or a Napoleon."[1]

He was afterward a member for four years of
the United States Senate, and although defeated in
a gubernatorial contest in Mississippi, he rose
rapidly in the esteem of the people of his own section; and now, at the age of forty-five, he was the
"leader of the Southern people, and successor of
John C. Calhoun." He was leader a few years
later in the Battle of the Giants, fought so bitterly
in Mr. Buchanan's time.

[1] J. F. Rhodes's "History of the United States," Vol. I. p. 390.

Of Mr. Caleb Cushing I knew less than I did of Mr. Davis and Mr. Marcy. He had great learning, great ability, wide experience in public life. He has been described as a "scholar, author, lawyer, statesman, diplomatist, general, and judge." He was one of the rare class of men who are precocious in childhood and youth, and who go intellectually from strength to strength as long as they live. He was graduated from Harvard when only seventeen years of age. He was a most attractive man in manner and address, and a fascinating public speaker. He could quote the "Iliad" from beginning to end, and could speak to each one of the foreign ambassadors in his own tongue.

Mr. Cushing sent an editorial nearly every day to the *Washington Union*, of which my husband was associate editor. No compliment upon his own articles which my husband ever received was more gratefully appreciated than one from Mr. Cushing. A serious difference of opinion had arisen with the senior editor, because of a paper upon the Anglo-Russian war, in which my husband warmly advocated the side of Russia. He declined retracting his words (which were copied and translated abroad), and finally gave up his position on the paper rather than express sentiments other than his own. Mr. Cushing applauded him, and bade him stand fearlessly by an argument, "unanswered and unanswerable."

Shortly after this Mr. Pierce appointed my husband special Minister to Greece. I longed to go with him to Athens, but my mother's health was

frail, and I felt I could not leave her. So I returned to my home in Virginia with my children,
and their father went on his mission alone. When
it was accomplished, the Pierce administration was
drawing to a close.

My temporary home was near Charlottesville,
and thither, on his way South, came the President
to spend a day and to visit Monticello, the home
of the Father of Democracy. He wrote to me,
inviting me to spend the evening with him and a
few friends at his hotel. We had a delightful evening. He told me all I wished to know of the exile
far away in Greece, expressed warm friendship for
him and his, and presented me with two gorgeous
volumes, bound sumptuously in green morocco,
and inscribed, from my "friend Franklin Pierce,"
in his own fine handwriting. I played at his request, he sitting the while beside the piano. I
selected Henselt's " L'Elisire d'Amour " and " La
Gondola," to the great delight of the President. The
other day I read, from the pen of some irreverent
critic, of the "lilting puerilities of the innocuous
Henselt." All the same, these puerilities pleased
the President, and will charm the world until the
end of time.

I feel that I have said too little of Mr. Pierce in
this sketch of the men we knew. I cannot hope to
convey an adequate conception of his captivating
voice and manner. Surely its source was in genuine
kindness of heart. I knew nothing of him as a
politician. It was urged against him that he was
extremely partial to the South. I know the South

honored and loved him always. It was said that " Franklin Pierce could not say ' No ' " — a weakness which doubtless caused him a world of trouble in his political relations, but to which he may have owed something of the indescribable charm for which he was conspicuous. Mr. Seward, his political opponent, wrote to his wife: " The President has a *very* winning way in his manners." I can fully understand the beautiful friendship between him and Nathaniel Hawthorne. How exquisite the answer of the author when chidden because he had dedicated a book to the President, after the latter had become unpopular: " Unpopular, is he? If he is so exceedingly unpopular that his name is enough to sink the volume, there is so much the more need that an old friend should stand by him."

Hawthorne had then arrived at the height of his own popularity, while his friend, on account of his fancied Southern sympathies, had lost the friendship of his own people. A bitter lot for a sensitive patriot, who had done his best! " An angel can no more ! "

My residence in Washington during the Pierce administration was too short to afford me more than a brief glimpse of the social life of the city, but I keenly enjoyed that glimpse. I had the good fortune to find favor, as I have said, with the old residents, and also with the Hon. W. W. Corcoran, at whose house the best of the old and new could always be found.

There I met many distinguished people. I remember especially General Winfield Scott, Sam

Houston, and Washington Irving.   General Scott, grand, imposing, and ceremonious, never failed to tell everybody that he had been groomsman for my husband's father — he had been born in Petersburg, Virginia.   He addressed all young women as "fair lady."   He was a great hero and a splendid old fellow in every particular, and he never for a moment forgot his heroism and his splendor.   People called him "vain."   So great a man could not be accused of vanity — "the food of fools."   He had a reasonable pride in what he had achieved, but his was certainly not the kind of pride that apes humility.

As for old Sam Houston, he had had romance enough in his past life for a dozen heroes.   He had lived many years among the Indians, had fought in many wars, had achieved the independence of Texas — what had he not done?   Now he was Senator from Texas, very popular, and rather impatient, one might judge, of the confinement and restraints of his position.   It was amusing to see the little pages of the Senate Chamber providing him with small bundles of soft pine sticks, which he would smuggle into his desk with a rather shamefaced expression.   Doubled up over this desk, his face almost covered with his hanging eyebrows and iron-gray whiskers, he occupied himself in whittling sticks as a safety-valve for unrest while listening to the long speeches, lasting sometimes until midnight.   He would prove afterward in his brilliant conversation that he had not lost a word. Sometimes the pine under his knife would take shape in little crosses, amulets, etc.   He was known, now and then, to draw from the pocket of his tiger-skin vest an exquisitely carved heart and present it to some young lady whose beauty attracted him.

Then there was Washington Irving, — an old man with but a few years to live. He died before the end of the administration. One would never think him old, — so keen and alert was he, — but for his trick of suddenly falling asleep for a minute or two in the middle of a conversation. A whisper, " Sh-h-h," would pass from one to another, " Mr. Irving is asleep;" and in a moment he would wake up, rub his hands, and exclaim, " Well, as we were saying," taking up the conversation just where he had left it.

My little sister worshipped Mr. Irving. " Only let me see him," she pleaded; " only let me touch the hand that wrote the ' Sketch Book.' "

I repeated this when I introduced her, and he said : " Ah, yes, yes! I know! I have heard all that before — many times before. And just as I am getting happy over it, here comes a young fellow, some whipper-snapper who never wrote a line, and [mimicking] it's ' Good evening, Mr. Irving, I am glad to have met you.' "

It happened that my sister had not heard. She was already distraite. Her favorite friend had appeared, and she at once echoed, " Good evening, Mr. Irving, I am glad to have met you," to the old gentleman's infinite delight and amusement. I was proud to have had even a word with " America's most celebrated writer : exquisite in courtesy and fidelity and of lofty purity of character." He died in 1859 —

the heart which had ached so long for the death of
an early love failing him suddenly at "Sleepy
Hollow," his home on the Hudson.   His country
scarcely noticed his death!   That country, crazed
on the subject of slavery, was writing columns on
columns about John Brown.

One morning, when I was passing the corner of
Fifteenth Street, below President Square, my steps
were arrested by a large crowd which had assembled
in front of the bank of Corcoran & Riggs.   "Dear
me," I thought, "has the bank failed?"   But the
green blinds of the plain two-storied building were
all open, and presently through the opening door,
escorted by Mr. Riggs himself, came a slight little
maid in a Connemara cloak and hood.   Mr. Riggs
put her in a waiting carriage, slammed the door, and,
with a look which said plainly to the waiting crowd,
"No more this time," reëntered the house.

The little lady was Adelina Patti — just sixteen
— and Mr. Riggs's guest during the few days she
spent in Washington on her way to meet Southern
engagements.   Congressmen tendered her a complimentary benefit, and she sang in a small hall, supported by a few local musicians.   She stood before
us in a simple muslin slip, her dark hair bound with
a narrow blue velvet ribbon, — a Scottish "snood,"
— and never, in all her brilliant life, was she more
appreciated, more admired.

I could remember a time of musical dearth in
Virginia, relieved only by rare occasions when the
dimly lighted concert rooms would be filled by eager
listeners to wandering minstrels: the Hutchinson

family, Anna Bishop, the Orpheans, Parodi, and
Amalia Patti. After a while Strakosch appeared with
an infant phenomenon. She looked precisely like a
French doll, with her little round face, pink cheeks,
and big black eyes, dressed in short frocks of rose-
color or blue silk. But she sang like a linnet on
a bough ; and it was comical to see her in her duets
inclining her small head toward her contralto, after
the manner of other divas. This was the ten-year-
old Adelina Patti!

"What does she keep in her throat?" asked a
little girl near her own age — adding comfortably,
"Never mind, we will find out when she dies!"

Maurice Strakosch accompanied her on a square
piano placed upon the floor, the platform being often
too narrow to admit it. He played, frequently turning his face to the audience, nodding and smiling, as
if to say : —

"See this little marvel I have discovered! Is she
not a darling?"

The midget had an uncertain temper in those days.
Travelling once in the same car with a lady who took
her fancy, she found an opportunity to free her mind
of her opinion of her troupe : Amalia was jealous of
her ; Amalia would shake and pinch her behind the
scenes if the audience applauded her ; Strakosch was
utterly horrid — just observe his great hands! Not
for worlds would she sing for him were it not for the
sugar-plums!

At the end of the journey Strakosch approached
the little girl and held out his hand to take her to
her sister.

"I am not going with you," said Adelina, "I am going home with this lady."

"Ah, but impossible!" said Strakosch.

"I will!" said the small rebel. "You know I always do things when I say 'I will.'"

"Why not?" said the lady (she was Mrs. Glasgow, the lovely mother of Ellen Glasgow, the authoress). "Why not? Let her come with me! I will take good care of her."

Strakosch shrugged his shoulders. A scene was imminent. "If I consent, Adelina," he said at last, "will you be sure to be ready when I come for you for rehearsal? Will you be sure to sing?"

"Will *you* be sure to bring me back?"

"Sure — I promise."

"How much candy?" was the next excited question.

"A whole pound."

"No — not enough!"

"Two pounds," said Strakosch, glancing around to satisfy himself that the scene attracted admirers and possible concert goers.

"Not enough," persisted Adelina, shaking her head.

"A hatful!" cried Strakosch, and won the day.

Mrs. Glasgow devoted herself to the little girl for the four days of her stay. On the last evening she invited ten or fifteen child neighbors to a dolls' party with Adelina Patti. At the end of the evening she said: "Now, Adelina, these little girls have been very kind to you. They have brought you lovely flowers — I wish you to sing one little song for them."

D

A shrewd look possessed the tiny face.   "*Sing —
for — them!* Sing without money! Mais non! J'ai
toujours beaucoup des fleurs."

She disappeared for a while from public view. I saw
her no more until her visit to Washington.   Later,
if I may anticipate, during Mr. Buchanan's administration, she made her début in " Lucia di Lammer-
moor."   People fought for seats and boxes.   Three
rival beauties secured the three best — tiny, comfort-
less stalls — at ninety dollars each.   It was something to see Miss Harriet Lane, Mrs. John R.
Thompson, and Mrs. Stephen A. Douglas in those
three boxes! Each was filled with beautiful women,
and the Cabinet officers and Senators stood behind.

" What is all this about?" asked Judge Douglas,
the " Little Giant."

" The opera follows Scott's ' Bride of Lammer-
moor,'" I gently suggested.

" Whose bride was she?   Where did she live?"
asked the mighty man, the famous Senator who came
so near being President.

" I doubt whether she lived at all," I told him.
" She is a creature of pure imagination, I'm afraid."

" Oh!" said the Senator, contemptuously, and
gave no more attention to the stage nor to the divine
artist upon it.

As I had come to Washington from Virginia,
where everybody's great-grandfather knew my great-
grandfather, where the rules of etiquette were only
those of courtesy and good breeding, I had many a
troubled moment in my early Washington life, lest
I should transgress some law of precedence, etc.   I

wisely took counsel with one of my "old residents," and she gave me a few simple rules whereby the young chaperon of a very young girl might be guided : "My dear," said this lady, "My dear, you know you cannot always have your husband to attend you. It will be altogether proper for you to go with your sister to morning and afternoon receptions. When you arrive, send for the host or the master of ceremonies, and he will take you in and present you. Of course, your husband will take you to balls ; if he is busy, you simply cannot go ! I think you would do well to make a rule *never*, under any circumstances, to drive in men's carriages. There are so many foreigners here, you must be careful. They never bring their own court manners to Washington. They take their cue from the people they meet. If you are high and haughty, they will be high and haughty. If you are genially civil but reserved, they will be so. If you talk personalities in a free and easy way, they will spring some audacious piece of scandal on you, and the Lord only knows where they'll end."

Now, it so happened that I had just received a request from a Frenchman who had brought letters, to be allowed to escort Madame and Mademoiselle to a fête in Georgetown. We were to drive through the avenue of blossoming crab-apples, and rendezvous at a spring for a picnic. I forget the name of our hostess, but she had arranged a gay festival, including music and dancing on the green. I had accepted this invitation and the escort of M. Raoul, and received a note from him asking at what hour

he should have the honor, etc., and I immediately
ran home and wrote that " Madame would be happy
to see M. Raoul *à trois heures* "—and that Madame
asked the privilege of using her own horses, etc.   I
made haste to engage an open carriage and congratu-
lated myself on my clever management.

The afternoon was delicious.   Monsieur appeared
on the moment, and we waited for my carriage.
The gay equipages of other members of the party
drove up and waited for us.   Presently, rattling
down the street, came an old ramshackle " night-
hawk," bearing the mud-and-dust scars of many
journeys, the seats ragged and tarnished, raw-boned
horses, with rat-eaten manes and tails, harness tied
with rope, — the only redeeming feature the old
negro on the box, who, despite his humiliating
entourage, had the air of a gentleman.

What could I do?   There was nothing to be
done !

Monsieur handed me in without moving a muscle
of his face, handed in my sister, entered himself, and
spoke no word during the drive.   He conducted us
gravely to the place of rendezvous, silently and
gravely walked around the grounds with us, silently
and gravely brought us home again.

I grew hot and cold by turns, and almost shed
tears of mortification.   I made no apology — what
could I say ?   Arriving at my own door, I turned
and invited my escort to enter.   He raised his hat
and, with an air of the deepest dejection, dashed with
something very like sarcastic humility, said he
trusted Madame had enjoyed the afternoon —

thanked her for the honor done himself — and only regretted the disappointment of the French Minister, the Count de Sartiges, at not having been allowed to serve Madame with his own state coach, which had been placed at his disposal for Madame's pleasure!

As he turned away my chagrin was such I came near forgetting to give my coachman his little "tip."

I began, "Oh, Uncle, how *could* you?" when he interrupted: "Now, Mistis, don't you say nothin'. I knowed dis ole fune'al hack warn't fittin' for you, but der warn't nar another kerridge in de stable. De boss say, 'Go 'long, Jerry, an' git 'er dar!' — an' I done done it! An' I done fotch 'er back, too!"

I never saw M. Raoul afterward. There's no use crying over spilt milk, or broken eggs, or French monsieurs, or even French counts and Ministers. I soon left for Virginia, and to be relieved of the dread of meeting M. Raoul softened my regret at leaving Washington.

CHAPTER III

TWO days after Mr. Buchanan's inauguration, the nominations for the Cabinet were sent to the Senate. The venerable Lewis Cass, with many years of honorable service behind him, was Secretary of State, — selected, the "Old-Line Whigs" said, because the President meant really to be Secretary of State himself, and he wished an amiable first assistant. Moreover, he liked to say "old Lewis Cass," as though he were himself so much younger. Hon. Howell Cobb of Georgia had the Treasury Department. He was a man of political ability, "frank and genial," sagacious and conservative, "qualities fitting him well to dominate his associates." Mr. Floyd, who "belonged to the first families of Virginia," was the Secretary of War. Mr. Toucey of Connecticut was Secretary of the Navy, Mr. Jacob Thompson of Mississippi, Secretary of the Interior, Mr. Brown of Tennessee, Postmaster-General, and Judge Jeremiah Black, Attorney-General, — three from the North, four from the South. The new Cabinet, people said, was far inferior in capacity to the retiring one.

The new President was a bachelor. Despite his years and his cold, reserved manner, his fidelity to the memory of beautiful Miss Coleman, to whom he had been affianced in his youth, invested him with the interest which attaches to romance.   This was enhanced by his devotion to his niece, Miss Harriet Lane.   In her affection he found the only solace of his lonely life.   For her sake he condescended to unbend in public ; and to brighten the atmosphere around her, he sometimes became quite a jaunty old bachelor.   She was his confidante in all matters political and personal.   A stately etiquette ruled between the two.   She was always addressed as " Miss Harriet," and to her he was " The President "—never " Uncle Buchanan," except on the rare occasions when she considered it worth her while to coax him in order to carry a point.

Washington was never gayer than during this administration, more memorable than any other except Washington's and Lincoln's.   The mighty giants of the House and Senate were there, the men who must be held largely responsible for that most unnecessary, cruel, and wicked war — the war between the Northern and Southern states of America. Washington was the storm centre, charged with the electric forces so soon to burst in fury upon the country.

But before we enter upon these troubled times, we will live over again some of the happy, care-forgetting months of our life in Washington.

My husband who had succeeded Mr. Ritchie as one of the editors of the *Richmond Enquirer* was now a member of Congress.   He had accomplished his mission to Greece to the satisfaction of his government and to his own pleasure and profit. With a good courier and a generous country at his back, he had traversed Europe, had seen Venice rise from the sea, had revelled in the grandeur that was — and is — Rome, had beheld the mosques and minarets of the Byzantine city from the waters of the Golden Horn, had looked into the inscrutable eyes of the Sphinx, and had finally taken up his abode under the shadow of the Acropolis. There he had met the " Maid of Athens," now stout, middle-aged Mrs. Black, so the poor American Minister, who was young and romantic, — in order to understand the passionate entreaty of Byron to return the wandering heart of him or else take the rest of him, — was constrained to think of the poem, and look the while at a dark-eyed Greek beauty named " Elpis " — at least this was the explanation made to me of his frequent allusions in his letters to the latter. There, too, he had charmed Queen Mathilde with a description of the night-blooming cereus of this country and had stricken the court of King Otho dumb with amazement by outrageous American boasting.

" Kindly tell us, your Excellency," inquired the king at a state banquet, " what subject most interests your country at the present moment."

" The problem, may it please your Majesty, of how we shall govern our superfluous territory and invest our superfluous treasure."

This may not have pleased his Majesty, but it certainly astounded him. Little Greece was, at the moment, hemmed in by organized bands of brigands and sorely pressed for the means of existence.

Our envoy had the honor, too, of attending, with Madame le Vert, the ball at the Hôtel de Ville, and of witnessing the opening quadrille, danced by Victoria and Albert, Louis Napoleon and his sister Mathilde, the empress being ill.   Both queen and princess seemed young and happy, both attired in white satin flounced with point lace, and wearing a prince's ransom in jewels.

The weather was fearfully hot, and the royal party danced but once.   The queen did not step a stately measure, dancing " high and disposedly " ; — but she entered into the spirit of the hour heartily, and, although the mother of eight children, danced with the glee of a young girl, growing withal very red in the face like any ordinary mortal.

At one of the gala days of the Exposition in Paris, a very large woman attracted much attention.   She was neither young nor handsome, but had a comfortable, well-to-do air of content.   A profusion of light curls clustered around her rotund face.   These ringlets were all that was left of the beauty of the Countess Guiccioli !   Alas, there was no " Elpis " at hand for consolation.   All these things and more would have appeared in a charming volume but for the secession of South Carolina, as will be seen later on in my story.

I never regretted the loss of this beautiful opportunity in my life.   My mother had been nursed back to bless me and mine a few years longer.   Moreover, I found myself enriched.   I had pictures, ravishing pictures, Raphael's " Belle Jardinière," a priceless Raffaello Morghen's proof impression of the " Ma-

donna della Seggiola," Guido's "Aurora" with its
glorious women — the most glorious being (if she
would only turn around) the one with her back
to the world.   I had many others, Titian, Domeni-
chino, Murillo, Leonardo da Vinci.   I had amber
from Constantinople, curios and antiques from
Egypt, corals and cameos from Naples and Florence, silks from Broussa (afterward swallowed up
by an earthquake), silks and velvets from Lyons,
laces from Brussels, perfumes from the land of
Araby the blest, — things mightily consoling to a
woman in her early twenties.

We found a large house on New York Avenue
and filled it with good Virginia servants.   Admonished by experience, we secured horses and a careful coachman.

We had come to stay!   My husband represented
the old district of his kinsman, John Randolph of
Roanoke, and his constituents were devoted to him.
They would never supplant him with another.   Of
that we might be sure.   God granting life and
health, we were going to be happy young people.

The market in Washington was abundantly
supplied with the finest game and fish from the
Eastern Shore of Maryland and Virginia, and the
waters of the Potomac.   Brant, ruddy duck, canvasback duck, sora, oysters, and terrapin were
within the reach of any housekeeper.   Oysters,
to be opened at a moment's notice, were planted
on the cellar floors, and fed with salt water, and the
cellars, as far as the mistress was concerned, were
protected from invasion by the large terrapins kept

there — a most efficient police force, crawling about with their outstretched necks and wicked eyes.

Such dainties demanded expert cooking. We found in our house a portly family servant, " Aunt Susan," who had been left as caretaker with permission to remain or not as the new tenant should please, or as she herself should please. I fell in love with her on sight and found her willing to engage with me.

" Can you cook, Aunt Susan?" I imprudently inquired.

" No'm, I don't call myself a cook, but I know a hogfish from a yellow-bellied perch, and a canvasback duck from a redhead. I could cook oysters to suit my own white folks."

We had brought with us a number of servants who had lived with us in Virginia. They were free. We never owned slaves; this one free family had served us always.

A serious difficulty immediately arose in the kitchen. Susan felt her dignity insulted. She had supposed I would bring " gentlefolks' servants from the Eastern Sho'." She had not " counted on free niggers to put on airs an' boss her in her own kitchen."

My Virginia servants protested absolute humility and innocence. But that was not all. A French woman, Adele Rivière, was sewing in the nursery, and an Englishman, George Boyd, was coachman. Susan wanted " only one mistress," she had " not counted on working for furriners. By the time she had pleased that Frenchwoman and Englishman and them free niggers" she "wouldn't have enough sperrit left to wipe her foot on the door-mat."

A compromise was effected, however. Susan was to be queen on her own premises; and if she *must* occasionally "put on airs" herself and "boss" somebody, why she might always "boss" me.

"I think," said my friend Agnes, "you have very neatly arranged to have as much trouble as possible. The question of caste will crop up every hour of the day. If the worst comes to the worst, let them all go except Susan! Harriet Martineau gives fine advice, for an old maid: 'Never *nag* your servants — but if occasion demands, come down upon them like the day of judgment.'"

"I stand by Susan," I assured her, "whatever she does. I am dreadfully opposed to capital punishment, but if anybody kills a cook, he needn't bring his case to our office."

Susan had offended, by her assumption of superiority, all the members of my household except myself, to whom she was most kind and respectful. The boy James had been brought by his aunts, who promised to train him for my service. He soon developed an ingenuity in teasing the cook amounting to inspiration. Matters between them reached a crisis one morning. I was reading my paper in the office adjoining the breakfast-room when I heard Susan's raucous voice: "What do you mean coming in this kitchen hollerin' out 'Susan, Susan'? Whar's your manners?"

"I loant 'em to de cook dis mornin', Susan — leastways Miss Moss! I always disremembers yo' entitlements."

"Well, you just get out of this kitchen! I can
send breakfast up on the dumb waiter. You stay
in your own place."

"I kin make myse'f skase, Miss Moss, but dat
ain't de pint. Cose de dumb waiter can't talk, an' I
has to speak about clean plates an' —"

"Get out o' here, I tell you. *Clean*, indeed! And
your face not washed this morning! An' you all
pizened up with scent like —"

"*Lawd*, Miss Moss! *Don't* say what I'se like!
An' what I gwine fling water in my face for? I ain'
no house afire."

In a few minutes Susan, her ample figure endowed
with a fresh white apron, and her bandanna turban
tied to a nicety, presented herself, dropped a courtesy,
and said with perfect politeness : —

"Honey, I hate to worry you, but I'm afraid the
time has come when you must choose between me
and the free nigger. I think too much of myself
to mind his impudence, but everything smells and
tastes of his strong scents — which I know will never
suit you nor the master. I, for one, can't stand
'em."

"Then James must leave at once," said I, firmly.
"He knows the perfume is forbidden, and I have
myself heard his disrespectful language to you."

But James had no idea of leaving Washington
and returning to the position of knife-cleaner in the
Petersburg hotel, whence I had taken him. He
experienced a total change of heart. He surrendered
in magnificent style. I was too skilful a general not
to press my advantage. Then and there I confis-

cated his entire stock of spurious attar of rose. It
could not be buried, because the court was paved;
it could not be emptied in the waste-water pipes, lest
we remember it forever; but I opened the doors of
Susan's kitchen range, and laid it, a burnt-offering
to her offended dignity, upon the glowing coals.
I then went calmly in to my coffee, which had a
distinctly Oriental flavor that morning.

Things went smoothly after this. The prevailing
spirit of secession found its way only as far as the
nursery, when pretty Adele Rivière entered a con-
vent (with but one expressed regret, that the bonnets
were so unbecoming), and a dear little genius, Annie
Powers, took her place, — coming regularly for fifty
cents a day, and making me independent of the elu-
sive dressmakers who lorded and queened it over
my unhappy friends.

And just here I feel constrained to apologize to
my friend who has, at this moment, this page before
him, for recording so many trifling incidents; but in
painting a faithful picture of any time, the little lights
and shadows cannot be left out. Nothing is unim-
portant. Even

> " To the God that maketh all
> There is no great — there is no small,"

words which I quote with no fear of being deemed
irreverent; since the couplet has been discovered by
a sojourner in the Orient to have been a petty larceny
of Emerson's from the book of a Brahmin, and is not
a quotation from the pen of inspiration, as we understand inspiration.

CHAPTER IV

WE attended Dr. Gurley's church and found that the President also had taken a seat in that church. Our own was near the door, and for many Sundays before I knew him, I was interested in seeing him enter the church and walk briskly up to his pew near the pulpit (while the bell was ringing), buttoned in his broadcloth coat, wearing no overcoat in the coldest weather. Immediately after the benediction he would walk rapidly down the aisle, the congregation standing until he passed. Miss Lane attended St. John's Church, and the President was accompanied only by his secretary, Mr. Buchanan Henry. After I knew him quite well, I always spoke to him when he passed me near the door, and I sometimes ventured, " A good sermon, Mr. President ! " he never failing to reply, " Too long, Madam, too long."

I was leading a very happy domestic life, busy with my little boys and my housekeeping, proud of my self-constituted office as my Congressman's private secretary, much exercised in sending documents, seeds, and cuttings (we were introducing tea-culture in Virginia) to his constituents, when I was called to order by our dear old friend, Mr. Dudley Mann, an old politician, diplomat, and "society man."

"Madam, did you come to Washington to live in your own house and write letters to farmers?"

"What better could I do?"

"The President does not agree with you. He admires your husband and wonders why you were not at the Levee. He has asked me to see that you come to the next one."

"I shall be on a committee that night," said my Congressman, hastily, — he was usually on a committee when a reception was to the fore.

"I will take her myself," said Mr. Mann. "Now, wear a pretty evening dress of silk or velvet. Can it be lavender? And I will call precisely at nine."

I appreciated the honor of Mr. Mann's escort, and, wishing to please him, procured the lavender silk. Our evening gowns were cut straight across the neck, and finished with a bertha of lace. The full skirt was distended over a large hoop. An elaborate headdress of flowers or marabout feathers was *de rigueur* for a levee, which, however, demanded simpler attire than a ball or a dinner. Our white gloves were short and were finished at the wrist with a fall of lace three or four inches wide, and a band of ribbon and rosette.

Mr. Mann approved my attire and gave me a very good time. The crowd was great and the amplitude and length of the ladies' robes filled me with anxiety.

"Dear Mr. Mann," I said, "pray be careful not to tread on the trains."

" My child," he answered, " I haven't lifted my feet for twenty years ! "

The President detained us for a few courteous words, and we were passed on to Miss Lane, standing, not beside him, but in a group with other ladies. Thence we found our way to the East Room, and a great many ladies and gentlemen were introduced to me, as I stood on the arm of my courtly escort.

Such a number of cards came to us after this that the housekeeping, the writing, the little boys, the seeds, and the tea-culture in Virginia were likely to suffer.

The reign of the "afternoon tea" was not yet — at least not in Washington; but entertainments included morning receptions, evening receptions, dinners, musicales, children's parties, old-fashioned evening parties with music and supper, and splendid balls. So many of these were crowded into a season that we often attended three balls in one evening.

The first time I dined with the President I made early and elaborate preparation. When the great day arrived, all my paraphernalia, rosetted slippers, gloves, fan, dress, and wrap were duly laid out on my bed and sofa. In the evening I seated myself at a dressing table and submitted my head to François' hands. The evening coiffure was elaborate and troublesome. The hair in front was stiffened with bandoline, and formed into sleek, smooth bandeaux, framing the face. Behind, all the hair was tightly tied, low at the nape of the neck, then divided into two parts, and each woven with many strands into a wide braid. These were curved from ear to ear

E

to form a basket, and within the basket were roses, or pond-lilies, or violets, with long trailing vines floating behind.

François was a very agreeable talker. He had dressed Rachel's hair and was leisurely giving a charming lecture on Rachel's art. Suddenly my husband burst in: "The carriage is at the door! Hurry, hurry! We've only ten minutes to reach the White House."

I literally leaped into my gown, had no time for flowers or jewels, snatched up my gloves, left everything else, and ran! We entered the green room just as Mr. Buchanan Henry was arranging the guests for dinner. Luckily I was low down on his list.

I was miserably heated, and very uncomfortable lest I should not be able to conceal my Congress gaiters, having had no time to change them. My gloves were on, but not buttoned. To add to my misfortunes I found I was to be taken in by a Southern Congressman who was already — well, not exactly himself. To my horror he winked at Miss Lane when he drank wine with her. When a side dish was handed, he said audibly: "Now look here, Joe! Is that the same old thing you gave me here last year? Because if it is, I don't want any of it." After we returned to the parlor I confided my miseries to the lady who had been placed next him at dinner, and she reassured me: "Oh, that's nothing! Such things happen here any day — nobody notices these people from the rural districts."

This was worse than the ramshackle carriage.

Could I bear to be classed with "people from the rural districts?" I was never a moment late afterward.

Dinners at the White House were much less elaborate in their appointments than were dinners at the homes of the wealthy Cabinet officers and Senators. Mr. Buchanan set an example of Republican simplicity. Few flowers were placed in the drawing rooms. In the centre of the Blue Room there was a divan surrounding a stand of potted plants and surmounted by a small palm. The dinner table was not ornamented with flowers, nor were bouquets at the covers. A long plateau, a mirror edged with a hunting scene (gilt figures in high relief), extended down the middle, and from the centre and at the two ends rose epergnes with small crystal dishes for bonbons and cakes.

One evening the President said to me, "Madam, what is this small shrub I find always placed before me?"

"If the berries were white, Mr. President, it would be *Ardisia alba.*"

"Ah," he answered, "I am all right! My berries are red — I have '*Ardisia rufa!*' Miss Harriet has the *alba!*"

There were no other floral decorations on the table.

I once ventured to send the President a Virginia ham, with particular directions for cooking it. It was to be soaked, boiled gently three or four hours, suffered to get cold in its own juices, and then toasted. This would seem simple enough, but the executive cook disdained it, perhaps for the reason that it was so simple. The dish, a shapeless, jellylike mass, was placed before the President. He took his knife and fork in hand to honor the dish by carving it himself, looked at it helplessly, and called out — "Take it away! Take it away! Oh, Miss Harriet! You are a poor housekeeper! Not even a Virginia lady can teach you."

The glass dishes of the epergne contained wonderful "French kisses" — two-inch squares of crystallized sugar wrapped in silver paper, and elaborately decorated with lace and artificial flowers. I was very proud at one dinner when the President said to me, "Madam, I am sending you a souvenir for your little daughter," and a waiter handed me one of those gorgeous affairs. He had questioned me about my boys, and I had told him of my daughter Gordon, eight years old, who lived with her grandmother. "You must bring her to see Miss Harriet," he had said — which, in due season, I did; an event, with its crowning glory of a checked silk dress, white hat and feather, which she proudly remembers to this day. Having been duly presented at court, the little lady was much "in society" and accompanied me to many brilliant afternoon functions.

She was a thoughtful listener to the talk in her father's library, and once when an old politician spoke sadly of a possible rupture of the United States, surprised and delighted him by slipping her hand in his and saying, "never mind! *United* will spell *Untied* just as well" — a little *mot* which was remembered and repeated long afterwards.

Mr. Buchanan's kind notice of her is gratefully recollected. It was said that he was influenced by the Southern Senators and Representatives. I only know he was most kind to us, and I refuse to believe we were of consequence enough to make this kindness a matter of policy. I would fain think he really liked us, really desired to add to our happiness.

It cannot be said that his niece, Miss Harriet Lane, although universally admired, was a popular woman. She lacked magnetism. She followed a prescribed rule of manner from which she never deviated, no matter with whom she was thrown. This was, perhaps, fortunate. Always courteous, always in place, silent whenever it was possible to be silent, watchful, and careful, she made no enemies, was betrayed into no entangling alliances, and was involved in no contretemps of any kind.

She was very handsome, a fair, blue-eyed, self-contained young woman. She was dignified — as indeed all women had to be, in gesture at least, when they wore great hoops! The "curtsy" was a perilous duty. "How does she do it? She never makes a cheese of herself," said one, looking on at a morning reception. Miss Lane's courtesy was the perfection of deference and grace. And she had exquisite taste in dress. She never wore many ornaments, many flowers, nor the billows of ruffles then in fashion. I remember her in white tulle, with a wreath of clematis; in soft brown or blue silk; in much white muslin, dotted and plain, with blue ribbons run in puffs on skirt and bodice.

She was very affable and agreeable, in an unemotional way — the proper manner, of course, for her. I imagine no one could take a liberty with her then, but I risked the experiment some years ago when we spent a summer together at Bar Harbor. A handsome widow, with silver hair, she was even more *distingué* than she had been in the White House. I recalled, to her genuine amusement, two incidents of her life there. When she took her place as mistress of the Executive Mansion, the President had given her but one rule for her conduct: never under any circumstances to accept a present. "Think of my feelings," she had said to me, "when the lovely lacquered boxes and tables the Japanese Embassy brought me were turned from the door, to say nothing of the music-boxes and these fascinating sewing-machines they have just invented."

A party was once made up for a visit to Mount Vernon. Mr. Augustus Schell of New York accompanied Miss Lane. He was a fine-looking fellow and very much in love with her. As they walked along the banks of the Potomac, she picked up a handful of colored pebbles. Mr. Schell requested them of her and put them in his pocket. He took them to Tiffany, had them beautifully polished, set with diamonds, and linked together in a bracelet, and sent them as "a souvenir of Mount Vernon" to Miss Lane for a Christmas gift.

She carried them for a week in her pocket, trying to get her own consent to give them up. The more she looked at them the better she liked them. One day the President was in fine spirits. He liked to rally

her about Lord Lyons, which she did not fancy
overmuch.   But this time she humored him, and at
last ventured to say, " Uncle Buchanan, if I have
a few pretty pebbles given me, you do not object to
my accepting them ? "

" Oh, no, Miss Harriet !   Keep your pebbles !
Keep your pebbles," he exclaimed, in high good
humor.

" You know," Miss Lane said, in telling me the
story at the time, " diamonds are pebbles."

There was an impression that she never condescended to the rôle of a coquette, but I could testify
to the contrary.

Mr. Porcher Miles, Congressman from South
Carolina, was one of her train of devoted admirers.
He accompanied me once to an evening reception
at the White House.   Miss Lane stood in front of
the flower-trimmed divan in the Blue Room.   Mr.
Miles and I paid our respects, lingered awhile, and,
having other engagements, sent for our carriage.

As we stood at the door waiting, he talked of
Miss Lane's beauty and charm — " Look at her
where she stands !   Is she not the personification of
a high-bred lady from head to foot ? "

Miss Lane perceived we were talking about her,
— and while she gave her right hand to the arriving
guests she passed her left behind her and plucked a
spray of mignonette.   We saw her beckon a servant,
who immediately found us, and gave the flowers to
Mr. Miles, " with Miss Lane's compliments."

I repeated these two little stories to her when her
head was silvered, — less by age than by sorrow, —

and awoke one of those rare moonlight smiles which her friends remember so well.

No one who observed Mr. Buchanan could fail to perceive the rapid change in him after he became President. Having committed himself to the policy of rotation in office, he was overwhelmed with the persistence of place hunters. " They give me no time to say my prayers," he complained. They exhausted him in listening to their petty interests at a time when the most important problems that ever confronted the head of the nation clamored for his consideration.

Toward the last, when the older men almost gave up hope, his only prayer was that the catastrophe of conflict might not come in his day. He cannot be blamed above others for hesitation, vacillation. The problems were too mighty for one man's wisdom, too mighty for the collective wisdom of many.

Lord and Lady Napier were interesting members of Washington society. They occupied the house built by Admiral Porter on H Street, near Fourteenth, now the residence of the French Embassy. They had succeeded Mr. Crampton, and were themselves succeeded in 1859 by Lord Lyons — so we had three British Ministers within a few years. Lord and Lady Napier gave delightful entertainments — dinners, musicales, receptions, evening parties. My Lady was more admired than were any of her predecessors. She was lovely in person, gentle, cultivated, most affable and approachable. At her receptions, and even at her balls, her sons, charming boys of ten and twelve, were always present to help her receive

LADY NAPIER AND HER SONS.

From a photograph by Brady, 1850.

her guests. Everything she did, everything she said, seemed wisest, virtuosest, discreetest, best. We have had no representative from the court of St. James who did so much for the entertainment of our own people as Lord and Lady Napier.

They gave a splendid ball in 1858 in honor of the queen's birthday. Lady Napier was superb in a tiara of diamonds and emeralds. Lord Napier and all the foreign Ministers shone forth in all the splendor of court dress; and everybody must concede — Mr. Marcy to the contrary notwithstanding — that the glitter of gold lace and gems, the distinction of orders, the imperial stars and decorations, do add to the interest of such an occasion. They mean much. They mean honor achieved, services recognized.

A recording Jenkins of this ball dilates upon the elegance of the supper, " this vista of gold and silver plate and the more than epicurean daintiness of the delicacies, the age and vintage of the wines."

The most interesting ball of the season was that given by the Senators and Representatives to Lord and Lady Napier just before they returned to England.

We were early arrivals at this ball, because we wished to see the sanded floor of the ball room, representing in colors St. George and the Dragon, before it should be effaced by the dancers.

Lord and Lady Napier were seated on a dais at the head of the room, and we passed in review before them. Lady Napier was attired in rich white satin, embroidered with pearls, with a close

" Juliet cap " of pearls on her hair.   No lofty throne
could make her less gracious than was her wont.

Dion Boucicault gave me his arm at the door, and
after our obeisance walked around the room to show
me the portraits and paintings.   On the right of
Lord and Lady Napier was a full-length portrait of
young Victoria in her ermine robe and crown, and
on the left, one of Washington.   " Alas, alas," said
Mr. Boucicault, " that so great a man should have
been painted with cramp in his fingers ! "   My escort
was altogether charming.   I discovered he was " putting in time " with me, for presently here came little
Agnes Robertson, just from the theatre, where she
had been playing in the " Siege of Lucknow," and I
lost Mr. Boucicault !   He married her soon afterward.   And *afterward!*   Ah, well !   That is none
of the business of this story.

When we entered the banquet hall, Lady Napier's
exclamations were enthusiastic.   " Look, George,"
she cried, " there is the knight and his dragon again
— all in sugar !   And here are the English arms
and — oh, George ! here are our own arms ! "   Gautier had excelled himself.   There were glittering
haystacks of spun sugar ; wonderful Roman chariots, drawn by swans, and driven by Cupids ; pyra-
mids of costly bonbons ; dolphins in a sea of rock
candy ; and ices in every form from a pair of turtle
doves to a pillared temple.   Gautier spread all his
tables in this fashion, the grosser dishes of game,
terrapin, and canvasback being served from a buffet.

Washington suppers in the fifties were superb.
One wondered if we might not some day return

to the feasts of the Roman emperors, the tables of cedar and ivory incrusted with jewels, the movable ceilings representing the celestial spheres, the showers of violets and roses which rained down on the guests in the intervals between the courses of peacocks' brains and nightingales' tongues, the trumpets which greeted the appearance of the stuffed peacocks with spread plumage. Time has really changed our supper fashions less than we imagine. Music, delicate wines, confectionery in fanciful forms, silver dishes, flowers, perfumed water for the fingers, were all fashionable in the fourteenth century. We smile to read of the flocks of living birds and the stuffed fowls that adorned the boards of the Neapolitan kings. But it has not been many years since, at a banquet given in New York to Ex-President Cleveland by the Manhattan Club, a tank was placed in the middle of the table where living terrapins crawled about and were thoughtful spectators of the fate of the *terrapine à la Maryland*. And at intervals around the board, stuffed pheasants contemplated the flight of the *faisan roti* down Democratic throats. Benedetti Salutati in 1476 never did better than this. And, compared with these ancients and moderns, M. Gautier was extremely refined, and only a bit anachronistic with his Roman chariots, Cupids, and swans.

People were wont to remark upon the atmosphere the lovely Lady Napier seemed to bring with her everywhere. Those who were admitted into her *sanctum sanctorum*, her little boudoir, fancied they could explain it. Upon her table was much silver marked with her coronet and initials, and beside these was a rosewood book rack containing half a dozen volumes — a Bible, a " Treatise on Practical Religion," " The Mount of Olivet," " Paradise of the Christian Soul," " The Christian Year," " Child's Catechism," " Life of Dean Ramsey." These were the pure waters from which Lady Napier drank daily. " Ninia Napier " was written in a delicate Italian hand on the fly-leaf of each volume.

My acquaintance with Lord Napier was slight. Judge Douglas introduced him to me at a ball. He stood some seconds without speaking. At last he raised his cold blue eyes and asked, " Have you been long at this place ? " I answered, " No, my Lord ! " Ten words had passed between us, with which he seemed to be satisfied. But Lady Napier I knew well. She returned all visits, and mine among the rest.

England and Russia had been at war, and peace had recently been concluded. Of all the foreign Ministers I knew best the English and Russian. Baron Stoëckle, then the Russian Envoy, and Baron Bodisco, his predecessor (I am not sure about the " Baron "), I knew very well, and I cordially liked their wives. This does not imply that their wives, both American, liked each other.

Madame Bodisco, laden with diamonds, looked with disfavor upon Madame Stoëckle, young, blue-eyed, and in simple attire. The latter was from Massachusetts ; the former had been a beautiful Georgetown girl, whom the baron, passing her father's orchard, had spied in a blossoming apple tree, and to whom he had forthwith lost his Russian and baronial heart.   Madame Bodisco was an enthusiastic Southern sympathizer.   At Madame Stoëckle's own table, after she had related an amusing anecdote, Madame Bodisco whispered to me, " Will you listen to that Yankee woman with her ' *says she's* ' and ' *says I's* ' ! "

Of course politics, in this seething time, were never alluded to in any company, least of all in the presence of our foreign envoys.   It required skill ; but we kept the talk upon " literature and flowers," the birds and fishes of different lands, anything, everything, except the topic of all-consuming interest.   But at one of Baron Stoëckle's very genial dinners, one of us, to test his ingenuity, said : " Come now, Baron !   Here we are, Republican and Democrat !   Show your colors !   Where do you belong? " " Alas, dear lady," said the wily diplomat, " I am an orphan !   I belong nowhere !   I am an *Old-Line Whig*."   This party had just become extinct.

One of the exciting events during the Buchanan administration was the arrival in Washington of the first embassy from Japan — the Japan which for hundreds of years had been governed by the dominant idea: " to preserve unchanged the condition of the native intelligence " and to " prevent the introduction of new ideas."   The government had maintained a rigid policy of isolation, " living like frogs in a well," until 1853, when they were rudely awakened from their dream of peace and security by Commodore Perry sailing into the harbor of Yokohama with a squadron of United States war vessels. By dignity, resolution, argument, and promise, he extorted a treaty in 1854 — and thus Japan entered the family of nations.

We had much curiosity about the Japanese. We read Perry's " Expedition" with keen interest, and were delighted with the prospect of receiving the embassy from the new land. Arrangements were made for a series of entertainments, invitations were already issued — one to the White House to witness the presentation of credentials and the reception of the President.

At last we heard that the strangers had landed and would soon arrive. I was in the gallery of the Senate Chamber with an intimate friend. We were doubtful about going out with the crowd of citizens to meet the Japanese, and were hoping that the Senate and House would adjourn. Presently a member rose and said: " Mr. President, the first Ambassadors from the venerable country of Japan are about to arrive. I move the Senate do now adjourn to meet and welcome the Japanese."

Immediately another Senator was on his feet, not to second the motion, but to say sharply, " Mr. President, I humbly trust the Senate of the United States of America will not adjourn for every show that comes along." That settled it. My friend and I hurried to our carriage, and meeting the cortège, turned just in time to drive side by side with the first landau containing the Ambassadors.

Our progress was slow and often interrupted — and we had abundant time to observe the two dignitaries close beside us in the first carriage. They sat,

fanning themselves, without looking to right or left.
The one next me was extremely wrinkled and withered — doubtless the greater man — and he was so
wooden, so destitute of expression that I — oh, this
is *much* worse than the episode of the ramshackle
hack! How can I confess that I "lost my head."
The old creature, with his wrinkled, yellow face,
turban, short gown, and petticoats looked so very
like my old mulatto mammy, the darling of my
childhood, that — I leaned over and put my pearl-
handled fan on his knee, motioning to him to give
me his in exchange. The old gentleman looked
startled for an instant, but he soon understood, and
I became the first possessor of a Japanese fan. But
then a strange thing happened! I was suddenly
overwhelmed with confusion and sank back beside
my companion, pulling her parasol well over my face.
"Was it so dreadful?" I implored. "I'm afraid it
was," said she. "Hide your fan from the others.
We will never tell." Presently she added, thought-
fully, "I wonder what your Aunt Mary would say?"
I did not wonder. I knew perfectly well what my
Aunt Mary would say.

All of which goes to prove that it was lucky my
husband had not taken his wife to Greece, and had
not accepted the mission to Persia which was offered
him. He had a wife, unfortunately, who might on
provocation lose her head.

The next morning we repaired to the White
House to help receive the Japanese Embassy. Mr.
Buchanan would have done well to select his guests
with regard to their slimness. The East Room was

packed.   Ranging on either side according to our rank, the Congressmen found themselves near the wall.   We mounted our smallest representative, Mr. Boyce, on the low mantelpiece behind some palms with instructions to peep and tell us everything he saw.   "What are they doing now, Mr. Boyce?" "Oh, it's grand! They bow, and then they bow again!"   "Well, what are they saying?   What are they doing now?"   "They are still bowing, and 'old Buck,' God bless him, is bowing too."   The ceremony was long.   The murmured voices were low.   One might have imagined one's self at a funeral.

The Belgian Baron de Limbourg gave a fine garden party to the strangers.   The Baron considered himself on the entertainment committee as he had recently married the daughter of our Secretary of State, Mr. Cass.   There were large grounds around his residence, and these he lighted with Japanese lanterns, dotting the lawn all over with pretty tents, in which young girls costumed to represent the peasants of various countries served ices and confections.   The large area in the rear was converted by carpets, hangings, and divans into a luxurious Turkish smoking den.

The Japanese always presented a pretty work-box, filled with curious silks, to the ladies who entertained them.   They would then range themselves on the seats prepared for them and look on silently, with half-shut eyes and expressionless faces.   The dancing delighted them.   "How much are the women paid?" ventured one, and was amazed to find they danced for pleasure only. A tiny, round-faced boy was always of the party. We sometimes spoke to him, and he invariably answered " all right," until he was known as " Little All Right," and, as he was the only gracious one of the whole party, he became a favorite.

The Prince de Joinville attended Madame de Limbourg's fête. During the afternoon our host sent for me, and I was conducted to an alcove where the Prince, Miss Lane, Lord Lyons, and some of the Cabinet ladies were gathered around a little bottle of wine, which was, we were told, old, old Rose wine — costing so much that now, what with interest and compound interest, every drop was worth — I forget how much! And we were to drink Miss Lane's health. " And I ! " — she protested. " I cannot drink my own health ! Am I to have no wine? " Whereupon she was conjured to think her own toast — and we would, not knowing her thought, drink it with her.

It was supposed that Lord Lyons was her suitor, and we were persuaded that the President desired her to marry him. But nobody knows the heart of the king, nor the heart of the President (who fills in some sort a king's position), still less the heart of the President's pretty niece — least of all the heart of a wily diplomat! We only know she married one of her own countrymen — and as to Lord Lyons, we lost him for good and all when the dreadful war came.

F

CHAPTER V

THE rolls of the Supreme Court, Senate, and House of Representatives presented a list of great names in 1854–1860. It would seem that our country, knowing herself to be in mortal danger, had summoned the wisest of her sons for conference and council: Rufus Choate, Curtis, Seward, Douglas, Jefferson Davis, Salmon Chase, Sumner, Hale, Toombs, Hunter, Robert J. Walker, and the brilliant men of the lower House; all these were present at the great consultation.

Of these men the most interesting, picturesque, and prominent was undoubtedly Stephen A. Douglas. His political career is known to a world which is still divided in opinion of him. Was his fevered life the result of patriotism, or of personal ambition? The world still assumes the power to read, with a magnifying glass, the inner workings of the human mechanism, and to put its discerning finger on the spring of human actions. Who has ever seen the heart of another? Who knows his own? By their works ye shall know them, not by their impulses, not by their struggles with the diverse machinery within them.

One who liked not Stephen A. Douglas has thus

described him. "Erect, compact, aggressive. A personage truly to be questioned timidly, to be approached advisedly. Here indeed was a lion, by the very look of him master of himself and of others. By reason of its regularity and masculine strength, a handsome face. A man of the world to the cut of the coat across the broad shoulders. Here was one to lift a youngster into the realm of emulation, like a character in a play, to arouse dreams of Washington and its Senators and great men. For this was one to be consulted by the great alone. A figure of dignity and power with the magnetism to compel moods. Since, when he smiled you warmed in spite of yourself, and when he frowned the world looked grave."

This was Stephen A. Douglas. The picture is a true one. What wonder that he should have captivated my husband and myself, scarcely more than half his age? The warmest friendship grew up between us.

I remember well my own first interview with him in Washington. At a crowded ball, I had found a chair outside the crush, when he approached with a bottle of champagne and a glass in his hands. "I need no introduction, Madam," he said. "I am sure you cannot have forgotten the man who met you a few years ago in the little Petersburg hotel and told you how like you are to the Empress Eugénie. No? I thought not," laughed the judge, "and yet she isn't a priming to our own women! Now," he added, bending down and speaking gravely, "I shall send Mrs. Douglas to see you. I wish you to be friends. Not pasteboard friends, with only a bit of cardboard passing between you now and then, but real good friends, meeting often and being much together." Just here, as he poised his bottle to fill my glass, his elbow was jostled, and down came the foaming champagne, over my neck and shoulders and the front of my dress. The friendship was christened — the bottle broken on the new ship! " Don't worry about the gown! You have excuse now to buy another," said the judge, as I gasped when the icy flood ran down my bosom.

He had lately married his second wife, the belle of Washington, beautiful Adèle Coutts; tall, stately, and fair exceedingly. She was a great-niece of Dolly Madison. We met often, and it came to pass that " the soul of Jonathan was knit with the soul of David."

She did not impress one as having what we call "depth of character," what is commonly implied in the term " superior," not a woman to assume to lead and teach other women — a character less lovable often than the woman who knows herself to be of like weaknesses with ourselves. But she was beautiful as a pearl, sunny-tempered, unselfish, warm-hearted, unaffected, sincere. She was very attentive to her " little giant." When he made those terribly long speeches in the Senate, on the Lecompton Constitution, on the Kansas-Nebraska Bill, on popular sovereignty, she would wait in the gallery and hurry down to wrap his overcoat around him, as he stood in the hall dripping with perspiration.

She imbibed enough political lingo to rally and amuse him. Some workmen having arrived to erect a platform in his ball room for musicians, she exclaimed: "Oh, Judge Douglas! What is a platform? They are going to bring one into this house, and we shall be flayed alive or murdered in our beds!"

I said to her once: "You know you are not really handsomer than the rest of us! Why do people say so?"

"Because I never trick myself out in diamonds, or have more than one color in a gown. An artist told me once that all those things spoiled a picture."

She would have liked the diamonds as well as the rest of us, and once said so to her husband. "Oh, no!" he answered, "diamonds are the consolation of old wives, a diamond for a wrinkle!"

Mrs. Douglas was the first of the Washington ladies who adopted the fashion of closing her shutters in the early afternoon and lighting her rooms with gas. She was delighted as a child with the effect and indulged in a preliminary waltz with me before the company arrived. "O dear!" she exclaimed, suddenly, "what am I to do with this *awful* picture of Judge Douglas's? I daren't take it away because he bought it for his first wife; and when old Mrs. Martin pounces down upon us to see how we are spending her grandchildren's money, she will miss it, and think I've sold it! But isn't it *awful?* Do spread out your flounces in front of it as well as you can." The noonday lighting of her rooms was a great success. Lord Lyons looked up

and spoke of the beauty of the starlit night, adding
"and there's a fine moon out of doors." John G.
Saxe was one of the guests — and his merry hostess
introduced him as "deserving capital punishment
for making people laugh themselves to death."

I have had occasion to allude so often to the
costumes of the ladies of Mr. Buchanan's administration, that I have resolved boldly to ask my reader
to accompany me for a few minutes to Vanity Fair,
as, guided by society reports of the period, I
describe the dresses worn by the leaders of fashion.
I suppose the journals of our day would not print
columns on columns describing the gowns worn at
balls, unless there were some sure to read. Costume
has always interested the world. It is still a question
whether costume influences character, or *vice versa*.
And yet one regrets to treat charming women as
though they were lay figures.

There will be a great deal of sorrowful record in
this book. Let us linger awhile on the flowery
brink, before we reach the time when the noise of
angry waters will be too loud to be hushed by the
frou-frou of a lady's silken gown. Moreover, there
are always mistakes and misconceptions to be cor-
rected and set right. Have I not just read in a
New York daily paper of the ugly fashions of the
Washington of the times just before the war — the
"great hoops, gowns of reps, the hideous tints of
red, the Congress gaiters; how nobody wore a ball
gown costing more than $55," etc., etc.? The Con-
gress gaiters must be acknowledged, the hoops also,
but perhaps they may all come again; and then

MRS. STEPHEN A. DOUGLAS,

née ADÈLE COUTTS.

From a portrait by G. P. A. Healy, 1865.

some beauty like the empress of the French may arise to make them beautiful. They *were* large! Beside them Queen Elizabeth's farthingale was an insignificant circumstance. The belle in the fifties lived in an expansive time. There was still plenty of room in the world. Houses were broad and low, carriages were broad and low, furniture was massive. Even a small pier glass was broadened by great scrolls of mahogany. Drawing-rooms were filled with vast arm-chairs, sofas, and tables. The legs of pianos were made as massive as possible.

Ladies wore enormous hoops, and because their heads looked like small handles to huge bells, they widened the coiffure into broad bandeaux and braids, loaded it with garlands of flowers, and enlarged it by means of a wide head-dress of tulle, lace, and feathers, or crowned it with a coal-scuttle bonnet tied under the chin with wide ribbons. In this guise they sailed fearlessly about, with no danger of jostling a neighbor or overturning the furniture. They had not then filled their rooms with spider-legged chairs and tables, nor crowded the latter with frail toys and china. Now that so many of these things are imported, now that the world is so full of people, — in the streets, cars, theatres, at receptions, — milady has found she must reef her sails. Breadth was the ambition of 1854 — length and slimness the supreme attainment of 1904. What would the modern belle look like, among all these skyscrapers, in a hoop? Like a ball — nothing more.

Finding herself with all this amplitude, milady of the fifties essayed gorgeous decoration. She had stretched a large canvas; she now covered it with pictures — bouquets and baskets of flowers appeared on the woollens for house dresses; on the fine gauzes and silks one might find excellent representations of the Lake of Geneva, with a distant view of the Swiss mountains.

When a lady ordered a costume for a ball, her flowers arrived in a box larger than the glazed boxes of to-day in which modistes send home our gowns. The garniture included a wreath for the hair, with bunches at the back from which depended trailing vines. The *bouquet de corsage* sometimes extended to each shoulder. Bouquets were fastened on gloves at the wrist, wreaths trailed down the skirt, wreaths looped the double skirt in festoons. Only one kind of flower was considered in good taste. Milady must look like a basket of shaded roses, or lilies, or pomegranates, or violets. Ropes of wax beads were sometimes substituted for flowers.

I once entered a milliner's shop — not my dear Madame Delarue's — and in the centre of the room, suspended by a wire from the ceiling, was one of these huge garnitures — all tied together and descending down to the floor. "This, Madame," I said, "is something very *recherché*?"

"Yes, Madame! That is the rarest parure I have. There was never one like it. There will never be another."

I scrutinized the flowers, and found nothing remarkable in any way.

"That, Madame," continued the milliner, "was purchased from me by the wife of Senator ——!

She wore it to Mrs. Gwin's ball, and returned it to me next day. I ask no pay! I keep it for the sake of Mrs. Senator ——, that I may have the honor of exhibiting it to my patrons."

There is no reason, because we sometimes choose to swing back into the ghastly close-fitted skirt, or to wrap ourselves like a Tanagra figurine, that we should despise a more spacious time. Nor is it at all beneath us to attach enough importance to dress to describe it. Witness the recent "Costumes of Two Centuries," by one of our most accomplished writers. Witness the teachings of a theologian eighteen hundred or more years ago, who condescended to illustrate his sermon by women's ways with dress! Says Tertullian: "Let simplicity be your white, charity your vermilion; dress your eyebrows with modesty, and your lips with reservedness. Let instruction be your ear-rings, and a ruby cross the front pin in your head; submission to your husband your best ornament. Employ your hands in housewifely duties, and keep your feet within your own doors. Let your garments be of the silk of probity, the fine linen of sanctity, and the purple of chastity."

"How does that impress you for a nineteenth-century costume?" I asked Agnes my bosom friend, to whom I read the passage aloud. "Well," she replied, "I should be perfectly willing to try the ruby hairpin as a beginning — and get Clagett to order the new brand of silk, which sounds as if it might be a very pure article indeed and warranted to wear well; but if you are seeking my honest opinion of Tertullian, I frankly confess that I think our clothes and our behavior to our husbands are none of his business."

Society letters of 1857 give us strictly accurate description of toilettes, which may interest some of my readers : [1] —

"The wealth of the present Cabinet, and their elegant style of living, sets the pace for Washington soirées — equal in magnificence to the gorgeous fêtes of Versailles.

"At the Postmaster-General's the regal ball room was lined with superb mirrors from floor to ceiling. In the drawing-rooms opposite the host, hostess, and daughter and Miss Nerissa Saunders occupied the post of receiving.

"Mrs. Brown was dressed in rose-colored brocade, with an exquisite resemblance of white lace stamped in white velvet, a point lace cape, and turban set with diamonds. Miss Brown wore a white silk tissue embroidered in moss rosebuds, a circlet of pearls on her hair, and natural flowers on her bosom. Lady Napier wore white brocaded satin, with head-dress of scarlet honeysuckle. Madame de Sartige's gown was of white embroidered crêpe, garnished with sprays of green. The wife of Senator Slidell was costumed in black velvet, trimmed with fur. Her head-dress was of crimson velvet, rich lace, and ostrich feathers. A superb bandeau of pearls bound her raven hair. Miss Nerissa Saunders was exquisite in a white silk, veiled with tulle, the skirts trimmed with rose-

---

[1] "Life in Washington, 1858–1859," by M. Windle.

colored quilling. Mrs. Senator Clay wore canary satin, covered all over with gorgeous point lace. Mrs. John J. Crittenden was superb in blue moire antique, with point lace trimmings. Mrs. General McQueen of South Carolina appeared in a white silk with cherry trimmings, her head-dress of large pearls fit for a queen. Mrs. Senator Gwin wore superb crimson moire antique with point lace, and a head-dress of feathers fastened with large diamonds. Mrs. Stephen A. Douglas, a white tulle dress over white silk — the overdress looped with bunches of violets and grass, similar bunches on breast and shoulder, and trailing in her low coiffure. Mrs. Senator Faulkner from Virginia was attired in blue silk and Mechlin lace, her daughters in white illusion. Mrs. Reverdy Johnson was superb in lemon satin and velvet pansies. Mrs. Pringle of Charleston wore a velvet robe of lemon color; Mrs. Judge Roosevelt of New York velvet and diamonds; Mrs. Senator Pugh of Ohio crimson velvet with ornaments of rubies and crimson pomegranate flowers."

This last lady, Mrs. Pugh, wife of the Senator from Ohio, was *par excellence* the beauty of the day. To see her in this dress was enough to "bid the rash gazer wipe his eye." Her eyes were large, dark, and most expressive. Her hair was dark, her coloring vivid. Mrs. Douglas, Mrs. Pugh, and Kate Chase were the three unapproached, unapproachable, beauties of the Buchanan administration. The daughter of Senator Chase was really too young to go to balls. She was extremely beautiful, "her complexion was marvellously delicate, her fine features seeming to be cut from fine bisque, her eyes, bright, soft, sweet, were of exquisite blue, and her hair a wonderful color like the ripe corn-tassel in full sunlight. Her teeth were perfect. Poets sang then, and still sing, of the turn of her beautiful neck and the regal carriage of her head." She was as intellectual as she was beautiful. From her teens she had been initiated into political questions for which her genius and her calm, thoughtful nature eminently fitted her. When she realized that neither party would nominate her father for President in 1860, she turned her energetic mind to the formation of plans and intrigues to obtain for him the nomination of 1868! She failed in that, she failed in everything, poor girl. She wrecked her life by a marriage with a wealthy, uncongenial governor of Rhode Island, from whom she fled with swift feet across the lawn of the beautiful home at Canonchet, and hand in hand with poverty and sorrow ended her life in obscurity.

It is going to be a long time before we again visit Vanity Fair; and lest it linger too delightfully in our memories, we must try to find some rift in the lute, some fly in the amber — not daring, however, to look beneath the surface.

And so we are fain to acknowledge that the evening gowns of these fair dames were liberal only in their skirts. The bodice was *décolleté* to the extremest limit — as I suppose it will always be. And then, as now,— as always,— there was no lack of wise men, usually youthful prophets, to preach against

it, to read for our instruction Solomon's disrespectful allusions to jewels in the ears of fair women
without discretion, and St. Paul's well-known remarks upon our foibles. "The idea of quoting
Solomon as an authority on women," said my
friend Agnes one day, as we walked from church.
" I *never* quote Solomon! He knew a good many
women without discretion, some hundreds of them;
but he didn't live up to his convictions, and he
changed his mind very often. He was to my thinking not at all a nice person to know."

"But how about St. Paul?" I ventured.

" I consider it very small in St. Paul to think
so much about dress anyway! One would suppose the thorn in his own flesh would have made
him tender toward others; and Timothy must have
been a poor creature to be taken in by 'braided hair,'
'gold and pearls, and costly array.' Now, of course,
we have a few of those things, and like to wear our
hair neatly; but I don't see why they are not suitable
for us so long as we don't live for them, nor seek to
entangle Timothy."

"Well," I replied, "I never can feel it is at all
my affair. I hear it often enough! But somehow
St. Simeon Stylites, preaching away on his pillar,
seems a great way off, and not to know the bearings
of all he talks about. We listen to him dutifully;
but I fancy if we amend our ways we will do it of
our own selves, and not because of St. Simeon."

" I wouldn't mind St. Simeon," said my irate friend
(she had worked herself up to a pitch of indignation);
" probably he was old and venerable, and to be tol-

erated; but it hurts me to be preached to by a young thing like that minister to-day, as if I were a Baby-lonish woman! We don't 'walk haughtily with stretched-forth necks, walking and mincing as we go, making a tinkling with our feet.' And as to our 'changeable suits of apparel,' and the 'crimping pins,' do we live for these things? Our maids make a living by taking care of them while we are at church hoping to hear of something better than crimping pins."

The lady who expressed these heretical sentiments was, as I have remarked, my most intimate friend; and although not older than herself, I considered it my duty to reason with her. "But you see, my dear Agnes," I said, "we are obliged to be on the side of our young preacher, whether we like it or not. He is the white-plumed champion riding forth from the courts of purity and beauty of behavior. We wouldn't like to be the sable knight who emerges from the opposite direction."

"I would!" declared my young rebel. "Infan-tile clergymen should keep to the sins of their own sex. Nobody criticises men's dress. They are ex-empt. They may surround their countenances with Henry VIII ruffs, which make them look like the head of John the Baptist on a charger, — nobody calls them ridiculous. They wear the briefest surf costumes — nobody says they are indecent."

"But, my dear — "

"But, my dear, I know all about the matter of evening dress. I've studied it up. It is a time-honored fashion (I can show you all about it in my

new encyclopædia). You remember I let you air
your learning and quote old Tertullian. Did I look
bored?"

"Not at all. You may tell me now. You can
finish before we get home."

"Well, then, the *décolleté* bodice is not a new
expression of total depravity. It is an old fashion,
appearing in 1280, with stomacher of jewels. It
reached England from Bohemia, but was then the
fashion in Italy, Poland, and Spain. Those times
were not conspicuous for sentiment, but were quite
as moral as the times of the Greek chiton, or the
Roman tunic, or the Norman robe, or the Saxon
gown."

"But," I interrupted, "it was out of fashion in
the high-necked days of Queen Elizabeth."

"Oh, she had her own reasons for disliking to
see a suggestive bare throat! Queen Bess was not
conspicuous for purity. Don't interrupt me — I'll
prove everything by the book — lots of good women
have worn low dresses. Madame Recamier was a
pretty good woman, and so were our grandmothers,
and so were the ladies of the Golden Age in Virginia
who reared the boys that won our independence."

"All of which proves nothing," I declared; but
we had reached our door on New York Avenue, and
went in for our Sunday dinner. My friend did not
inflict the encyclopædia. She had already quoted
it. What was the use? We may be sure of one
thing: no fashion has ever yet been discarded because it was abused. No Damascus blade has ever
been keen enough to lop off an offending fashion.

CHAPTER VI

THERE were many brilliant and beautiful women who escaped the notice of the society newsmonger of the day.

Mrs. Cyrus McCormick, recently married to the inventor of the great reaping machine, was one of these. Mr. McCormick, then a young man, was destined to be decorated by many European governments and to achieve a great fortune. His wife, just out of Miss Emma Willard's school, was very beautiful, very gentle, and winning. No sheaves garnered by her husband's famous reaper can compare with the sheaves from her own sowing, during a long life devoted to good deeds.

Then there were Mrs. Yulee, wife of the Senator from Florida, and her sisters, Mrs. Merrick and Mrs. Holt, all three noted for personal and intellectual charm ; and beautiful Mrs. Robert J. Walker, who was perhaps the first of the coterie to be called to make a sacrifice for her country, exchanging the brilliant life in Washington for the hardships of Kansas — "bleeding Kansas," torn with dissensions among its "squatter sovereigns," and with a climate of stern severity, where food froze at night and must be broken with a hatchet for breakfast. Mrs.

Walker shrank from the ordeal, for she was well
fitted for gay society; but the President himself
visited her and begged the sacrifice for the good of
the country.   She went, and bore her trials.   They
were only a little in advance of sterner trials or-
dained for some of her Washington friends.   Nor
must we fail to acknowledge the social influence of
Mrs. Jefferson Davis, one of the most brilliant
women of her time — greatly sought by cultivated
men and women.

But the wittiest and brightest of them all was
Mrs. Clay, the wife of the Senator from Alabama.
She was extremely clever, the soul of every company.   A costume ball at which she personated
Mrs. Partington is still remembered in Washington.
Mrs. Partington's sayings could not be arranged
beforehand and conned for the occasion.   Her mal-
apropos replies must be improvised on the moment,
and must moreover be seasoned with wit to redeem
them from commonplace dulness.   Mrs. Clay rose
to the occasion, and her Mrs. Partington became
the Mrs. Partington of the future.

The reader will not fail to observe the number
of Southern women who were prominent in Mr.
Buchanan's court.   A correspondent of a leading
New York paper[1] has recently written an interesting article on this subject.   He declares that the
Southern women (before Lincoln's day) had long
controlled the society of Washington.   " With their
natural and acquired graces, with their inherited
taste and ability in social affairs, it was natural that

---

[1] *New York Herald*, February 7, 1904.

the reins should fall to them.   They represented
a clique of aristocracy; they were recognized leaders
who could afford to smile good-naturedly at the
awkward and perplexed attempts of the women
from the other sections — Mrs. Senator This, Mrs.
Congressman That — to thread the ins and outs
of Washington's social labyrinth.   To none of
these ladies was the thought pleasant of secession
from the Union and consequent giving up whatever of social dominion she had acquired."

I wish I could give some idea of the "days at
home" of these court ladies in Washington in 1858.
The large public functions were all alike then as
now, with this exception, that nearly every man
present was Somebody, and every woman Somebody's wife.   It was not necessary for these people
to talk.   The men made little effort.   It was well
known what they had said yesterday in the House
or the Senate Chamber; but we dared not express
opinions in public (and not freely in private),
such was the tense feeling at that time.   Conversation had been always, at the South, an art carefully
cultivated.   Conversation suffered at a time when
we were forced to ignore subjects that possessed us
with absorbing interest and to confine ourselves to
trivialities.

Excusing the silence of one famous man, somebody remarked : " Oh, well, you know brilliant men
do not of necessity talk well.   Thrilled by their
utterances in their speeches and writings, we are
surprised, when we meet them, at their silence."
A " famous man's " eye twinkled.   " Ask Galt,"

he said, "why he doesn't give away his gems. Probably he might answer that he proposes to sell them," an ingenious way of avoiding the remotest hint that silence was the result of preoccupied thought on the grave questions of the hour.

For some inexplicable reason the wives of great men are apt to be quiet and non-committal — little moons revolving around a great luminary. Moon-like, one side only is turned to the world. How is it on the other side? We have a glimpse of it over the *demi-tasse* in the drawing-room after dinner, or at our informal "at homes" in our own houses.

At these times of unbending in Washington we were wont to begin in a rather stilted manner, sipping our coffee and liqueurs in a leisurely way, and steering widely clear of politics and politicians. We talked of art and artists, galleries in Europe, shops in Paris, — anything except what we were all thinking about. The art of conversation suffered under such circumstances. But some interesting books were just out in England, and everybody was discussing them. Thackeray had recently given "The Virginians" to the world. Tennyson was turning all the girls' heads with "Elaine." A new star was rising — George Eliot. Dickens, we were, at the moment, cordially hating because of his "American Notes." Bulwer was well to the fore. Two valued members of our own special coterie were Randolph Rogers and Thomas Crawford the sculptor, whose genius, differently expressed, lives to-day in his gifted son, Marion Crawford. Thomas

Crawford had been commissioned by the state of
Virginia to execute a colossal statue of Washington
for the Capitol Square in Richmond, a great work,
— including statues of Virginia's statesmen, — which
was happily completed in 1861, and from which I
heard Jefferson Davis's inaugural address, February 22,
1862, upon his taking the oath as permanent President of the Confederacy.   It was a black day of
rain and snow; the new government, destined never
to flourish in sunshine, was born in storm and
tempest.

Thomas Crawford, born in New York in 1814,
was now at the height of his fame.   He had studied
and worked with Thorwaldsen.   Apart from his
peculiar genius he was a charming companion, full
of versatile talk.   The younger man, Randolph
Rogers, was also most interesting.   He brought to
us his sketches and drawings for the bronze doors
of the Capitol before they were submitted to the
committee, and came again when they were accepted, to tell us of his good fortune.

The army and navy people were especially interesting.   They never discussed politics.   Their positions were assured and there were consequently no
feverish society strugglers among them.   They had
no vulgar respect for wealth, entertaining charmingly
within their means.   Admiral Porter and his family
were there, General Winfield Scott was there, the
admiral (then commander) forty-four years old, and
the noble old veteran nearer seventy-four.   Both
were delightful members of Washington society.
Nobody esteemed wealth or spoke of it or thought

MRS. CYRUS HALL McCORMICK.

From a portrait by Cabanel.

of it.   Office, position, talent, beauty, and charm
were the requisites for men and women.

On one day, I remember, I had gone the rounds
of Cabinet receptions, had taken my chocolate from
the generous urn of the Secretary of State, and
had dutifully looked in upon all the other Secre-
taries.   I knew a dear little lady, foreign, attached
to one of the legations (I really never knew whether
she was Russian or Hungarian), who had invited
me for the " end of the afternoon."   Her husband
had not a prominent place in the embassy, nor she
in society, but she knew how to gather around her
tea-kettle a choice little company, every one of whom
felt honored to be included.   I found her seated at
a small round table, and she welcomed me in the
English that gained from a musical voice, and the
deliberate enunciation of syllable which always seems
to me so complimentary and respectful in foreigners.

The fashion of the low tea-table had just been
introduced.   One could have tea, nothing else.
One could always find behind the silver urns " 'igh
and 'aughty " butlers serving chocolate, wine, and
every conceivable dainty at the houses of the great
Senators, Ministers, and Cabinet officers.   Things
were much more *distingué* at this lady's tea-table.
A few early spring flowers, crocuses, hyacinths, or
purple heather, were blooming here and there about
the room.   Our hostess was gowned in some white
stuff, and there was a bit of classic suggestion in
her attire, in the jewelled girdle, and an order or
medal tucked under a ribbon.   A little white-
capped maid welcomed and ushered us, and man-

aged to hover about for all the service we were likely to require. The impression grew upon me that all this had been done for me especially, and I found myself thinking how fortunate it was I had happened to come. That lovely woman would have been so sorely disappointed had I stayed away!

But presently other guests arrived. They were all foreigners, but perceiving the American presence they spoke only English. The hostess put into motion the most musical conversation. How has she done it? She has made no effort " to entertain." Conversation had come unbidden. Russian tea? Why, certainly! Do we ever care for other than Russian tea? She was deliberate. We forgot we were sorely pressed this day with seventeen names on our list. We gave ourselves up to the pleasure of observing her.

She lighted her silver lamp; and, although she wished us to see the great shining samovar which descended to her from her grandmother, she said it was good, very good indeed, in the camp or on journeys when one had only charcoal; but here in America the fairy lamp to light the wax taper and the alcohol burner beneath the kettle are best. She poured the water, which had bubbled, but not boiled (boiling water would make the tea flat), over delicious tea, paused a moment only, then poured the steaming amber upon two lumps of sugar, two slices of lemon, and one teaspoonful of rum, and we pronounced it a perfect cup of tea. But our enchantress said No, that some day ladies will grow tea in their own conservatories, and then only will it be perfect in this country; for the ocean voyage spoils the delicacy of the sensitive herb.

Glancing around the table, our hostess grasped the situation. Here was a Russian lady with a proud head, there two dark-eyed Bohemians, one Greek beauty, an English woman, and our own stiff, heavy, uncompromising American self!

She is to make these people happy for the five minutes they are around her little board. How does it come to pass that these strangers find a common ground upon which they can hold animated conversation?

They talked of genius and geniuses, — how they are not created by opportunity or culture, but are inspired; how that, apart from their gifts, they are quite like other people, not even cleverer always. "Yes," said the Greek girl, with an exalted look in her dark eyes, "they are chosen, like the prophets, to speak great words or compose immortal music, or build symphonies in stone; and what they do is outside themselves altogether." "It is literally true," said the Englishwoman, "that people have 'a gift' apart from their ordinary selves. Does not George Eliot say that his novels grow in him like a plant. No amount of work and study can create a genius!" And then everybody marvels at the wonderful young man (for nobody knows it is a woman) who has just written "Adam Bede" and "The Mill on the Floss."

Or perhaps the hostess has bribed some one of the foreign legation to come to her "at home." Novels on Washington life hint of such a possibility. Or

perhaps some prince of good talkers among our own
Ministers is home for a brief holiday, or returned
from a mission, and a circle gathers around him.

Our Minister, sent to France by Mr. Pierce, once
honored me by his presence and told us the following story. Everybody who remembers the genial
John Y. Mason will easily imagine how he told it,
and how his own magnetism possessed his listeners.
Not a tea-cup rattled during the narration. " I
lived," said Mr. Mason, " at a hotel for a few
weeks after receiving my appointment as Minister
Plenipotentiary — while my house was being made
ready to bring my family. The house was crowded,
and my landlord was forced to divide one of his
offices by a thin partition to receive me at all.

" One night I was awakened by a stifled sob on
the other side of the partition. Rising on my
elbow, I listened. The sob was repeated — then
I heard abusive language and oaths in English — I
fancied I heard a blow! Leaping to my feet, I
struck smartly on the partition, and all was still.

" The next morning I asked the clerk about my
neighbors and complained that they disturbed me.
He shrugged his shoulders and said, ' Mais, Monsieur! they are Americans!' as if that explained
everything. However, he informed me that they
had left the hotel that morning.

" A few days later I was sitting in my room at the
legation, when I received a visitor — a slender female
closely veiled, who said in a troubled whisper that
she had come to claim protection of the French
government. I told her I could not confer with

her while she was disguised, and she slowly raised her hand and held her veil aside. I never saw a lovelier face.

"She could not have been older than eighteen years. Her features were delicate, her eyes large and expressive, her brow shaded by golden-brown hair. She was deathly white. I never saw such pallor. 'What can I do for you, my child?' I asked. Well, it was a sad story. Married to a dissipated young fellow, away on her wedding journey; threatened, and in terror of losing her life. She wished the protection of the police. She said she should never have had the courage to ask it alone, but that she knew I had slept near her at the Maison Dorée. I had heard! I could understand. I was the American Minister, and I could help.

"'But think,' I said, 'I heard nothing but harsh language. We cannot go with this to the *préfet*. He will not consider it cause for action against your husband.'

"The girl hesitated. Finally, with a burst of tears, she unfastened her gown at the throat, turned it down, and disclosed the dark print of fingers on the delicate skin.

"It was enough. She had been choked into silence — this frail American girl — on the night when I heard the smothered sob.

"Of course you may imagine my zeal in her behalf. I had daughters of my own. I arranged to accompany the young wife at once to the office of the *préfet*, and having ascertained the address of her bankers I resolved to make arrangements to get her out of Paris in case she felt her life to be in danger.

"Well, I waited long at the office of the *préfet*. Finally our turn came. I rose and made my statement. Imagine my feelings when my fair client threw back her veil, and with a surprised look said:

"'I think the American Minister has been dreaming!'

"I felt as if a tub of ice-water had been poured over me. Of course my position was perfectly ridiculous. Before I could recover she had slipped through the crowd and was gone. While we waited she had changed her mind!"

"The wretch!" exclaimed one of the listeners. "That just proves that women are always attracted by brutality."

"Really?" said Mr. Mason.

"Not exactly, perhaps, but there was once an English countess who explained a divorce suit of one of her relatives thus: —

"'You see, Ermentrude was one of those women who needed kicking down the stairs, and Ferdinand was gentle; he was not up to it!'"

An agreeable function, no longer in vogue in this country, was the evening party. Lady Napier gave one of these parties to present her friends to Edward Everett.

These parties were arranged that pleasant people might meet distinguished strangers and each other. As this was the prime object of these occasions, there were no blatant bands to make conversation impossible, but there was no lack of delightful music.

Miss Nerissa Saunders played exquisitely upon the
harp; Mrs. Gales's niece, Juliana May, sang divinely; many young ladies had cultivated voices.
Nobody thought of hiring entertainment for guests.
The guests were bright talkers and could entertain
each other.   If a ball room were attached to the
salon, dancing was expected; but the parlors were
distant and people could talk!   Of course it is always stupid to collect a lot of dull people together,
but the wives of the brilliant men of Mr. Buchanan's
administration understood entertaining.   There were
always gifted conversationalists present who liked
talking better than eating, with cleverness enough
to draw out, and not forestall, the wit of others.
This art could not be claimed by the great talkers
of old English society, Johnson, Macaulay, Cole-
ridge, De Quincey, and the rest.   We should not now,
I am sure, care much for these monopolists.   Sheridan, for instance, must have been rather a quenching
element at an evening party; for in addition to his
own witty creations, he had a trick of preserving the
bon mots of others, leading conversation into chan-
nels where they would fit in, and using them accordingly.   Thus in talking with Sheridan his friends
had a dozen wits to cope with withal.

Our Washington hostesses always gave a supper
— not a fine supper — a *good* supper, where the old
family receipt book had been consulted, especially
if our hostess had come from Kentucky, Maryland,
or Virginia.   The canvasback ducks, terrapin, and
oysters were unlike Gautier's.   We all know that
rubies are now less rare in this country than good

cooks. We may essay the triumphs of the old Washington of the fifties, but beneath our own fig tree they become failures and shabby makeshifts. There are mysteries in cooking unattainable to any but the elect — and of the elect were the sable priestesses of the Washington kitchens.

CHAPTER VII

THE THIRTY-SIXTH CONGRESS

WHEN the famous Thirty-sixth Congress met for its long session, December 5, 1859, the whole country was in ferment over the execution of John Brown. "An indiscreet move in any direction," wrote ex-President Tyler from his plantation, "may produce results deeply to be deplored. I fear the debates in Congress, and above all the Speaker's election. If excitement prevails in Congress, it will add fuel to the flame which already burns so terrifically."[1] He, and all patriots, might well have been afraid of increased excitement. It was evident from the first hour that the atmosphere was heavily charged. The House resolved itself into a great debating society, in which the only questions were: "Is slavery right or wrong? Shall it, or shall it not, be allowed in the territories?" The foray of the zealot and fanatic aggravated the fury of the combatants.

The member from Mississippi—L. Q. C. Lamar (afterwards Supreme Court Justice of the United States) — threw an early firebrand by announcing on the floor of the House, "The Republicans are not guiltless of the blood of John Brown, his co-

---

[1] Rhodes's "History of the United States," Vol. II, p. 417.

conspirators, and the innocent victims of his ruthless vengeance." Lawrence Keitt of South Carolina declared: "The South asks nothing but its rights. I would have no more, but as God is my judge, I would shatter this republic from turret to foundation-stone before I would take a tittle less." Thaddeus Stevens of Pennsylvania retorted: "I do not blame gentlemen of the South for using this threat of rending God's creation from foundation to turret. They have tried it fifty times, and fifty times they have found weak and recreant tremblers in the North who have been affected by it, and who have acted from those intimidations." Such were a few, by comparison with those that rapidly followed, of the wild utterances of the hour. This occurred on the second day of the session. The House was in an uproar! Members from their seats crowded down into the aisles, and the clerk was powerless to preserve order. "A few more such scenes," said one, "and we shall hear the crack of the revolver and see the gleam of brandished blade."

In this spirit Congress proceeded to ballot for its Speaker, and balloted for two months (until February 1), before Mr. Sherman was abandoned (having withdrawn his name) and a compromise effected by the election of Mr. Pennington, who represented neither extreme of party.

During these two months everything was said that could be said to fan the flame. Hot disputes were accentuated by bitter personal remarks. One day a pistol accidentally fell from the pocket of a member from New York, and, thinking it had been drawn with the intention of using it, some of the members were wild with passion, crying excitedly for the sergeant-at-arms, and turning the House into a pandemonium.   John Sherman, who had been the unlucky bone of contention, made this remarkable statement: " When I came here I did not believe that the slavery question would come up; and but for the unfortunate affair of Brown at Harper's Ferry I do not believe that there would have been any feeling on the subject.   Northern men came here with kindly feelings, no man approving the foray of John Brown, and every man willing to say so, every man willing to admit it as an act of lawless violence."

Four years before this stormy election, Banks had been chosen Speaker after a contest longer by a few days than this.   Then, as now, slavery was the point at issue; but " good humor and courtesy had marked the previous contest where now were acrimony and defiance. . . .   Then threats of disunion were received with laughter; now they were too manifestly sincere to be treated lightly."   In four years the breach between North and South, once only a rift in the rock, had become a yawning chasm.   What might it not become in four years more?

Not foreseeing the rapid change of public sentiment, the Democrats had, four years before, selected Charleston for the meeting of the convention to name their candidate for the presidency.   Accordingly, on April 23, the party was convened in the " hotbed of disunion."

The Northern Democrats had heard much of the

splendor and elegance in which Charlestonians lived, and of the Arabian hospitality of the South, which could ignore all animosities over the bread and salt. But Charleston turned a cold shoulder to its guests from the North. All hearts, however, and all homes were opened to the Southerners. They dined with the aristocrats, drove with richly dressed ladies in gay equipages, and were entertained generally with lavish hospitality. All this tended to widen the breach between the sections.

When the delegates left their fair entertainers for the sessions of the convention, the ladies repaired to old St. Michael's Episcopal Church, where prayers, specially ordered for the success and prosperity of the South, were daily offered. "At the same time fervent abolition preachers at the North were praying for a disruption of the Charleston convention."

Judge Douglas had written a platform that was not acceptable to the South. After its adoption seven delegates from Southern states declared their purpose of secession. The convention, seeing that it was impossible to reach any result, adjourned May 3, to meet at Baltimore the 18th of June. The seceders resolved to meet at Richmond the second Monday of May. This initial movement awakened the alarm of at least one devoted son of the South. Alexander Stephens wrote to a friend : " The leaders intended from the beginning to rule or ruin. . . . Envy, hate, jealousy, spite — these made war in heaven, which made devils of angels, and the same passions will make devils of men. The Secession movement was instigated by nothing but bad pas-

sions. Patriotism, in my opinion, had no more to
do with it than love of God had with the other
revolt." [1] In conversation with his friend Johnston,
shortly after the adjournment of the Convention,
Stephens said, " Men will be cutting one another's
throats in a little while. In less than twelve months
we shall be in a war, and that the bloodiest in history.
Men seem to be utterly blinded to the future." [2]

The nomination of Lincoln and Hamlin on a
purely sectional platform aroused such excitement
all over the land, that the Senate and House of
Representatives gave themselves entirely to speeches
on the state of the country. Read at this late day,
many of them appear to be the high utterances of
patriots, pleading with each other for forbearance.
Others exhausted the vocabulary of coarse vituperation. " Nigger thief," " slave driver," were not
uncommon words. Others still, although less unre-
fined, were not less abusive. Newspapers no longer
reported a speech as calm, convincing, logical, or
eloquent,—these were tame expressions. The terms
now in use were : " a torrent of scathing denuncia-
tion," " withering sarcasm," " crushing invective,"
the orator's eyes, the while, " blazing with scorn and
indignation." Young members ignored the saluta-
tion of old Senators. Mr. Seward's smile after such
a rebuff was maddening ! No opportunity for scorn-
ful allusion was lost. My husband was probably
the first Congressman to wear " the gray," a suit of
domestic cloth having been presented to him by his

[1] " Life," by Johnston and Browne, p. 365.
[2] Rhodes's " History of the United States," Vol. II, p. 453.

H

constituents.   Immediately a Northern member said, in an address on the state of the country, " Virginia, instead of clothing herself in sheep's wool, had better don her appropriate garb of sackcloth and ashes." In pathetic contrast to these scenes were the rosy, cherubic little pages, in white blouses and cambric collars, who flitted to and fro, bearing, with smiling faces, dynamic notes and messages from one Representative to 'another.   They represented the future which these gentlemen were engaged in wrecking — for many of these boys were sons of Southern widows, who even now, under the most genial skies, led lives of anxiety and struggle.   Thoroughly alarmed, the women of Washington thronged the galleries of the House and the Senate Chamber.   From morning until the hour of adjournment we would sit, spellbound, as one after another drew the lurid picture of disunion and war.

Our social lines were now strictly drawn between North and South.   Names were dropped from visiting lists, occasions avoided on which we might expect to meet members of the party antagonistic to our own.   My friend Mrs. Douglas espoused all her husband's quarrels and distinctly " cut " his opponents.   There were very few boxes to be had at our little theatre — and the three best were usually secured by Mrs. Douglas, Miss Harriet Lane, and Mrs. John R. Thompson.   The feud between the President and Judge Douglas was bitter, and Mrs. Douglas never appeared at Miss Lane's receptions in the winter of 1859–1860.   One evening we were all in our theatre boxes, Miss Lane

next to us, and I the guest of Mrs. Douglas. Mr.
Porcher Miles, member from South Carolina, who
had opposed Judge Douglas's nomination, appeared
at the door of our box. Instantly Mrs. Douglas
turned and said, " Sir, you have made a mistake.
Your visit is intended for next door ! " " Madam,"
said Mr. Miles, " I presumed I might be permitted
to make my respects to Mrs. Pryor, for whom my
call was intended."   I had the benefit, of course, of
the private opinions of each, and was able to be
the friend of each.   " This, I suppose, is Southern
chivalry," said my fair friend.   " It savors, I think,
of ill-bred impertinence."   " I had supposed her a
lady," said Mr. Miles, " or at least a woman of the
world.   She behaved like a rustic — an *ingénue*."

I could but receive their confidences in silence,
perfectly well knowing that both were in the wrong.
Both were betrayed by the mad passions of the hour
— passions which caused older heads to misunder-
stand, mislead, and misbehave! " I am the most
unpopular man in the country," said Judge Douglas
(one of the presidential candidates) ; " I could walk
from Boston to Chicago by the light of my own
burning effigies, — and I guess you all know how
much Virginia loves me."

I had the good fortune to retain some of my
Northern friends.   The family of the Secretary of
State was loyal to me to the end.   When my husband was once embroiled in a violent quarrel, growing out of sectional feeling, General Cass sent his
granddaughter, pretty Lizzie Ledyard (my prime
favorite), with his love to bid me " take heart," that

"all would turn out right." Mrs. Douglas never
abated one jot of her gentle kindness, although she
knew we belonged to a party adverse to her husband.
Mrs. Horace Clarke's little brown ponies stopped
as often as ever at my door to secure me for a drive
down the avenue and a seat beside her in the House.
She had been a Miss Vanderbilt and was now wife
of a member from New York. All of them were
prompt to congratulate me upon my husband's
speech on "the state of the country," and to praise it
with generous words as "calm, free from vituperation,
eloquent in pleading for peace and forbearance."

The evening after this speech was delivered, we
were sitting in the library on the first floor of our
home, when there was a ring at the door-bell. The
servants were in a distant part of the house, and such
was our excited state that I ran to the door and answered the bell myself. It was snowing fast, a carriage stood at the door, and out of it bundled a mass
of shawls and woollen scarfs. On entering, a man-
servant commenced unwinding the bundle, which
proved to be the Secretary of State, General Cass!
We knew not what to think. He was seventy-seven
years old. Every night at nine o'clock it was the
custom of his daughter, Mrs. Canfield, to wrap him
in flannels and put him to bed. What had brought
him out at midnight? As soon as he entered, before
sitting down, he exclaimed : " Mr. Pryor, I have been
hearing about secession for a long time — and I would
not listen. But now I am frightened, sir, I am
frightened! Your speech in the House to-day gives
me some hope. Mr. Pryor! I crossed the Ohio

when I was sixteen years old with but a pittance in my pocket, and this glorious Union has made me what I am. I have risen from my bed, sir, to implore you to do what you can to avert the disasters which threaten our country with ruin."

Never was a spring more delightful than that of 1860. The Marine Band played every Saturday in the President's grounds, and thither the whole world repaired, to walk, or to sit in open carriages, and talk of everything except politics. Easy compliments to the ladies fell from the lips of the men who could apply to each other in debate abuse too painful to remember. Sometimes we would be invited for the afternoon to sit on the veranda of the White House — and who could fail to mark the ravages of anxiety and care upon the face of the President! All the more because he insistently repeated that he was never better — that he slept finely and enjoyed the best health. Nevertheless, if one chanced to stand silently near him in a quiet corner, he might be heard to mutter, "Not in my time — not in my time." Not in his time let this dear Union be severed, this dear country be drowned in blood.

On other afternoons we visited Mr. and Mrs. Robert E. Lee at Arlington, or drove out to Georgetown through the fragrant avenue of blossoming crab-apples, or to Mrs. Gales's delightful house for tea, returning in the soft moonlight. Everybody in Washington dined early. Congress usually adjourned at four o'clock, and my little boys were wont to be on the roof of our house, to watch for

the falling of the flag over the House of Representatives, the signal that we might soon have dinner.
The evening meal was late, usually handed.   It was
considered not "stylish" to serve it at a table.   A
servant would enter the drawing-room about eight
o'clock, with a tray holding plates and little doilies.
Another would bring in buttered biscuits and
chipped beef or ham, and a third tray held cups of
tea and coffee.   Some delicate sweet would follow.
Little tables of Chinese lacquer were placed between
two or more ladies, and lucky was the man who
would be invited to share one of them.   Otherwise
he must improvise a rest for his plate on his trembling knees.   "Take care!   Your plate will fall,"
I said to one.   "Fall!   I wish it would — and
break!   The only thing that worries me is when
the blamed thing takes to rolling.   Why, I have
chased plates all around the room until I thought
they were bewitched or held the secret of perpetual
motion!"   These suppers were very conversational,
and one did not mind their being so light.   There
would be punch and sandwiches at eleven.

Such were the pleasant happenings that filled our
days — clouded now by the perils which we could
not ignore after the warnings to which we listened at
the Capitol.   We were conscious of this always in
our round of visits, receptions, dinners, and balls,
with the light persiflage and compliments still in
our ears.

But when late evening came, the golden hour of
reunion in the library on the first floor of our home
was marked by graver talk.   There would assemble

R. M. T. Hunter, Musco Garnett, Porcher Miles, L. Q. C. Lamar, Boyce, Barksdale of Mississippi, Keitt of South Carolina, with perhaps some visitors from the South. Then Susan would light her fires and show us the kind of oysters that could please her " own white folks," and James would bring in lemons and hot water with some choice brand of old Kentucky.

These were not convivial gatherings. These men held troubled consultations on the state of the country — the real meaning and intent of the North, the half-trusted scheme of Judge Douglas to allow the territories to settle for themselves the vexed question of slavery within their borders, the true policy of the South. The dawn would find them again and again with but one conclusion — they would stand together: " Unum et commune periclum una salus ! "

But Holbein's spectre was already behind the door, and had marked his men ! In a few months the swift bullet for one enthusiast, for another (the least considered of them all), a glorious death on the walls of a hard-won rampart — he the first to raise his colors and the shout of victory; for only one, or two, or three, the doubtful boon of existence after the struggle was all over ; for *all* survivors, memories that made the next four years seem to be the sum of life — the only real life — beside which the coming years would be but a troubled dream.

The long session did not close until June, and in that month Abraham Lincoln was chosen candidate by the Republican party for the presidency, and

Stephen A. Douglas by the Democrats. The South had also a candidate, and hoping to make things better, the ruffled-shirt gentry — the Old-Line Whigs — had also named their man.

My little boys and I were glad to go home to Virginia. A season of perfect happiness awaited them, with their sisters and the dear old people whom they called grandfather and grandmother. Under the shade of the trees, and in the veranda covered with Lamarque roses, who could dream of war?

In the hot and bitter campaign that ensued we are told that "Douglas took the *unusual course* for a presidential candidate of visiting different parts of the country and discussing the political issues and their personal bearings. Speaking on all occasions, from the platform of the railroad car, the balcony of the hotel, at monster mass-meetings, he said much that was trivial and undignified, but he also said much that was patriotic, unselfish, and pregnant with constitutional wisdom. Coldly received at the South, where he was looked upon as a renegade, he aroused great enthusiasm at the North, and his personal presence was the only feature that gave any life to the struggle against the Republicans." [1]

The words "irrepressible conflict" were much in evidence during this campaign. Seward adopted them, and made speeches characterized as his "Irrepressible Conflict Speeches." [2] Seward reaffirmed almost everywhere the declaration of the "irrepressible conflict," and when challenged because of the

---

[1] Rhodes, Vol. II, p. 493.   [2] *Ibid.*, Vol. II, p. 495.

term, he "maintained that the Republicans simply reverted to the theory and practice of their fathers," giving no hint of a quotation.

The authorship of these words has always been credited to Mr. Seward. Their true origin may be found in the address of Mr. Lincoln, delivered at Cincinnati, Ohio, in September, 1859. On page 262 of the volume published by Follett, Foster, & Co. in 1860, entitled "Political Debates between Hon. Abraham Lincoln and Hon. Stephen A. Douglas," may be found the following extract from Mr. Lincoln's speech : —

"I have alluded in the beginning of these remarks to the fact that Judge Douglas has made great complaint of my having expressed the opinion that this Government 'cannot endure permanently half slave and half free.' He has complained of Seward for using different language, and declaring that there is an 'irrepressible conflict' between the principles of free and slave labor. [A voice : 'He says it is not original with Seward. That is original with Lincoln.'] I will attend to that immediately, sir. Since that time, Hickman of Pennsylvania expressed the same sentiment. He has never denounced Mr. Hickman ; why ? There is a little chance, notwithstanding that opinion in the mouth of Hickman, that he may yet be a Douglas man. That is the difference ! It is not unpatriotic to hold that opinion, if a man is a Douglas man.

"But neither I, nor Seward, nor Hickman is entitled to the enviable or unenviable distinction of having first expressed that idea. That same idea was expressed by the *Richmond Enquirer* in Virginia, in 1856, quite two years before it was expressed by the first of us. And while Douglas was pluming himself that in his conflict with my humble self, last year, he had 'squelched out' that fatal heresy, as he delighted to call it, and had suggested that if he only had had a chance to be in New York and meet Seward he would have 'squelched' it there also, it never occurred to him to breathe a word against Pryor. I don't think that you can discover that Douglas ever talked of going to Virginia to 'squelch' out that idea there. No. More than that. That same Roger A. Pryor was brought to Washington City and made the editor of the *par excellence* Douglas paper, after making use of that expression, which in us is so unpatriotic and heretical."

Before we returned to Washington Mr. Lincoln was elected President of the United States.

CHAPTER VIII

MEMORABLE DAYS IN THE HISTORY OF THE COUNTRY

A MOMENTOUS day in the history of this country was November 6, 1860 — on that day the extreme party of the North elected its candidate, with a Vice-President, making the Executive purely sectional. But few people expected the fulfilment of the evils so insistently threatened as a consequence of this election.

Not for one moment had we seriously entertained the thought of secession. The question of slavery in the territories was still unsettled, and the stormy scenes in the House might possibly be reënacted. Like General Cass, we had heard all our lives rumors of possible secession, possible war. Nobody believed these rumors — any more than we believed that every threatening cloud would burst in a devastating tempest. It was part of the routine, "the order of the day," to enliven things by warm discussions and spicy personalities.

My husband had been unanimously reëlected, and our delightful Washington life was assured to us — certainly for three winters — probably for all time.

We were so deeply concerned about the state of the country at large, that his election excited us but little. When the polls closed at sunset, one of his political friends came to me and said there would be a torch-light procession in his honor, that the crowd would call at his residence, and the house must be illuminated. "Illuminated!" I exclaimed. "Impossible! There are not half a dozen candles in the house, and the stores are all closed. Besides, the babies will be asleep. It is bad for babies to be roused from their first sleep."

My friend seemed to appreciate this reasoning; but later in the evening I received a bushel of small white turnips and a box of candles, with a pencilled note saying that I must cut holes in the vegetables, and I would find them admirable candlesticks. The little boys and servants went to work with a will, and when the drum announced the near approach of the cavalcade, every window was blazing with a double row of lights, one row on the window-sill, the other midway, on the top of the lower sash.

My young Congressman was considered a brilliant speaker, and his talents were sometimes called into use in Washington. Some matter of municipal interest was supported by him, and another torch-light procession gathered late one night around the door of the house on New York Avenue.

"You are not to listen," he said to me, as he descended to the front door to speak to the crowd; "I shall say a few words only." I threw a shawl over my night-dress and crouched down in a little balcony just over his head. To my prejudiced mind, his speech was the most graceful and charming thing I had ever heard. I was in a delightful trance of happiness when he closed, and was rudely awakened when, in response to shouts of " Go on, go on, we could listen all night," the daring young orator deliberately turned and pointed to the balcony above him: " Go on, my friends? Go on, exposed to the criticism of one from whose criticism I am always trying to escape? "

I fell back out of sight on the floor. I never listened afterward!

And among the pleasant happenings of these golden days, so soon to be shut in by darkness and sorrow, was the presentation to my young Congressman of a beautiful service of silver from his Democratic friends of Virginia in recognition of " brilliant talents, eminent worth, and distinguished services."

Mr. Galt made this splendid service, and I record it here because it became part of the history of the next years of trouble. I should have lost it once (in a dark hour), but Mr. Galt bade me keep it — that brighter days were in store for me and mine, a prophecy which he lived to see fulfilled.

We were all in our places in November, setting our houses in order, several weeks before the assembling of Congress. We were warmly welcomed into our pleasant home by Susan, whose authority, now fully established and recognized, kept us in perfect order. Everything promised a season of unusual interest. We now knew everybody — and what is more I, for one, liked everybody. It takes so little to make a woman happy!

In Washington our social life did not begin

before New Year's Day. Among our first cards
this winter was an invitation to the marriage of
Mr. Bouligny, member from Louisiana, and Miss
Parker, daughter of a wealthy Washington grocer.
Rumors reached us of unusual plans for this wedding. Mr. Parker's large house was to be converted
into a conservatory filled with blossoming roses
and lilies. Fountains were to be introduced, new
effects in lighting. The presents were to be magnificent, the bridal dress gorgeous.

Upon arriving at the house (I think it was an
afternoon wedding) I found the President seated in
an arm-chair at one end of the drawing-room, and
the guests ranging themselves on either side. A
crimson velvet curtain was stretched across the other
end of the room. Presently the curtain parted, and
the bridal tableau appeared in position behind it.
After the ceremony the crowd waited until the
President went forward to wish the bride and her
husband "a great deal of happiness." Everybody
remained standing until Mr. Buchanan returned to
his seat. I stood behind his chair and observed that
he had aged much since the summer.

He had had much to bear. Unable to please
either party, he had been accused of cowardice,
imbecility, and even insanity, by both parties.
"The President is pale with fear," said General
Cass. "He divides his time equally between praying and crying. Such an imbecile was never seen
before," said another. A double-leaded editorial in
the *New York Tribune* of December 17 suggested
that he might be insane. On the day of the wed-

ding, December 20, he stoutly denied that he was ill. " I never enjoyed better health nor a more tranquil spirit," said the hard-pressed President. " I have not lost an hour's sleep nor a single meal. I weigh well and prayerfully what course I ought to adopt," he had written on that day.

The crowd in the Parker drawing-room soon thinned as the guests found their way to the rooms in which the presents were displayed. The President kept his seat, and I stood behind him as one and another came forward to greet him. Presently he looked over his shoulder and said, " Madam, do you suppose the house is on fire?   I hear an unusual commotion in the hall."

" I will inquire the cause, Mr. President," I said. I went out at the nearest door, and there in the entrance hall I found Mr. Lawrence Keitt, member from South Carolina, leaping in the air, shaking a paper over his head, and exclaiming, " Thank God! Oh, thank God! " I took hold of him and said : " Mr. Keitt, are you crazy ?   The President hears you, and wants to know what's the matter."

" Oh! " he cried, " South Carolina has seceded! Here's the telegram.   I feel like a boy let out from school."

I returned and, bending over Mr. Buchanan's chair, said in a low voice : " It appears, Mr. President, that South Carolina has seceded from the Union.   Mr. Keitt has a telegram." He looked at me, stunned for a moment.   Falling back and grasping the arms of his chair, he whispered, " Madam, might I beg you to have my carriage called?" I met his secretary and sent him in without explanation, and myself saw that his carriage was at the door before I reëntered the room. I then found my husband, who was already cornered with Mr. Keitt, and we called our own carriage and drove to Judge Douglas's. There was no more thought of bride, bridegroom, wedding cake, or wedding breakfast.

This was the tremendous event which was to change all our lives — to give us poverty for riches, mutilation and wounds for strength and health, obscurity and degradation for honor and distinction, exile and loneliness for inherited homes and friends, pain and death for happiness and life.

The news was not known, except in official circles, until the evening. The night was dark. A drizzling rain was falling; the streets were almost impassable from mud.

At the house of a prominent South Carolina gentleman a crowd soon collected. The street was full of carriages, the house brilliantly lighted.

Admiral Porter, then a lieutenant, had heard the startling news, and called at this house to tell it. He found the mistress of the mansion descending in cloak and bonnet, and as soon as she saw him she exclaimed: "Oh, Captain, you are just the man I want. I'm going to the White House to tell the President some good news. The horses are sick and I'm going to walk over." [1]

"It is impossible for you to walk through the rain and mud," said the Lieutenant. "There are

[1] "Anecdotes and Incidents of the Civil War," Porter.

ten or twelve hacks at the door, and I will press one into your service." So saying, he called a carriage and helped her to enter it, getting in after her.

"I was under the impression," he said, as they started, "that you were having a party at your house, it was so brilliantly lighted up, and I thought I would venture in uninvited."

"No, indeed," she replied; "but we have received glorious news from the South, and my husband's friends are calling to congratulate him. South Carolina has seceded, and, oh, Captain, we will have a glorious monarchy, and you must join us."

"And be made Duke of Benedict Arnold?"

"Nonsense!" she exclaimed, "we will make you an admiral."

"Certainly," said Lieutenant Porter, "Admiral of the Blue. For I should feel blue enough to see everything turned upside down, and our boasted liberty and civilization whistled down the wind."

"What would you have?" she inquired. "Would you have us tamely submit to all the indignities the North puts upon us, and place our necks under their feet? Why, this very day my blood boiled while I was in Congress, and I could scarcely contain myself. An old black Republican was berating the Southern people as if they were a pack of naughty children. However, Mr. Rhett took the floor and gave the man such a castigation that he slunk away and was no more heard from."

Just then they reached the White House. "Come in," said the lady, "and hear me tell the President the good news."

I

Lieutenant Porter preferred returning to her house. There he found a crowd around a generous bowl of punch. When he had an opportunity, he asked the host if he thought it possible the Southern states would secede. "What more do they want?" he inquired. "They have a majority in the Senate and the House, and, with the Supreme Court on their side, they could make laws to suit themselves."

"True," his host replied, "most people would be satisfied with that. 'Better to bear the ills we have than fly to others that we know not of.' But *you* will join us? *You must!* We will have a navy to be proud of, and we'll make you admiral."

"There's one comfort," said an old society dame who now joined the party. "South Carolina is a fickle young thing and may change her mind! She declared herself ready once before to walk out, — you all remember it, — and changed her mind. She took off her things and concluded to stay a little longer."

"She has gone for good and all this time, depend upon it," said the host. "She was only giving warning then! Her time is up now and she is off."

Meanwhile the lady of the house was telling the President news that was no news to him. He was fully prepared to receive it calmly and gravely. I had preceded her by some hours.

Lieutenant Porter little dreamed of the good fortune the secession of South Carolina would bring to him. From a poor lieutenant with anxious cares about a large family, he was speedily raised by Mr.

Lincoln to the proud position of rear-admiral of the United States.

His own comment upon the enthusiasm of his Southern friends is amusing. He declared that if the capital and its surroundings had been less stupid, that if those vivacious Southerners could have had a court, theatres, and opera-houses, the catastrophe which overwhelmed North and South might have been prevented. "The Romans understood these things better than we. They omitted nothing to keep the people amused; they even had the street fountains at times run with wine, and the investment was worth the money spent." "But what," said Admiral Porter, "could one expect at a court presided over by an old bachelor whose heart was dead to poetry and love; who sat at dinner with no flowers to grace the festive board, and never even had a *boutonnière* on his coat lapel?" which was one way, at least, of accounting for things.

Of course, we all paid our respects to the President on the next New Year's Day, and joined the motley crowd of men and women of every degree who were admitted after the starred and beribboned dignitaries from foreign lands had been received. "Here I am, Mr. President," said one of the witty Southern women, "and my cook will be here in a few minutes! I left her dressing to come."

The day that ushered in the eventful year 1861 was gloomy out of doors, but within the Executive Mansion flowers, music, gay attire, and bright smiles ruled the hour. " I wish you a happy New Year, Mr. President," fell from every lip, but in every heart there was a gloomy foreboding of impending disaster. What would the year bring to the "wayward sister," whose sons had all gone home? How we missed them! — Mr. Porcher Miles, Mr. Boyce, Mr. and Mrs. Keitt, always so delightful a part of our Washington social life. Some of us might expect to return; but this was adieu, not *au revoir*, to our President. This was his last New Year's Day in the White House, not his last day of perplexity and trouble. Very soon more wayward sisters would depart, and the hour he had dreaded would " come in his time."

There is no time at the President's New Year's reception to gather in corners for private talk. We must hurry on our rounds to the houses of the Cabinet and of the foreign Ministers. Sending the gentlemen of our party forward to visit the Senators' wives, we hastened home to our own punch-bowl.

I brewed a mighty bowl that last New Year's Day. Dr. Garnett and Judge Scarborough presided over the mixing, to be sure that the arrack was proportioned rightly, and that there were just as many and no more toasted crab-apples than there should be. I was assisted by my friend Agnes, whom I love to quote, and whose full name I should like to give, except for the reason that she is now living, and, being a respectable lady of the old school, is averse from seeing her name in print. In the society journal occasionally, apropos of the opera or reception, perhaps, but in a book! I should never be forgiven.

Late in the afternoon my rooms were thronged —
with Virginians and Southerners mainly, but with
some Northern friends as well, for Virginia was not
yet classed.   Like Touchstone, I was "in a parlous
state," lest some of my guests who had already honored many punch-bowls should venture on forbidden
subjects.   More than one came in on the arm of
James, but it took a better man than James to conduct him out again and into his carriage.   My
friend who had distinguished himself at my first
President's dinner was in high feather, as were some
grave judges I knew.

There was but one thought in every mind, gay
or sober.   " Is this a meeting of the Girondists?"
queried one.

> "When shall we three meet again ? "

quoted another.

> "When the hurly-burly's done —
> When the battle's lost and won,"

was the prompt answer.   "Sh-h-h!" said an old
army officer.   "It is not lucky to talk of lost battles
on New Year's Day, nor of Girondists' feasts on the
eve of a revolution."

The season which was always ushered in on New
Year's Day resolved itself literally this year into a
residence in the galleries of the Senate Chamber and
the House of Representatives.

Before the 1st of February, Mississippi, Florida,
Alabama, Georgia, Louisiana, and Texas had dis-
solved their bonds with the Federal Union.   The

farewell addresses of the Representatives of the seceded states became the regular order of the day.
Jefferson Davis's final farewell closed with these
solemn words: " May God have us in His holy
keeping, and grant that, before it is too late, peaceful counsels may prevail."

Virginia, had she retained her original colonial
bounds, could have dictated to the rest. Now,
should she elect to join the Southern Confederacy,
the states she had given to the Union — her own
children — would be arrayed against her.

Virginia now essayed to arbitrate. Her Peace
Commission met in Washington, but without result,
except that it was for her a fleeting moment of
enthusiasm.

Mr. Kellogg of Illinois said: " She has thrown
herself into the breach to turn aside the tide of disunion and revolution, and she says to the nation, ' Be
united and be brothers again.' God bless the Old
Dominion!" Said Mr. Bigler of Pennsylvania, January 21: "Pennsylvania will *never* become the enemy of Virginia! Pennsylvania will never draw the
sword on Virginia."

Apprehension was felt lest the new President's
inaugural might be the occasion of rioting, if not
of violence. We were advised to send our women
and children out of the city. Hastily packing my
personal and household belongings to be sent after
me, I took my little boys, with their faithful nurse,
Eliza Page, on board the steamer to Acquia Creek,
and, standing on deck as long as I could see the
dome of the Capitol, commenced my journey home-

ward.   My husband remained behind, and kept his
seat in Congress until Mr. Lincoln's inauguration.
He described that mournful day to me — differing
so widely from the happy installation of Mr. Pierce.
" O'er all there hung a shadow and a fear."   Every
one was oppressed by it, and no one more than the
doomed President himself.

We were reunited a few weeks afterward at our
father's house in Petersburg; and in a short time
my young Congressman had become my young
colonel — and Congressman as well, for as soon
as Virginia seceded he was elected to the Provisional
Congress of the Confederate States of America, and
was commissioned colonel by Governor Letcher.

I am afraid the evening is at hand, when we must
bid adieu to the bright days — the balls, the merry
hair-dresser, the round of visits, the levees, the charming " at homes."   The setting sun of such a day
should pillow itself on golden clouds, bright har-
bingers of a morning of beauty and happiness.
Alas, alas! " whom the gods destroy they first
infatuate."

CHAPTER IX

RAPID PROGRESS OF EVENTS AT THE SOUTH

WHEN it was disclosed that a majority of the Virginia Convention opposed taking the state out of the Union, the secessionists became greatly alarmed; for they knew that without the border states, of which Virginia was the leader, the cotton states would be speedily crushed. They were positively certain, however, that, in the event of actual hostilities, Virginia would unite with her Southern associates. Accordingly, it was determined to bring a popular pressure to bear upon the government at Montgomery to make an assault on Fort Sumter. To that end my husband went to Charleston, and delivered to an immense and enthusiastic audience, a most impassioned and vehement speech, urging the Southern troops to " strike a blow," and assuring them that in case of conflict, Virginia would secede " within an hour by Shrewsbury clock." The blow was struck; Mr. Lincoln called upon Virginia for a quota of troops to subdue the rebellion, and the state immediately passed an ordinance of secession.

Mr. Pryor, with other gentlemen, was deputed by General Beauregard to demand the surrender of the fort, and in case of the refusal which he foresaw, to direct the commandant of battery, Johnson, to open fire. When the order was delivered to the commandant, he invited my husband to fire the first shot; but this honor my husband declined, and instead suggested the venerable Edmund Ruffin, an intense secessionist, for that service. It was the prevalent impression at the time, that Mr. Ruffin did "fire the first gun"; at all events he fired, to him, the last; for on hearing of Lee's surrender, Cato-like, he destroyed himself.

I have often wondered what would have been the effect upon the fortunes of our own family, had my husband fired the shot that ushered in the war. Even had his life been spared, he certainly would not have become an eminent lawyer in the state of New York and a justice of its Supreme Court.

Fort Sumter was reduced on April 12, and Virginia was in a wild state of excitement and confusion.

The deputation sent to Washington in the interests of peace had failed in its mission. The Convention of 1861 was in session at Richmond as early as April 11 — sitting with closed doors. The people were wrought to the highest pitch of anxiety lest the conservative spirit of the older men should triumph and should lead them to prefer submission, which would mean dishonor, to secession, which could mean nothing worse than death.

Business was practically suspended in Richmond and Petersburg; men crowded the streets to learn the latest news from the North, and were inflamed by reports of the arrest and incarceration in Fort

Lafayette of Southern sympathizers.   As crowds gathered in different localities the advocates of secession addressed them in impassioned speeches which met with hearty response from the people.

On April 16, a body, calling itself the Spontaneous People's Convention, met and organized in the Metropolitan Hall at Richmond.   The door was kept by a guard with a drawn sword in his hand.   David Chalmers of Halifax County was president, and Willoughby Newton, vice-president.

Patrick Henry Aylett, grandson of Patrick Henry, made a noble speech, urging moderation and delay; warmer speeches followed.   A Southern flag was raised on the capitol amid shouts of applause, but at midnight the governor had it removed, for the convention had not yet passed the ordinance of secession, and those who rose with the dawn of the next eventful day found the state flag calmly floating in its place.

I was a guest of the government house at this time, and in the calm and seclusion of Mrs. Letcher's rooms I missed much of the excitement.   She was a motherly, domestic woman, who chose to ignore outside disturbances for the sake of present peace. We talked together of family matters, as we sewed upon little gowns and pinafores, indulged in reminiscences of the Washington life which we had enjoyed together, and said very little of the troubles of the hour.   Mrs. Letcher thought the political storm must pass.   It was hard to bear; the governor was nervous and sleeping badly, but quiet would surely come, and when it did — why, then,

we would all go down to Old Point Comfort for
June, bathe in the sea, and get strong and well.
As for fighting — it would never come to that!

On the memorable day of the 17th the "Spontaneous Convention" again met to discuss a new
political organization of the state. While they
argued and struggled, Lieutenant-Governor Mon-
tague entered the hall with momentous news. An
ordinance of secession had been passed by the
State Convention. This announcement was followed by a thrilling moment of silence succeeded
by tears of gladness and deafening shouts of applause.
The venerable ex-President Tyler made a stirring
address. He gave a brief history of the struggles of
the English race from the days of the Magna Charta
to the present time, and solemnly declared that at
no period of the history of our race had we ever
been engaged in a more just and holy effort for the
maintenance of liberty and independence than at the
present moment. The career of the dominant party
at the North was but a series of aggressions which
fully warranted our eternal separation; and if we
performed our duty as Christian patriots, the same
God who favored the cause of our forefathers in the
Revolution of 1776 would crown our efforts with
success. Generations yet unborn would bless those
who had the high privilege of participating in the
present struggle. A passionate speech followed from
ex-Governor Wise. He alluded to a rumor that
one of his children had been seized and held as hostage at the North. "But," he said, "if they suppose hostages of my own heart's blood will stay my

hand in the maintenance of sacred rights, they are mistaken. Affection for kindred, property, and life itself sink into insignificance in comparison with the overwhelming importance of public duty in such a crisis as this. Virginia is smitten with blindness, in that she does not at once seize Washington before the Republican hordes get possession of it." The Hon. J. M. Mason and others followed in the same strain. Governor Letcher appeared, and pledged himself to discharge his whole duty as executive of the state in conformity with the will of the people and the provisions of the constitution. The ordinance could not become a law until it was ratified by the people — and they would be called to vote upon it on May 23. "Not until then," said an ex-Congressman," will those fellows in Washington know we are Secessionists!" "*Never* as Secessionists!" said another; "I detest the word. We are revolutionists, — rebels, as our fathers were." "But perhaps," ventured one of the old Washington coterie, to Mr. Hunter, "perhaps the people will not vote us out of the Union after all." "My dear lady," said the ex-Senator, proudly, "you may place your little hand against Niagara with more certainty of staying the torrent than you can oppose this movement. It was written long ago in the everlasting stars that the South would be driven out of the Union by the North."

The fate of Virginia had been decided April 15, when President Lincoln demanded troops for the subjugation of the seceding states of the South. The temper of Governor Letcher of Virginia was precisely in accord with the spirit that prompted Governor Magoffin of Kentucky to answer to a similar call for state militia: "Kentucky will furnish no troops for the wicked purpose of subduing her sister Southern states!" Until this call of the President, Virginia had been extremely averse from secession, and even though she deemed it within her rights to leave the Union, she did not wish to pledge herself to join the Confederate States of the South. Virginia was the Virginian's Country. The common people were wont to speak of her as "The Old Mother." "The mother of us all," a mother so honored and loved that her brood of children must be noble and true.

Her sons had never forgotten her! She had fought nobly in the Revolution and had afterward surrendered, for the common good, her magnificent territory. Had she retained this vast dominion, she could now have dictated to all the other states. She gave it up from a pure spirit of patriotism — that there might be the fraternity which could not exist without equality, — and in surrendering it, she had reserved for herself the right to withdraw from the Confederation whenever she should deem it expedient for her own welfare. There were leading spirits who thought the hour had come when she might demand her right. She was not on a plane with the other states of the Union. "Virginia, New York, and Massachusetts had expressly reserved the right to withdraw from the Union, and explicitly disclaimed the right or power to bind the hands of posterity by any form of government whatever."

And so the question of the hour with Virginia was not the right to introduce slavery into the territories. Nothing was said or thought about slavery. The question was of states' rights only.

One need but go back to the original treaties with France and England in 1778 and 1783, to understand the origin and root of this feeling with the Virginians of 1861. France had made her treaty of perpetual alliance with the "Thirteen United Colonies," naming each one separately as one of the contracting parties. The king of England had named each one separately to be "free, sovereign and independent states" and "that he treated with them as such."

Said old John Janney, a Union man and president of the Convention of 1861, when taxed with having taken sides with Virginia against the Union, "Virginia, sir, was a nation one hundred and eighty years before your Union was born."

Another strong party was the "Union Party," sternly resolved against secession, willing to run the risks of fighting within the Union for the rights of the state. This spirit was so strong, that any hint of secession had been met with angry defiance. A Presbyterian clergyman had ventured, in his morning sermon, a hint that Virginia might need her sons for defence, when a gray-haired elder left the church and, turning at the door, shouted "Traitor!" This was in Petersburg, the birthplace of General Winfield Scott.

And still another party was the enthusiastic secession party, resolved upon resistance to coercion; the men who could believe nothing good of the North, should interests of that section conflict with those of the South; who cherished the bitterest resentments for all the sneers and insults in Congress; who, like the others, adored their own state and were ready and willing to die in her defence. Strange to say, this was the predominating spirit all through the country, in rural districts as well as in the small towns and the larger cities. It seemed to be born all at once in every breast as soon as Lincoln demanded the soldiers.

The "overt act" for which everybody looked had been really the reënforcement by Federal troops of the fort in Charleston Harbor. When Fort Sumter was reduced by Beauregard, "the fight was on."

On May 23 Virginia ratified an ordinance of secession, and on the early morning of May 24 the Federal soldiers, under General Winfield Scott,[1] crossed the Potomac River and occupied Arlington Heights and the city of Alexandria. "The invasion of Virginia, the pollution of her sacred soil as it was termed, called forth a vigorous proclamation from her governor and a cry of rage from her press." General Beauregard issued a fierce proclamation, tending to fire the hearts of the Virginians with anger. "A reckless and unprincipled host," he declared, "has invaded your soil," etc., etc.

General Scott, our father's groomsman, was knocking at the doors of the "fair ladies" he loved, with the menace of torch and sword.

[1] Rhodes, Vol. III, p. 435.

And now there was a mighty gathering of the sons of " The Old Mother !" She raised her standard, " *Sic semper tyrannis*," and from every quarter of the globe they rallied to her defence, not scurrying home for shelter from the storm, but coming to place their own breasts between her and the blast, — descendants of men who had won freedom in 1776, of Light Horse Harry Lee, of Peter Johnson, Ensign of the Legion, — Robert E. Lee, Joseph E. Johnston, Thomas Jackson, " Jeb " Stuart, A. P. Hill, Musco Garnett, Roger A. Pryor, Austin Smith from far San Francisco, Dr. Garnett from Washington, Bradfute Warwick from Naples, Powhatan Clark from Louisiana, Judge Scarborough from the Court of Claims at Washington, Judge Campbell, Associate Justice of the Supreme Court at Washington, and multitudes of others ! " The very earth trembled at the tramp of the Virginians as they marched to the assize of arms of the Mother of them all. From every continent, from every clime, from all avocations, from the bar, the pulpit, the counting-room, the workshop, the Virginians came.

> " ' Theirs not to reason why,
> Theirs but to do and die ! ' " [1]

Among them was a descendant of old Sir Humphrey Gilbert, — him of the sinking ship on his way to Virginia, — who cried as he went down : " Be of good cheer, my friends ! It is as near heaven by sea as by land."

[1] " Life of Joseph E. Johnston," by General Bradley Johnson, p. 32.

And among them were some who quoted old Sir George Somers of the *Sea Venture*, who drew around him his crew and exhorted them to " be true to duty and to return to Virginia."

General Bradley Johnson says these words of the old knight rang like a trumpet all over the country in the early days of the war wherever there was a Virginian. " Be true to duty and return to Virginia ! " And few, very few, failed to obey the call.

It is well known that General Lee did not approve the hasty, ill-considered action of the early seceders from the Union. He foresaw the perils and doubtful results of such action. He knew that war — as my own husband had so earnestly said in Congress — " meant widows and orphans, the punishment of the innocent, the ruin of the fortunes of all." Still, the " Old Mother " had been forced to accept it at the hands of others. The simple question was : " With or against blood and kin ? For or against the Old Mother ? " And the question answered itself in the asking.

I am sure that no soldier enlisted under Virginia's banner could possibly be more determined than the young women of the state. They were uncompromising.

" You promised me my answer to-night," said a fine young fellow, who had not yet enlisted, to his sweetheart.

" Well, you can't have it, Ben, until you have fought the Yankees," said pretty Helen.

" What heart will I have for fighting if you give me no promise ? "

K

"I'll not be engaged to any man until he has fought the Yankees," said Helen, firmly. "You distinguish yourself in the war, and then see what I'll have to say to you."

This was the stand they took in Richmond and Petersburg. Engagements were postponed until they could find of what mettle a lover was.

"But suppose I don't come back at all!" suggested Ben.

"Oh, then I'll acknowledge an engagement and be good to your mother, — and wear mourning all the same — *provided* — your wounds are all in front."

A few days before the vote was taken upon the ordinance of secession we had a fine fright in Richmond. An alarm was rung in the Capitol Square, and thousands of people filled the streets to learn the cause of its warning. Presently notices were posted all over the city that the *Pawnee* — a war-ship of the United States — was steaming up the James River with the purpose of shelling the mansions on the banks, and of finally firing on Richmond. We had friends living in those fine colonial mansions all along the river, — at Claremont, Upper and Lower Brandon, Shirley, Westover, — dear old ladies who were unprotected, and would be frightened to death. For ourselves in Richmond and Petersburg there would be no personal danger, we could escape; but our mills and shipping would be destroyed.

I think I am within the bounds of truth when I say that every man and boy capable of bearing gun or pistol marched with the soldiers and artillery down to the riverside, determined to defend the city. There they waited until the evening, the howitzers firing from time to time to forewarn the war-ship of their presence.

A little after sunset the crowd turned its face homeward. News had been received that the *Pawnee* had steamed up the river a short distance, had thought better of it, and had turned around and gone back to her mooring. All the same one thing was certain, the war-ship " bristling with guns " was there. She *could* steam up the river any night, and probably would when it pleased her so to do.

When I returned to my father's home in Petersburg, I found my friends possessed with an intense spirit of patriotism. The First, Second, and Third Virginia were already mustered into service; my husband was colonel of the Third Virginia Infantry. The men were to be equipped for service immediately. All of " the boys " were going — the three Mays, Will Johnson, Berry Stainback, Ned Graham, all the young, dancing set, the young lawyers and doctors — everybody, in short, except bank presidents, druggists, a doctor or two (over age), and young boys under sixteen.

To be idle was torture. We women resolved ourselves into a sewing society — resting not on Sundays. Sewing-machines were put into the churches, which became depots for flannel, muslin, strong linen, and even uniform cloth. When the hour for meeting arrived, the sewing class would be summoned by the ringing of the church bell. My dear Agnes was visiting in Petersburg, and was my faithful ally in all my work. We instituted a monster sewing class, which we hugely enjoyed, to meet daily at my home on Market Street. My Colonel was to be fitted out as never was colonel before. He was ordered to Norfolk with his regiment to protect the seaboard. I was proud of his colonelship, and much exercised because he had no shoulder-straps. I undertook to embroider them myself. We had not then decided upon the star for our colonels' insignia, and I supposed he would wear the eagle like all the colonels I had ever known. No embroidery bullion was to be had, but I bought heavy bullion fringe, cut it in lengths, and made eagles, probably of some extinct species, for the like were unknown in Audubon's time, and have not since been discovered. However, they were accepted, admired, and, what is worse, worn.

The Confederate soldier was furnished at the beginning of the war with a gun, pistol, canteen, tin cup, haversack, and knapsack — no inconsiderable weight to be borne in a march. The knapsack contained a fatigue jacket, one or two blankets, an oilcloth, several suits of underclothing, several pairs of white gloves, collars, neckties, and handkerchiefs. Each mess purchased a mess-chest containing dishes, bowls, plates, knives, forks, spoons, cruets, spiceboxes, glasses, etc. Each mess also owned a frying-pan, oven, coffee-pot, and camp-kettle. The uniforms were of the finest cadet cloth and gold lace.

This outfit — although not comparable to that of

the Federal soldiers, many of whom had "Saratoga" trunks in the baggage train, was considered sumptuous by the Confederate volunteer.

As if these were not enough, we taxed our ingenuity to add sundry comforts, weighing little, by which we might give a touch of refinement to the soldier's knapsack.

There was absolutely nothing which a man might possibly use that we did not make for them. We embroidered cases for razors, for soap and sponge, and cute morocco affairs for needles, thread, and court-plaster, with a little pocket lined with a bank-note. "How perfectly ridiculous!" do you say? Nothing is ridiculous that helps anxious women to bear their lot — cheats them with the hope that they are doing good.

CHAPTER X

THE day came at last when our regiments were to march. They were to rendezvous at the head of Sycamore Street, and march down to the lower depot. Every old man and boy, matron, maiden, and child, every family servant, assembled to bid them God-speed.

The reigning belles and beauties of Petersburg were all there, — Alice Gregory, Tabb Bolling, Molly and Augusta Banister, Patty Hardee, Mary and Marion Meade, pretty Helen, and my own friend Agnes.

"We are not to cry, you know," said Agnes, laying down the law by right of seniority.

"Of *course* not!" said Helen, winking away her tears and smiling.

Just then the inspiring notes of "Dixie," with drum and clash of cymbal, rent the air — the first time I had heard that battle-song.

"Forward! March!" And they were moving in solid ranks, all of us keeping step on the sidewalk, down to the depot.

When the men were on board, and the wheels began to move, Ben leaned out of his window and whispered to Helen, just below him : —

" Can't I have the promise now, Helen?"

" Yes, yes, Ben — *dear* Ben, I promise!" and as the cars rolled away she turned and calmly announced, " Girls, I'm engaged to Ben Shepard."

" *I'm* engaged to half a dozen of them," said one.

" That's nothing," said another, " *I'm* engaged to the whole regiment."

Poor little Helen — but I must not anticipate.

After the soldiers left, silence and anxiety fell upon the town like a pall. What should we do next? This was the question we asked each other; and it was answered by one of our dear women.

" We will hold a prayer meeting in each other's houses, at four o'clock every afternoon. We can *pray*, if we cannot fight."

This meeting was held daily throughout the years of the war — and comfort through its influence came to many a sorrowful heart.

But the lull was of short duration. The South was sending troops to help old Virginia.

I think Beauregard's veterans can never forget their reception in Petersburg. We were forewarned of their coming. We sent our servants laden with trays of refreshments, we went ourselves to the depot with flowers. Beauregard, our idol, the gallant, dashing Beauregard, hurriedly shook hands with us and filled his arms with our flowers; then, — " All aboard," — and off again, to be heard from very soon at Bull Run.

Other regiments passed through town, and none left without being refreshed. The railroad whistles instructed us as to numbers.

It was a happy day for me when a telegram came from my Colonel at Norfolk: "Suppose you pay me a visit!" There could be but one answer.

When the day of my departure arrived I was at the depot of the train which was to take me to City Point, long before the time of starting; and when I reached the terminus of the short railroad, I was in terror lest the Richmond boat might have gone on its way without stopping for us. Would it never come? Surely something had happened! "Oh, Captain," I cried for the third time, as that functionary paced to and fro in front of his little engine, "do you think the boat —" "In a moment, lady," said the Captain, "the boat is just coming round the Point;" and sure enough, there she was, slowing up to pick up the happiest woman in the world.

I can imagine few journeys more delightful than a sail down the James River on a lovely summer day. The river itself is not a clear stream of silver like the Potomac. Every stream that enters it is yellow with the peculiar clay of the country through which it passes. But the James is, *par excellence*, the romantic river of our country, though not like the beautiful Hudson, misty with the dreams of Washington Irving. The historic James needs no imaginings to enhance its charm. Seated on the forward deck, one glides softly over enchanted waters. Could the veil which hides the future have been lifted from my vision on this glorious noonday, what would have been my sensations. Here at City Point, in the venerable ivy-clad home of the Epes family, General Grant would in three short years make his headquarters, and would entertain President Lincoln, General Sherman, and Admiral Porter.

Across the river the elegant colonial house of Shirley was basking in the summer sun. Here the Carters had lived since 1720. Here Light Horse Harry Lee had found his sweet wife, Anne Hill Carter. Here, too, was the fine portrait of Washington by Peale, and other Revolutionary treasures.

Next to Shirley, a little higher up the river, was Turkey Island, where the English explorers had rejoiced to find, in great numbers, the Christmas bird, known in the mother country as early as 1527. Here had lived the wealthy king's councilman, William Randolph, who had come to Virginia in the good times after King Charlie had returned to "enjoy his own again"; and here he had built a goodly house, with a portico on three sides, surmounted by a dome visible a great way off to navigators of the James River, the whole surmounted by an aërial structure called the "bird cage because many birds do hover and sing about it." Seven years were required to complete this mansion — and all these seven years, doubtless, its master was serving like Jacob, hoping to cage one fair bird for himself.

Just across the river, at Bermuda Hundred, lived Henry Isham, Gent: and his wife Dame Katherine; and thither came William Randolph to smoke with the master "a pipe of tobacco kept in a lily pot, cut on a maple block, lighted with a coal taken with silver tongs from a brasier of juniper" — for these were the incantations wherewith the early Virginian wooed the subtle influences of the new gift of the gods. And as they smoked, pretty Mary Isham played on her " cittern " to the soothing accompaniment of the lapping waves of the river. She was a fit mate for the young aristocrat. He could trace his lineage " from the great Earls Murray, nay, from royalty itself " ; but gentle Mary could boast on her family tree nobler fruit than these : the Dukes of Normandy — Longue–Epée and Sanspeur — Hugh Capet of France ; the Saxon kings of England ; the Magna Charta barons ; and that noble house of De Vere, which bore on its standard the lone star, because one of their blood, hard pressed in a battle of the Crusades, had seen in a vision a star fall from heaven and alight upon his shield. And so it came that William and Mary Randolph were parents of seven noble sons, and from them descended the great men of colonial and Revolutionary Virginia — Thomas Jefferson, Richard Bland, Chief Justice Marshall, Robert E. Lee. In all these times, — prominent in council, in the college, in the halls of the Executive at Philadelphia, wearing the ermine, in the presidential chair, at the bar, in the pulpit of the Established Church, in the march, in the battlefield, — in every place where character, wisdom, and gallant bearing were needed, we find the descendants of William and Mary Randolph.

These were the things of which I proudly thought (for these were my Colonel's own people) as I was slowly borne along to other localities, — many of them where the Randolphs had lived, — all of them linked together in one chain of historic interest.   The old Randolph mansion still existed in part, although its fine dome and pillared porticoes had fallen into decay.   As I turned my reverent eyes to this Mecca, how would I have been cut to the heart had the future — the near future — been revealed to me.   In one short year McClellan would, before proceeding to Harrison's Landing, rest after the disasters of the Seven Days' Battles under the roof-tree at Turkey Island, and his gunboats would shell the old mansion and level it to the ground when it no longer sheltered their commander.

A bend of the river now revealed Jordan's Point, where lived in colonial and Revolutionary days Richard Bland, the antiquary, statesman, and patriot, over whose grave the " martial ranks of corn " were now waving, through the stupidity of a recreant descendant.   There was no house on Jordan's Point wherein the restless ghost of pretty Cicely Jordan might hold tryst with her many lovers, or where the wraith of the wise old antiquary might be discerned, bending over the books " which he studieth much." Pretty, rich, fascinating Cicely had in 1623 created so much disturbance in the colony by her utter inability to refuse a suitor, that she was the occasion of the famous law enacting punishment for women who promised marriage to more than one man at a time.   Here at "Jordan's" had lived another Mary — Mary Bland — and thence Henry Lee had borne her to Westmoreland; and Henry and Mary Lee were the grandparents of Light Horse Harry, the father of our beloved Robert E. Lee.   Here, too,

at Jordan's, Nathaniel Bacon had encamped his fol-
lowers, before leading them to avenge the outrages
of the Indians.

But as I mused of these things we were passing
Berkley, where lived Giles Bland, who was executed
for following Nathaniel Bacon; afterward the home
of the Harrison who signed the Declaration of Independence, the grandfather of "old Tippecanoe,"
President William Henry Harrison. If the veil
of the future had been lifted, I should have seen
General McClellan resting on the veranda here after
his retreat from Malvern Hills, the fields for miles
around covered with his tents, the waters alive with
war vessels and transports.

Now, as I passed, the tired cattle, gathered under
the shade of a great oak near the river, were chew-
ing in contentment the midday cud; and at an outhouse within sight, a woman was setting out her
newly washed milk pails to be sweetened by the sun
after her noonday dinner.

Next in interest came Westover — the fine house
built by Colonel William Byrd, to whose father my
children's ancestor had sold it. "The wise and
prudent Theodorick Bland" was sleeping there, I
knew, behind the tombstone which recorded his
wisdom and prudence, and on which his own and
his wife's arms were quartered, she having been
the daughter of the Colonial Governor Richard
Bennett. Near him in the graveyard lay the mortal
remains of Evelyn Byrd — whose restless spirit slept
not ever, but might be seen on moonlight nights
gliding among the roses.

Then " Pace's Pains," where lived the Christian
Indian Chanco, who revealed the plan for the wholesale massacre of the English in 1622, and who saved
Jamestown by a message at dawn to the authorities
of the town; and Argall's Point, where the settlers
were slain in the Indian massacre of 1619; and
Jamestown, where the good Mr. Hunt stretched a
sail between two trees for an altar, consecrating the
first church, floored by the leaves and flowers of the
forest and roofed by the blue sky of heaven.   And
Argall's — once called Paspahegh — where Nathaniel Bacon had halted his " tyred forlorne Body of
men " to rest them before marching on to Jamestown.

And so on and on — past Weyanoke and Brandon with its art treasures — and Martin's Hundred,
where the colonists were massacred in 1622.

How peacefully the old river glided between its
banks.   Now and then voices reached us from the
shores, or we paused at a busy landing to leave a
mail-bag, or to deliver packages and barrels for the
dwellers inland; or the gang-plank would be lowered
for some planter going home to his family, and soon
pulled up, the great paddle-wheels churning the thick
muddy water into a creamy froth, as we were off
again.

As late evening drew on the river became dark,
but less silent.   We passed numbers of little skiffs
with a single wing and a red eye astern, in which
the fisherman was hurrying home, sometimes singing as he sailed.   Overhead the homing birds flapped
their heavy wings.

A sense of peace and calm stole over me. War? Oh, surely, surely not! Something would prevent it. Surely, blood would not be shed because of those insulting words in the Senate and House. God was our Father — the Father of all. Were we not children of His covenant — His blessing promised to the third and fourth generation? Was not the blood of the saints in our veins?

If the veil could have been lifted, if one had said, "Behold, I shew you a vision — you may yet avert its fulfilment," how merciful would that have been! Could this have been vouchsafed me, I might have had unrolled before me, that fourteenth day of June, — just three years away, — when the man who was now drilling a small company of volunteers in Galena would be in these waters, crossing the James at the head of 115,000 men, sweeping for two days and nights over three lines of pontoons, marching horse, foot, artillery, and train, straight to the spot whence I had come in the morning of this day, going on their victorious way to lay siege to Richmond and Petersburg, and destined to overwhelm us in the end.

And now it was quite dark on the river. Phantom ships flashed now and then out of the darkness, and were swallowed up again. Was that the *Goodspeed*, or the *Susan Constant*, or perhaps the *Discovery?* Hark! was that a war-whoop?

Only the warning whistle of our own boat, as I discovered upon awaking. Before me stood the dignified old colored woman who held the proud position of stewardess of our boat, and beside her a young assistant who gently removed and began to fold the shawl I had tucked around my knees.

"Honey," said the old dame, "ain't you 'fraid you'll ketch cole out here so late? — it's time for you to go to bed. The cap'n sent me for you. Yo' state-room is nice an' cool now. The pote-hole been open ever since sundown."

I was awake and dressed by sunrise next day, our boat having arrived after midnight at the wharf in Norfolk — and in due time the clanking of spurs announced my Colonel! Very fine did he look in his uniform, with my eagles bristling on each shoulder.

There was to be a dress-parade that day, in the afternoon, and he desired me to join the ladies of the hotel in the drawing-room after breakfast and present with his compliments an invitation to the parade.

"Do you know when and where I can see the ladies of this hotel?" I asked my smiling colored chambermaid.

"Lor', lady, dey ain't fur off," she said. "Dey mostly sets all day in de shady side of de po'ch pickin' lint. Dey certainly makes a heap o' muss. Nobody can't say nuthin' to 'em; cause deyse guests of de hotel. An' 'tain't one bit o' use. Nobody gwine to git hurt, an' if dey does, what's de use of all dat sticky cotton?"

I found a number of ladies engaged in the veranda, but not as she had suggested. They were very glad to meet me, and accepted my invitation. They were making square bags out of bunting for cartridges. A gentle, blue-eyed woman joined us

and asked for work.   But when it was explained to
her, she colored, her lips quivered.   "Oh, I can't!
I can't!" she begged.   "Let me roll bandages for
wounds! I can't help with the cartridges! You see,
all my people live in Pennsylvania.   My husband
is going to fight them, I know; but don't ask me
to make the cartridges."

My Colonel came himself with his staff in the
afternoon to escort us to his headquarters at the
Marine Hospital.   On our way we passed an abandoned house, on the walls of which grew the most
glorious specimen of fuchsia I ever beheld.   I had
always heard that this was a marine plant, and I
now saw to what perfection it could be brought in
the sea air.   It reached to the second story and was
covered with a shower of great scarlet and blue bells.
" Dixie colors," said one of the ladies.   We gathered
gorgeous bunches and fastened them in our white
dresses.

The parade ground was a lovely stretch of green,
and beyond, the blue waters of the sea sparkled in
the afternoon sun, each little wave gemmed with a
diamond and set in sapphire.

A siege gun had just been mounted, and there
was to be practice-firing at a buoy for a mark.

I was standing with my group of friends when a
handsome officer approached with a military salute
and invited me to honor his company by firing their
first gun.   I went forward with him, and he put the
lanyard in my hands.

" Wait for the word of command, Madam," he
said.

" And then what ? " I inquired.

" Oh, then *pull* steadily," and with that he stepped back.

" Make ready !   Fire ! "

I pulled the lanyard — but I was unprepared for the result.   The great gun backed, leaped in the air and sent a mighty roar across the waters, — the first cannon fired by the Third Virginia Volunteers.   I received the congratulations and thanks of the Captain, and returned to my place — to be told that my eyes were congested by the concussion, and that I must return home and bathe and bandage them at once. Evidently I was not fit for artillery service.

L

CHAPTER XI

THE month of July, 1861, found me with my little boys at " The Oaks " — the residence of Dr. Izard Bacon Rice, in Charlotte County, seventy miles from Richmond, and miles away from the nearest railroad depot. There I might have enjoyed a peaceful summer with my kind host — a fine type of a Christian gentleman, sometime an Old-Line Whig and fierce Union man, now an ardent advocate of states' rights, and a stanch supporter of the New Confederacy. I might — as I had often done before — have revelled in the fine trees; the broad acres of tobacco in their summer prime, when the noble plant was proudly flinging out its banners before its fall; the old garden with its box-edged crescents, stars, and circles, — I might have dreamed away the summer in perfect contentment but for General Beauregard. Distant as was his army, a message from his guns reached my summer retreat more than a hundred miles away.

Dr. Rice lived in a large, old-fashioned house, on a plantation of two thousand acres or more. An oak grove, alive with chattering squirrels which had been held sacred for two generations, surrounded the house. The squirrels held conventions in the trees, and

doubtless expressed their opinions of the family below, whom they had good reason to consider inferior
beings, inasmuch as they were slow-motioned, heavy
creatures, utterly destitute of grace and agility, and
with small appreciation of hickory-nuts.

The Doctor cultivated tobacco, and when I arrived the fields stretched as far as the eye could
reach, now a vast level sea of green, now covering
the low, gently rounded, undulating hills as they
sloped down to the Staunton River. There was
never a season when these fields were not alive with
laborers of every age; for the regal plant so beloved
of men — and ranking with opium and hemp as a
solace for the ills of mankind — has enemies from
the hour it peeps from the nursery of the hot bed.
It can never be forgotten a moment. Children can
hunt the fly which seeks to line the leaf with eggs,
or destroy the unhatched eggs, or aid the great army
which must turn out in haste when the ravenous
worm is born. The earth must be turned frequently
at the roots, the flower buds pinched off, the shoots
or "suckers" removed. The Doctor's tobacco field
was an enlivening spectacle, and very picturesque
did the ebony faces of the little workers look,
among the broad leaves. No lady's garden was
ever kept so clean, so free from sticks, errant bits
of paper, or débris of any kind.

I do not claim that Dr. Rice (my uncle) was a
typical planter — as far as the government of his
slaves was concerned. He had inherited liberal
ideas with these inherited slaves. His grandfather,
David Rice, had written the first published protest

in this country against slavery as "inconsistent with
religion and policy." His father had ruled a plantation where severe punishment was unknown, where
the cheerful slaves rarely needed it. The old gentleman was considered eccentric — and eccentric it
surely was for a master to punish a fault by commanding the culprit to stand in his presence while
he recited a long passage from Homer or Virgil!
The punishment was effective. For fear of it, the
fault was rarely repeated.

It was my uncle's custom to assemble every slave
on his plantation on Sunday morning, and to speak
a few words to each one, commending the women if
their families appeared in clean, well-kept garments,
rewarding with a pair of shoes the urchins reported
by "Uncle Moses" as having been orderly and
useful, exchanging a pleasant jest here and there.

He presented a tight, comfortable house to every
newly married pair, with timber for the bridegroom
to add to it, or to enclose the piece of land for a
garden or a poultry yard which went with it. Every
mother at the birth of a child was presented with a
pig. The plantation, which was large and fruitful,
and from which nothing but tobacco and wheat was
ever sold, yielded vegetables, poultry, mutton, beef,
bacon in lavish abundance, while the orchards and
vines were equally productive.

Some hundreds of the negroes of the neighborhood were members of the Presbyterian church of
the whites. In the old church books may be seen
to-day records of their marriages and funerals, and
how (for example) "Lovelace Brown was brought

before the session for hog-stealing and suspended
for one month." But there were better records than
this. These Presbyterian negroes were at one time
led by an eminent patriarch, Uncle Abel, who de-
serves more than a passing notice. He had been
taught to read and had been well drilled in the
Shorter Catechism. But his marriage ceremonies
were always read from the Episcopal Prayer-book,
every word of which he held sacred, not to be
changed or omitted to suit any modern heresy.
" I M, take thee N," was the formula for Jack
or Peter, Dilsey or Dicey — and " with this ring
I thee wed" must be pronounced with solemnity,
ring or no ring, the latter being not at all essential.

My uncle's old family coach, punctual to the
minute, swept around the circle on the lawn every
Sunday morning, with Uncle Peter proudly guiding
the horses from his high perch. And high-swung
was the coach, to be ascended (as we ascended our
four-poster beds) by three carpeted steps, — in
the case of the carriage, folding steps, which were
tucked inside after we had disposed of ourselves,
with our ample hoops. There was plenty of room
inside. Pockets lined the doors, and these were
filled by my aunt with beaten biscuit and sugar-
cakes " for the little darkies on the road."

Arriving at the church, the gentlemen from the
adjacent plantations, who had been settling the
affairs of the nation under the trees, came forward
to hand us from our carriage, after the manner of
old-time cavaliers and sedan-chairs; and my aunt
and I would be very gracious, devoutly hoping in

our hearts that my uncle and his sons would not forget a reciprocal courtesy when Mrs. Winston Henry, Mrs. Paul Carrington, and Mrs. Sarah Carrington should arrive.

The women all seated themselves on the right side of the church, while the men, during the singing of a preliminary hymn, came in like a processional and took the left as their portion, — all of which (except the advertisements on the church doors) was conducted precisely according to the customs of Revolutionary times, when Patrick Henry and John Randolph, now sleeping a few miles away, were themselves (we trust) church-goers.

Church dinners at home were simple, but abundant, — so that if three or four carriages should arrive from distant plantations in the neighborhood, there could be welcome and refreshment for all, but on the great days when my uncle and aunt received the neighborhood, when the Carringtons and Patrick Henry's sons, John and Winston, came with their families to spend the day, the dinner was something to be remembered. Perhaps a description verbatim from an old family servant will be better than anything I can furnish from memory.

" Yes, sir ! We had fine dinners in them days. The butter was moulded like a temple with pillars, and a rose stuck in the top. There was a wreath of roses roun' all the dessert dishes. Viney biled the ham in cider. We had roas' pig, biled turkey, chickens fried an' briled, spring lam', ducks an' green goslin'. An' every cut-glass dish in the house was full of preserves, an' the great bowl full of ice-cream, an' floatin' island, an' tipsy-cake, an' cheese-cakes, an' green sweetmeats, an' citron.   John was bothered where to set all the dishes."

Our guests would remain late, that they might have the cool evening hours for their long drives. Mr. John Henry, with his family of gifted sons and beautiful daughters, lived at Red Hill, the home of his father, the great orator and patriot, under the trees his father had planted and near the grave where he sleeps.   Mr. Winston Henry had also an interesting family, and lived in an old colonial house not far away, surrounded by grounds filled in summer with pomegranates and gardenias, and with lemon and orange trees in tubs, also great *trees* of heliotrope, and vines of jessamine — a paradise of beauty and sweetness.   Rosalie Henry would bring her guitar to my uncle's and sing for us by the hour. She was so loved, so cherished by her parents, that they gave her a bedroom over their own, to which she ascended by a stairway from their own apartment — all that they might be near her.   But one morning early, pretty Rosalie changed gowns with her maid, put a pail on her head, and slipped past her trusting, adoring parents to join her lover in the jessamine bower, and in a bridal robe of linsey-woolsey was married at the next town!   Then it was that my good uncle had his opportunity.   The sublime teaching of forgiveness was respected from his kindly lips.

In the early summer of '61 Virginia planters were not all *d'accord* on political questions; and like Agag, it behooved us to "walk delicately" in conversation.   One thing they would not endure. Politics were to be kept out of the pulpit.   Never had the pastor such attentive congregations; they were watching him, keenly alive to the remotest hint or allusion to the war.   His business was with the spiritual kingdom of God.   He must not interfere with Cæsar's.   He found it expedient to omit for the present the warlike aspirations of David, in which he beseeches the Lord's attention to his enemies, and, among other things calculated to comfort and soothe his pious feelings, prays that they may be as "stubble before the wind," as "wood before fire," and be "rooted forever out of the land of the living."

"Enemies" were not to be alluded to in the pulpit.   Nor, indeed, not yet in private!   It was proper and in good taste to speak of them as "Federals"; but at no very distant day these same polite gentlemen called them "enemies" with a will; when scornfully disposed, they were "Yankees," and when they wished to be positively insulting, "Yanks."

Across the river from the Oaks was "Mildendo," the home of the Carrington family.   From this home went every man capable of bearing arms — Fontaine, the fine young surgeon so well placed in the United States Navy, and his brother, the grave head of the house upon whom everybody depended; and one, a cousin, leaving his bride at the altar. Patrick Henry's grandsons all enlisted.   Mr. Charles Bruce left his baronial castle on Staunton Hill near the Oaks, equipped the "Staunton Hill Artillery Company" at his own expense, placed himself at its head and shared all its hardships. His brother, Mr. James Bruce, cut up his rich carpets and curtains for the soldiers' blankets. These were but a few of the gallant neighbors of my uncle, who exchanged homes of luxury for the hardships of war — all of whom probably shared General Lee's keen sorrow at the necessity forced upon Virginia to withdraw her allegiance from the Union.

My uncle had a son already in the cavalry service — and another, Henry, a fine young fellow of sixteen, was at Hampden-Sidney College, Virginia. Presently a letter from the latter filled the family at the Oaks with — yes, anxiety — but at the same time a proud sense of how old Revolutionary "blood will tell." Henry was on the march! At the first tocsin of war the students of Hampden-Sidney had rushed to arms — most of them under age; and when their president, the venerable Rev. John Atkinson, found they would go, he placed himself at their head as their captain, despite his threescore years and physical infirmities. Military tactics had not been included in his theological training. Although he may not have been so dull but he could learn, nor yet so old but he might learn, certain it is he never *did* learn to drill his "Hampden-Sidney Boys." His orders of movement were given by pointing the way he wished his company to advance.

Notwithstanding the shortcomings of their captain, these boys, fresh from their college halls, were often publicly complimented by their colonel, as they headed the column in the long days' marches over the mountains of Virginia,—marches in which the old captain would fall asleep, and would be supported on either side.

When they were called to Richmond their patriotic ardor received a shock. Governor Letcher seriously took under consideration the propriety of sending them back to school on account of their youth. A committee from the company waited upon him, and he was finally prevailed upon to allow them to go to the front.

They soon learned what war was — these beardless college boys, and bore themselves gallantly in several engagements. But their military career was brief. McClellan flanked their position at Rich Mountain, July 12, 1861, and cut off every avenue of retreat. The whole command, after a sharp engagement, were made prisoners of war. For the time being the boys felt their military career to have been an inglorious failure.

While they were thus disappointed and depressed, a Federal officer, presumably a lieutenant, visited them in the prison camp. He said he had heard so much of the boy soldiers led by their college president that he wished to make their acquaintance.

The boys were not by way of being over anxious to receive visits from their victors. The officer asked, " Why in the world are you here ? "

" We are here to *fight!* " said they. " What do you suppose we came for ? "

" Well, boys," said the officer, pleasantly, " make

yourselves easy.   I'll send you home to your mothers
in a few days."

The officer was General McClellan!

The company was paroled, but was not exchanged
for a year.   This prolonged parole, they always
thought, was due to General McClellan's influence
in order to give them a whole year at college.

They all returned to the army after their exchange, but never as the " Hampden-Sidney Boys."
They never forgot the little interview with the General.   He won all their hearts.

Our own Hampden-Sidney boy, Henry Rice, soon
afterward wrote from a hospital in Richmond that
he was ill with fever.   My uncle ordered him home,
and I took the great family coach and Uncle Peter
and went to the depot, fourteen miles away, to fetch
him.   He looked so long, that I doubted whether
I could bestow him in the carriage ; and as he was
too good a soldier for me to suggest that he be
" doubled up," I entered the carriage first, had his
head and shoulders placed in my lap, then closed
the door and swung his long legs out of the window !

My uncle was a fine specimen of a Christian
gentleman — always courteous, always serene.   I
delighted in following him around the plantation on
horseback.   When he winnowed his wheat, Uncle
Moses, standing like an emperor amid the sheaves,
filled the hearts of my little boys with ecstasy by
allowing them to ride the horses that turned the
great wheel.   Finally the wheat was packed in bags,
and we stood on the bank of the river to see it piled
into flat-bottomed boats on the way to market.

The next morning Moses appeared at the dining room door while we were at breakfast.

"Good morning, Moses," said my uncle. "I thought you were going with the wheat."

"Dar ain't no wheat," said the old man. "Hit's all at de bottom of the river."

"How did that happen?"

"We jest natchelly run agin a snag; when de boat turn over, hit pulled all de others down. 'Cose you know, Marster, dey was tied together, an' boat ain' got no eyes to see snags."

"Well—get out your chains and grappling hooks, Moses, and save all you can. It will do to feed the chickens."

"Why, Uncle!" I exclaimed, "how calmly you take it."

"Certainly," said he; "because I've lost my crop is that any reason I should lose my temper? Here, Pizarro, have our horses saddled. We'll go down to the river and encourage Moses to resurrect his wheat." (Pizarro was John's son. John had studied with the boys of the family, and knew some history and Latin. One of the women bore the classic name of "Lethe"; others were "Chloe" and "Daphne"; another name, frequently repeated, was "Dicey"—a survival, according to Mr. Andrew Lang, of the myth of Orpheus and Eurydice, which was found among the Indians and the Virginia negroes of colonial times. Orpheus seems to have perished from their traditions, but Dicey is still a favorite name. The descendants of Lethe and Pizarro still live at the Oaks. A late achievement shows their progress under new conditions, the baptismal records having been enriched with "Hazel-Kirke-Florida-Bell-Armazinda-Hodge," more imposing if less suggestive than the "Homicide" and "Neuralgia" of a neighboring county.)

This precise type of a Virginia plantation will never appear again, I imagine. I wish I could describe a plantation wedding as I saw it that summer. But a funeral of one of the old servants was peculiarly interesting to me. "Aunt Matilda" had been much loved, and when she found herself dying, she had requested that the mistress and little children should attend her funeral. "I ain' been much to church," she urged, "I couldn't leave my babies. I ain' had dat shoutin' an' hollerin' religion, but I gwine to heaven jes' de same"—a fact of which nobody who knew Aunt Matilda could have the smallest doubt.

We had a long, warm walk behind hundreds of negroes, following the rude coffin in slow procession through the woods, singing antiphonally as they went one of those strange, weird hymns not to be caught by any Anglo-Saxon voice.

It was a beautiful and touching scene, and at the grave I longed for an artist (we had no kodaks then) to perpetuate the picture. The level rays of the sun were filtered through the green leaves of the forest, and fell gently on the dusky, pathetic faces, and on the simple coffin surrounded by orphan children and relatives, very dignified and quiet in their grief.

The spiritual patriarch of the plantation presided. Old Uncle Abel said : —

" I ain' gwine keep you all long.   'Tain' no use.
We can't do nothin' for Sis' Tildy.   All is done fer
her, an' she done preach her own fune'al sermon.
Her name was on dis church book here, but dat
warn' nothin', 'dout 'twas on de Lamb book too!

" Now whiles dey fillin' up her grave I'd like you
all to sing a hymn Sis' Tildy uster love, but you
all know I bline in one eye, an' de sweat done got
in de other; so's I can't see to line it out, an' I
dunno as any o' you all ken do it " — and the first
thing I knew, the old man had passed his well-worn
book to me, and there I stood, at the foot of the
grave, " lining out " : —

> " Asleep in Jesus, blessed sleep
> From which none ever wakes to weep," —

words of immortal comfort to the great throng of
negro mourners who caught it up, line after line, on
an air of their own, full of tears and tenderness, — a
strange, weird tune no white person's voice could
ever follow.

Among such scenes I passed the month of June
and the early part of July, and then General Beauregard reminded us that we were at war, and had no
right to make ourselves comfortable.

Dr. Rice, on the afternoon of the 21st, had be-
taken himself to his accustomed place under the
trees, to escape the flies, — the pest of Southern
households in summer, — and had lain down on the
grass for his afternoon nap.   He suddenly called
out excitedly : " There's a battle going on — a fierce
battle — I can hear the cannonading distinctly.

Here — lie down — you can hear it!" "Oh, no, no, I can't!" I gasped. "It may be at Norfolk."

Like Jessie, who had heard the pibroch at the siege of Lucknow, he had heard, with his ear to the ground, the firing at Manassas. The battle of Bull Run was at its height. We found it difficult to understand that he *could* have heard cannonading one hundred and fifty miles away. We had not then spoken across the ocean and been answered.

CHAPTER XII

W E had small faith in my uncle's wireless
telegraphy, but in a short time we had
confirmation of his news.

Then came the details of the first great battle of
the war. "Glorious news!" everybody said. A
glorious triumph for the South, — an utter rout of
the enemy; but my heart sank within me at the tale
of blood. How about those boys I had seen march
away? What would life hold for some of the wives
and mothers and sweethearts at home?

What was glory to the gallant Colonel Bartow,
lying in state at the capitol in Richmond? Could
glory dry his widow's tears or console his aged
mother? We gathered details of the last moments
of the men who fell. It was all so strange! *Could* it
be true that these things had actually happened in
Virginia?

Our men, when the bodies were brought home,
could tell many stories of officers — but how about
the boys in the ranks? Bartow had been unhorsed
in the fight, and his aide, young Lamar, dashed across
the field amid a hail of bullets to procure another
mount for his Colonel. Suddenly Lamar was seen
to fall with his horse. Extricating himself, and per-

ceiving that his horse was shot, he started to proceed
on foot; the wounded animal tried to rise and follow. Our men saw Lamar turn in that deadly fire,
stoop down, and pat the poor horse on the neck.
Another volley of bullets ended the noble animal's
life, and Lamar returned just in time to bear Bartow's body from the field.

I grew so restless and unhappy that I turned my
face homeward to Petersburg. My resolution was
taken. I steadily withstood all the entreaties of my
friends, and determined to follow my husband's regiment through the war. I did not ask his permission.
I would give no trouble. I should be only a help
to his sick men and his wounded. I busied myself
in preparing a camp equipage — a field-stove with a
rotary chimney, ticks for bedding, to be filled with
straw or hay or leaves as the case might be, a camp
chest of tin utensils, strong blankets, etc. A tent
could always be had from Major Shepard, our
quartermaster. News soon came that the Third Virginia had been ordered to Smithfield. McClellan
was looking toward the Peninsula, and Major-General Joseph E. Johnston was keeping an eye on
McClellan.

When I set forth on what my father termed my
"wild-goose chase," I found the country literally
alive with troops. The train on which I travelled
was switched off again and again to allow them to
pass. My little boys had the time of their lives,
cheering the soldiers and picnicking at short intervals all day.

But Smithfield would not hear of the camp outfit.

M

The great box was trundled away to the warehouse, and I was hospitably taken into one of the homes of the little town.

After a while things looked as if I would probably stay in Smithfield the rest of my natural life. So I rented a small furnished house, bought a cow, opened an account with Mr. Britt, the grocer, also with a fisherman who went out every night on Pagan Creek with a light in his boat, drew his blanket around him and dozed, while the fat little mullets jumped in for my breakfast. Until the mullet species becomes extinct nobody need starve in Smithfield.

The Third Virginia and its Colonel were giving themselves up to murmurs and discontent at being "buried in Smithfield" while gallant fighting was going on elsewhere, meanwhile studying Hardee and Jomini with all their might. Not one of the officers or men had ever before seen military service. The daily drill was the only excitement.

Here they were, fastened hand and foot, strong, ardent fellows, while so much was going on elsewhere, — Stonewall Jackson marching on his career of glory, Beauregard ordered to active service in the West, Fort Henry and Fort Donelson surrendered to the enemy, our army falling back from Manassas, the mighty Army of the Potomac divided and scattered. Then came news that General Lee, whose first appointment was from Virginia, was to have command of all the armies of the Confederacy.

Major-General Pemberton (the gallant hero who held Vicksburg against such odds) was then our commanding officer at Smithfield. His wife and her sister,

Miss Imogene Thompson, were our grand dames,
— deserving the admiration we accorded them. The
beauty of the town was Mary Garnett; the spirited
belle who wore brass buttons and a military cap,
Miss Riddick. Despite all the discouraging news,
these young people mightily cheered the spirits of
the officers and helped them to bear inglorious inaction with becoming fortitude.

General Pemberton varied our own routine somewhat by giving an occasional dinner party. Once
he invited us to an early morning drive to Cooper's
Point, opposite Newport News, where the warships *Congress* and *Cumberland* were anchored, with
whose guns (so soon to be silenced by the iron-clad
Merrimac) we were already familiar. We were a
merry party, assembled in open wagons on a frosty
morning, and we enjoyed the drive with fleet horses
through the keen air. Miss Imogene Thompson's
lover was a prisoner of war on board one of the
ships. "Look out for the ball and chain, Imogene!"
said the General, as we arrived in sight of the ships.
Through a glass we could see the brave fellows, so
soon to go down with their colors flying before the
relentless *Merrimac*, but not with pretty Imogene's
lover, who lived to make her happy after the cruel
war was over.

Another event of personal interest was the presentation to the Colonel by the ladies of Petersburg of a blue silken state flag. The party came
down the river in a steamboat, and we stood on
the river bank in a stiff breeze while the presentation speech covered the ground of all the possibili-

ties in store for the Colonel, ending with, " And, sir, if you *should* fall," and promises of tears and true faithful hearts to love and honor him forever. In his answer of thanks he expressed all the gratitude and chivalry of his heart, but craved sympathy for his present state of enforced idleness — " for the dearest sacrifice a man can make for his country is his ambition."

Soon afterwards he was called to Richmond to take his seat in Congress — and as there was nothing to keep him with the regiment, he left it with his Lieutenant-Colonel.

But I did not return with him. I had enlisted for the war! For some reason, which was not explained at the time, he suddenly returned, and my only knowledge of his coming was a peremptory official order to change my base — to leave Smithfield next morning at daybreak! The orderly who brought it stood before me as I read, and looked intensely surprised when I said : " Tell the Colonel it is impossible! I can't get ready by to-morrow morning to leave."

" Madam," said the man, gravely, " it is none of my business, but when Colonel Pryor gives an order, it is best to be a strict constructionist."

Mr. Britt proved a tower of strength. He closed his store and brought all his force to help me. My cow was presented with my compliments to my neighbor, Mrs. Smith, under promise of secrecy (for I knew I must not alarm the town by my precipitate departure), my camp equipage brought from the warehouse, my belongings all packed. As the sun

rose next morning, I greeted him from my seat on
a trunk in an open wagon on my way to Zuni, the
railway station fifteen miles away. I never saw a
lovelier morning. The cattle were all afield for their
early breakfast of dewy grass, a thin line of smoke was
ascending from the cottages on the wayside. The
mother could be seen within, preparing breakfast for
the children, who stood in the door to gaze at us
as we passed. The father was possibly away in the
army, although the times were not yet so stern that
every man became a conscript. These humbler
folk who lived close to the highway — what sufferings were in store for them from the pillage of the
common soldier! What terror and dismay for the
dwellers in the broad-porticoed, many-chambered
mansions beyond the long avenues of approach in
the distance! I could but think of these things
when I heard the boom of guns on the warships
at Newport News, sounds to which my ears had
grown accustomed, but which now took on, somehow, a new meaning.

I soon learned that the Third Virginia Regiment
moved the day after I received my own marching
orders.

McClellan had landed about one hundred thousand
efficient troops on the Peninsula for the movement
upon Richmond. General Joseph E. Johnston's
line of about fifty-three thousand men extended
across the narrow neck of land between the York
and the James. They gave McClellan battle May 5
at Williamsburg, captured four hundred unwounded
prisoners, ten colors, and twelve field-pieces, slept on

the field of battle, and marched off the next morning at their leisure and convenience. After this my Colonel was brevetted Brigadier-General.

The news of his probable promotion reached me at the Exchange Hotel in Richmond, whither I had gone that I might be near headquarters, and thus learn the earliest tidings from the Peninsula. There the Colonel joined me for one day. We read with keen interest the announcement in the papers that his name had been sent in by the president for promotion. Mrs. Davis held a reception at the Spotswood Hotel on the evening following this announcement, and we availed ourselves of the opportunity to make our respects to her.

A crowd gathered before the Exchange to congratulate my husband, and learning that he had gone to the Spotswood, repaired thither, and with many shouts and cheers called him out for a speech. This was very embarrassing, and he fled to a corner of the drawing-room and hid behind a screen of plants. I was standing near the president, trying to hold his attention by remarks on the weather and kindred subjects of a thrilling nature, when a voice from the street called out: " Pryor! *General* Pryor!" I could endure the suspense no longer, and asked tremblingly, " Is this true, Mr. President?" Mr. Davis looked at me with a benevolent smile and said, " I have no reason, Madam, to doubt it, except that I saw it this morning in the papers," and Mrs. Davis at once summoned the bashful Colonel: " What are you doing lying there *perdu* behind the geraniums? Come out and take your honors."

The next day my bristling eagles, which had faithfully held guard on the Colonel's uniform, retired before the risen stars of the Brigadier-General.

On May 31 " Old Joe " and " Little Mac," as they were affectionately called by their respective commands, again confronted each other, and fought the great two days' battle of Fair Oaks, or Seven Pines.

This battle was said to have been one of the closest, most hotly contested, and bloody of the war. A few miles from Petersburg the cannonading could be distinctly heard, and ten or twelve of the Federal observation balloons could be seen in the air.

McClellan had an army of one hundred thousand ; Johnston had sixty-three thousand. The afternoon and night before a terrible storm had raged, " sheets of fire, lightning, sharp and dreadful thunderclaps, were fit precursors of the strife waged by the artillery of man.

" All night long Zeus, the lord of counsel, devised them ill with terrible thunderings. Then pale fear gat hold upon them." [1]

The roads were deep with mud. With many disadvantages Johnston attacked, with vigor, the corps of Keyes and Heintzelman, drove them back, and came near inflicting upon them a crushing defeat. Near the end of the fight General Johnston was wounded and borne from the field, smiling and saying, " I'm not sure I am much hurt, but I fear that bit of shell may have injured my spine."

[1] Rhodes's " History of the United States."

He had already been wounded by a musket-ball, his enthusiasm having carried him nearer to the fight than a commanding officer has any right to be.

A little later he had observed one of his colonels trying to dodge the shell.

"Colonel," he said, "there is no use dodging! When you hear them, they have passed."

Just then he fell unconscious into the arms of one of his couriers. A shell had exploded, striking him on the breast. The moment he regained consciousness his unwounded hand sought his sword and pistols. They were gone!

"I would not lose my sword for ten thousand dollars," he exclaimed. "My father wore it in the war of the Revolution." The courier — Drury L. Armstead — dashed back through the storm of artillery, found both sword and pistols, brought them safely, and received one of the pistols as a token of the gratitude of his chief.[1]

In General George E. Pickett's report of this hard-won battle he says, "Pryor and Wilcox were on my right; our men moved beautifully and carried everything before them."

General Johnston was succeeded by General Lee. I did not know for a long time (for, so absorbing were the events that rapidly followed, the honors of battle were forgotten) that, after the capture at Fair Oaks of the Federal brigade under General Casey, "General Roger A. Pryor went around among the wounded, giving them whiskey and water, and told them it was a repayment of the kindness

[1] "Memoirs of J. E. Johnston," by General Bradley Johnson, p. 72.

with which the wounded Confederate prisoners were treated at ' Williamsburg,' " [1] — an incident which I hope I may be pardoned for relating, since the generous tribute affords an example of the spirit of that true Christian gentleman, General McClellan.

"He never struck a foul blow and never tolerated mean men or mean methods about him. His was a high ideal of war, a high sense of chivalry which is the duty of fighting the belligerent and sparing the weak. His conduct was keyed to the highest point of honor and generosity in war." When his march led him to the "White House," whence General Washington took his bride, Martha Custis, he ordered a guard to be placed around it; and finding himself alone in St. Peter's Church, where Washington was married, he records in his diary, "I could not help kneeling at the chancel and praying that I might save my country as truly as he did." This was just before the battle at Seven Pines, in which there were probably arrayed against him the near kindred of Martha Washington. What would they have thought of the invading general's prayer to "save the country"? And *his* country! And at the altar he held in especial homage because of their grandsire!

Like McClellan, Johnston had not the good fortune to be in accord with his Executive. "Not only," said an Old Virginian to him as he lay suffering from his severe wounds, "not only do we deplore this cruel affliction upon you, General, but we feel it to be a national calamity."

[1] "McClellan's Own Story," p. 338.

" No, sir," said Johnston, fiercely, rising suddenly upon his unbroken elbow. "The shot that struck me down was the best ever fired for the Southern Confederacy, for I possessed in no degree the confidence of this government, and now a man who does enjoy it will succeed me, and be able to accomplish what I never could."

The man who succeeded him, General Lee, wrote to the Secretary of War: "If General Johnston was not a soldier, America never produced one. If he was not competent to command the army, the Confederacy had no one who was competent." But even Lee could not control the opinions of the Executive. General Johnston was relieved from his command in 1864. General McClellan's treatment, as the world knows, was hardly less severe and quite as undeserved.

Richmond heard the guns of this bloody battle. As soon as the storm allowed them, crowds of anxious listeners repaired to the hills, from which the cannonading and rattle of musketry could be distinctly heard. The city waked up to a keen realization of the horrors of war. All the next day ambulances brought in the wounded — and open wagons were laden with the dead. Six thousand one hundred and thirty-four Confederate soldiers had been killed; the Federal loss was five thousand and thirty-one, — eleven thousand one hundred and sixty-five brave men gone from the country that gave them birth !

The streets of Richmond presented a strange scene — ambulances of wounded and dying men passed companies arriving on their way to the front, and each cheered the other. Batteries of artillery thundered through the streets; messengers and couriers ran hither and thither.

The streets were filled with a motley crowd, citizens hurrying to and fro, negroes running on messages, newsboys crying "extras" printed on short slips of the yellow Confederate paper; on one side of the street regiments arriving from the far South, cheering as they passed; on the other a train of ambulances bearing the wounded, the dead, the dying. Now and then a feeble cheer answered the strong men going in to win the victory these had failed to win, but for which they never ceased to look until death closed the watching eyes.

Every house was opened for the wounded. They lay on verandas, in halls, in drawing-rooms of stately mansions. Young girls and matrons stood in their doorways with food and fruit for the marching soldiers, and then turned to minister to the wounded men within their doors.

It has been estimated that five thousand wounded men were received in private houses and hospitals from the field of Seven Pines. The city was thrilled to its centre. The city had "no language but a cry"! And yet there was no panic, no frantic excitement. Only that Richmond, the mirth-loving, pleasure-seeking, was changed into a city of resolute men and women, nerved to make any sacrifice for their cause.

At all times during the war the Capitol Square was a rallying place where men met and received

news and compared chances of success.   They would
sit all day on the hills outside the city and congregate
in the square in the evening to discuss the events
of the day and the probable chances for the morrow.

My news of this battle was coupled with the
information that my General had fallen ill from
malarial fever, and had kept up until the army
approached Richmond, but that he was now lying
sick in his tent a few miles from the city.

There I found him.   It seemed strange to see
the daisies growing all over the ground on which his
little tent was pitched.   I obtained leave to move
him at once, and took him to the Spotswood Hotel
in Richmond.   " He wants nothing now," said kind
Dr. Dean, " except some buttermilk and good
nursing."

The hotel was crowded.   President and Mrs.
Davis were there, Mrs. Joseph E. Johnston, Mrs.
Myers, wife of the quartermaster-general, and
many, many more whose names are familiar in all
the war histories.   Everybody was on the alert and
on the *qui vive*.

From my windows I witnessed the constant arrival
of officers from every division of the army.   The
Louisiana Zouaves were an interesting company
of men.   Their handsome young French Colonel
Coppens was a fine example of grace and manly
beauty.   He would dash up to the door on his
handsome horse, dismount, run up the stairs for a
word with some official, run down again, vault
lightly into his saddle, and gallop down the street.
No one was more admired than Colonel Coppens.

I had not visited the drawing-room often before I became aware that a bitter feud existed between the three eminent ladies I have mentioned — indeed, the *Richmond Examiner* gave a most amusing account of one of their spicy interviews. Jealousy and consequent heartburning had possessed the bosoms of these ladies — do they not intrude into every court and camp? And here were court and camp merged into one. Had I remained idle I should probably have ranged myself on the side of my *ci-devant* commanding officer, Mrs. Johnston; but matters of tremendous importance soon filled every mind and heart.

CHAPTER XIII

THE SEVEN DAYS' BATTLES

THE intense heat of July 26th has been noted in many of the diaries and records of the day. I remember it because I had feared its unfavorable effect upon my husband, not yet discharged by his physicians, and now lying weak and listless upon his bed at the Spotswood Hotel in Richmond.

I was reading aloud to him the news in the morning papers, fanning him the while, when a peremptory knock at the door sent me to my feet. An ominous-looking note was handed in to " Brigadier-General Pryor." Upon reading it, my husband slipped to the side of the bed, and reached out for his cavalry boots. The note ran: " Dear General, put yourself *at once* at the head of your brigade. In thirty-six hours it will all be over. LONGSTREET." Before I realized the tremendous import of the order, he was gone.

McClellan was almost at the gates of the city. The famous " seven days' fight " was about to begin.

Several of the officers of our brigade were in the hotel, and I ran out to find their wives and learn

more news from them.   On the stair I met Colonel
Scott, and as he passed me, he exclaimed, " No time
until I come back, Madam ! "   Turning, he paused,
raised his hand, and said solemnly, " If I ever come
back."   The wife of Captain Poindexter came up at
the moment.   She was weeping, and wringing her
hands.   " Do you think," she said, " that we could
drive out to camp and see them once more before
they march ? "

We hurried into the street, found a carriage, and,
urging our driver to his utmost speed, were soon in
sight of the camp.

All was hurry and confusion there.   Ambulances
were hitching up, troops forming in line, servants
running hither and thither, horses standing to be
saddled, light army wagons loading with various
camp utensils.

Captain Whitner of the General's staff met me,
and said, as he conducted me to my husband's tent:
" The General will be so glad to see you, Madam !
He is lying down to rest a few minutes before we
move."

He opened his arms to me as I went in, but there
were no sad words.   We spoke cheerily to each
other, but, unable to control myself, I soon ran out
to find John and see that he had provided brandy
and cold tea, the latter a necessity lest good water
should be unprocurable.   Never have I seen such
a number of flies !   They blackened the land, cor-
rupted the food, and tormented the nervous horses.
When I returned, Mrs. Poindexter was standing
outside the tent waiting for me.   " I can see my

husband only at the head of his company," she said. " Look ! they are forming the line."

We stood aside as the brigade formed in marching order. The stern command, " Fall in ! Fall in !" reached us from company after company stretching far down the road. My husband mounted his horse, and, drawing his sword, gave the order to advance.

" Head of column to the right !" and with steady tramp they filed past us — past the only two women, of the many who loved them, who had known of their going and had come out to cheer and bless them.

We could not bear to remain a moment after they left. Finding our carriage, we were about to enter, when the driver pointed back with his whip. There, sure enough, rose the puffs of blue smoke from McClellan's guns — so near, so near !

We set our faces homeward, two stunned, tear-less women, neither yet able to comfort the other. Presently the carriage stopped, and the driver, dis-mounting, came to the door.

" Lady," said he, " there's a man lying on the roadside. We just passed him. Maybe he's drunk, but he 'pears to me to look mighty sick."

Fanny Poindexter and I were out of the carriage in less than a minute, eagerly embracing an oppor-tunity for action — the relief for tense feelings.

The man wore the uniform of a Confederate soldier. His eyes were closed. Was he asleep ? We feared the worst when we perceived a thin thread of blood trickling slowly from a wound in his throat, and staining his shirt.

We knelt beside him, and Fanny gently pressed

her handkerchief upon the wound, whereupon he opened his eyes, but was unable to speak. "What in the world are we to do?" said my friend. "We can't possibly leave him here!"

"I can tote him to the carriage," said the kind-hearted driver. "He ain' no heavy-weight, an' we can car' 'im to dat hospital jus' at de aidge of town. Come now, sir! Don't you be feared. I'll tote you like a baby."

We were terrified lest he should die before we reached the hospital. To avoid jolting, we crawled at a snail's pace, and great was our relief when we drew up at the open door of the hospital and summoned a surgeon. He ordered out a stretcher and took our patient in, and we waited in a little reception room until we could learn the verdict after an examination of his injuries.

"It is well for him, poor fellow," said the surgeon upon returning to report to us, "that you found him when you did. His wound is not serious, but he was slowly bleeding to death! Which of you pressed that handkerchief to it?" I had to acknowledge that my friend had rendered this service. She was one of those nervous, teary little women who could rise to an occasion.

"He had probably been sent to the rear after he was wounded, and had tried to find General Pryor's camp," said the doctor. "He missed his way, and went farther than necessary. It has all turned out right. He is able now to write his name — 'Ernstorff' — so you see he is doing well. When you pass this way, you must call and see him."

N

We never went that way again. Two years afterward I was accosted at a railway station by a handsome young officer who said he "had never forgotten, never would forget" me. He was Lieutenant Ernstorff!

All the afternoon the dreadful guns shook the earth and thrilled our souls with horror. I shut myself in my darkened room. At twilight I had a note from Governor Letcher, telling me a fierce battle was raging, and inviting me to come to the Governor's mansion. From the roof one might see the flash of musket and artillery.

No! I did not wish to see the infernal fires. I preferred to watch and wait alone in my room.

The city was strangely quiet. Everybody had gone out to the hills to witness the aurora of death to which we were later to become so accustomed. As it grew dark a servant entered to light my candles, but I forbade her. Did I not mean to go to supper? I would have coffee brought to me. God only knew what news I might hear before morning. I must keep up my strength.

The night was hot and close. I sat at an open window, watching for couriers on the street. The firing ceased about nine o'clock. Surely now somebody would remember us and come to us.

As I leaned on the window-sill with my head on my arms, I saw two young men walking slowly down the deserted street. They paused at a closed door opposite me and sat down upon the low step. Presently they chanted a mournful strain in a minor key — like one of the occasional interludes of

Chopin which reveal so much of dignity in sorrow. I was powerfully affected — as I always am by such music — and found myself weeping, not for my own changed life, not for my own sorrows, but for the dear city; the dear, doomed city, so loved, so loved!

A full moon was rising behind the trees in the Capitol Square. Soon the city would be flooded with light, and then! — would the invading host come in to desecrate and destroy? How dear the city had been to me always! I could remember when I was a very little child one just such night as this. The splendor, the immensity of the city had so oppressed me, coming, as I had come, from the quiet country, that I could not sleep. Hot and fevered and afraid, I had risen from my little bed beside my sleeping mother, and had stolen to the window to look out. Like to-night there was a solemn moon in the sky, like to-night an awful stillness in the city. Just below me a watchman had called out, "*All's well!*" Presently the cry was repeated at a distance "All's well!" Fainter and fainter grew the echo until it became a whisper, far away in the distant streets. The watchmen were telling me, I thought, telling all the helpless little babies and children, all the sick people and old people, that God was taking care of them; that "All's well, All's well."

Ah! forever gone was the watchman, forever silent the cry. Never, never again could all be well with us in old Virginia. Never could we stifle the memories of this bitter hour. The watchman on

the nation's tower might, some day, mark the
triumphant return of this invading host, and declare,
" All's well," — *our* hearts would never hear. Too
much blood, too much death, too much anguish !
Our tears would never be able to wash away the
memory of it all.

And so the night wore on and I waited and
watched. Before dawn a hurried footstep brought
a message from the battle-field to my door.

" The General, Madam, is safe and well. Colonel
Scott has been killed. The General has placed a
guard around his body, and he will be sent here
early to-morrow. The General bids me say he will
not return. The fight will be renewed, and will
continue until the enemy is driven away."

My resolution was taken. My children were
safe with their grandmother. I would write. I
would ask that every particle of my household
linen, except a change, should be rolled into bandages, all my fine linen be sent to me for compresses,
and all forwarded as soon as possible.

I would enter the new hospital which had been
improvised in Kent & Paine's warehouse, and would
remain there as a nurse as long as the armies were
fighting around Richmond.

But the courier was passing on his rounds with
news for others. Presently Fanny Poindexter, in
tears, knocked at my door.

" She is bearing it like a brave, Christian woman."

" *She!* Who ? Tell me quick."

" Mrs. Scott. I had to tell her. She simply
said, ' I shall see him once more.' The General

wrote to her from the battle-field and told her how nobly her husband died, — leading his men in the thick of the fight, — and how he had helped to save the city."

Alas, that the city should have needed saving! What had Mrs. Scott and her children done? Why should they suffer? Who was to blame for it all?

Kent & Paine's warehouse was a large, airy building, which had, I understood, been offered by the proprietors for a hospital immediately after the battle of Seven Pines. McClellan's advance upon Richmond had heavily taxed the capacity of the hospitals already established.

When I reached the warehouse, early on the morning after the fight at Mechanicsville, I found cots on the lower floor already occupied, and other cots in process of preparation. An aisle between the rows of narrow beds stretched to the rear of the building. Broad stairs led to a story above, where other cots were being laid.

The volunteer matron was a beautiful Baltimore woman, Mrs. Wilson. When I was presented to her as a candidate for admission, her serene eyes rested doubtfully upon me for a moment. She hesitated. Finally she said: "The work is very exacting. There are so few of us that our nurses must do anything and everything — make beds, wait upon anybody, and often a half a dozen at a time."

"I will engage to do all that," I declared, and she permitted me to go to a desk at the farther end of the room and enter my name.

As I passed by the rows of occupied cots, I saw a

nurse kneeling beside one of them, holding a pan
for a surgeon. The red stump of an amputated arm
was held over it. The next thing I knew I was
myself lying on a cot, and a spray of cold water was
falling over my face. I had fainted. Opening my
eyes, I found the matron standing beside me.

"You see it is as I thought. You are unfit for
this work. One of the nurses will conduct you
home."

The nurse's assistance was declined, however. I
had given trouble enough for one day, and had only
interrupted those who were really worth something.

A night's vigil had been poor preparation for hospital work. I resolved I would conquer my cul-
pable weakness. It was all very well, — these heroics
in which I indulged, these paroxysms of patriotism,
this adoration of the defenders of my fireside. The
defender in the field had naught to hope from me
in case he should be wounded in my defence.

I took myself well in hand. Why had I fainted?
I thought it was because of the sickening, dead odor
in the hospital, mingled with that of acids and dis-
infectants. Of course this would always be there —
and worse, as wounded men filled the rooms. I
provided myself with sal volatile and spirits of camphor, — we wore pockets in our gowns in those days,
— and thus armed I presented myself again to Mrs.
Wilson.

She was as kind as she was refined and intelligent.
"I will give you a place near the door," she said,
"and you must run out into the air at the first hint
of faintness. You will get over it, see if you don't."

Ambulances began to come in and unload at the door. I soon had occupation enough, and a few drops of camphor on my handkerchief tided me over the worst. The wounded men crowded in and sat patiently waiting their turn. One fine little fellow of fifteen unrolled a handkerchief from his wrist to show me his wound. " There's a bullet in there," he said proudly. " I'm going to have it cut out, and then go right back to the fight. Isn't it lucky it's my left hand ? "

As the day wore on I became more and more absorbed in my work. I had, too, the stimulus of a reproof from Miss Deborah Couch, a brisk, efficient middle-aged lady, who asked no quarter and gave none. She was standing beside me a moment, with a bright tin pan filled with pure water, into which I foolishly dipped a finger to see if it were warm ; to learn if I would be expected to provide warm water when I should be called upon to assist the surgeon.

" This water, Madam, was prepared for a raw wound," said Miss Deborah, sternly. " I must now make the surgeon wait until I get more."

Miss Deborah, in advance of her time, was a germ theorist. *My* touch evidently was contaminating.

As she charged down the aisle with a pan of water in her hand, everybody made way. She had known of my " fine-lady faintness," as she termed it, and I could see she despised me for it. She had volunteered, as all the nurses had, and she meant business. She had no patience with nonsense, and truly she was worth more than all the rest of us.

"Where can I get a little ice?" I one day ventured of Miss Deborah.

"Find it," she rejoined, as she rapidly passed on ;
but find it I never did.   Ice was an unknown
luxury until brought to us later from private houses.

But I found myself thoroughly reinstated — with
surgeons, matron, and Miss Deborah — when I
appeared a few days later, accompanied by a man
bearing a basket of clean, well-rolled bandages, with
promise of more to come.   The Petersburg women
had gone to work with a will upon my table-cloths,
sheets, and dimity counterpanes — and even the
chintz furniture covers.   My springlike green and
white chintz bandages appeared on many a manly
arm and leg.   My fine linen underwear and napkins
were cut, by the sewing circle at the Spotswood,
according to the surgeon's directions, into lengths
two inches wide, then folded two inches, doubling
back and forth in a smaller fold each time, until
they formed pointed wedges for compresses.

Such was the sudden and overwhelming demand
for such things, that but for my own and similar
donations of household linen, the wounded men
would have suffered.   The war had come upon us
suddenly.   Many of our ports were already closed,
and we had no stores laid up for such an emergency.

The bloody battle of Gaines's Mill soon followed
— then Frazier's Farm, within the week, and at once
the hospital was filled to overflowing.   Every night
a courier brought me tidings of my husband.   When
I saw him at the door my heart would die within me !
One morning John came in for certain supplies.

After being reassured as to his master's safety, I asked, " Did he have a comfortable night, John ? "

" He sholy did !   Marse Roger cert'nly was comfortable las' night.   He slep' on de field 'twixt two daid horses ! "

The women who worked in Kent & Paine's hospital never seemed to weary.   After a while the wise matron assigned us hours, and we went on duty with the regularity of trained nurses.   My hours were from seven to seven during the day, with the promise of night service should I be needed. Efficient, kindly colored women assisted us.   Their motherly manner soothed the prostrate soldier, whom they always addressed as " son."

Many fine young fellows lost their lives for want of prompt attention.   They never murmured.   They would give way to those who seemed to be more seriously wounded than themselves, and the latter would recover, while from the slighter wounds gangrene would supervene from delay.   Very few men ever walked away from that hospital.   They died, or friends found quarters for them in the homes in Richmond.   None complained !   Unless a poor man grew delirious, he never groaned.   There was an atmosphere of gentle kindness, a suppression of emotion for the sake of others.

Every morning the Richmond ladies brought for our patients such luxuries as could be procured in that scarce time.   The city was in peril, and distant farmers feared to bring in their fruits and vegetables. One day a patient-looking middle-aged man said to me, " What would I not give for a bowl of chicken broth like that my mother used to give me when I was a sick boy!" I perceived one of the angelic matrons of Richmond at a distance, stooping over the cots, and found my way to her and said: " Dear Mrs. Maben, have you a chicken? And could you send some broth to No. 39?" She promised, and I returned with her promise to the poor wounded fellow. He shook his head. "To-morrow will be too late," he said.

I had forgotten the circumstance next day, but at noon I happened to look toward cot No. 39, and there was Mrs. Maben herself. She had brought the chicken broth in a pretty china bowl, with napkin and silver spoon, and was feeding my doubting Thomas, to his great satisfaction.

It was at this hospital, I have reason to believe, that the little story originated, which was deemed good enough to be claimed by other hospitals, of the young girl who approached a sick man with a pan of water in her hand and a towel over her arm.

"Mayn't I wash your face?" said the girl, timidly.

"Well, lady, you may if you want to," said the man, wearily. "It has been washed fourteen times this morning! It can stand another time, I reckon."

I discovered that I had not succeeded, despite many efforts, in winning Miss Deborah. I learned that she was affronted because I had not shared my offerings of jelly and fruit with her, for her special patients. Whenever I ventured to ask a loan from her, of a pan or a glass for water or the little things of which we never had enough, she would reply, " I must keep them for the nurses who understand reciprocity. Reciprocity is a rule *some* persons never seem to comprehend." When this was hammered into my slow perception, I rose to the occasion. I turned over the entire contents of a basket the landlord of the Spotswood had given me to Miss Deborah, and she made my path straight before me ever afterward.

At the end of a week the matron had promoted me! Instead of carving the fat bacon, to be dispensed with corn bread, for the hospital dinner, or standing between two rough men to keep away the flies, or fetching water, or spreading sheets on cots, I was assigned to regular duty with one patient.

The first of these proved to be young Colonel Coppens, of my husband's brigade. I could comfort him very little, for he was wounded past recovery. I spoke little French, and could only try to keep him, as far as possible, from annoyance. To my great relief, place was found for him in a private family. There he soon died — the gallant fellow I had admired on his horse a few months before.

Then I was placed beside the cot of Mr. (or Captain) Boyd of Mecklenburg, and was admonished by the matron not to leave him alone. He was the most patient sufferer in the world, gentle, courteous, always considerate, never complaining. I observed he often closed his eyes and sighed. "Are you in pain, Captain?" "No, no," he would say gently. One day, when I returned from my "rest," I found the matron sitting beside him. Tears were running down her cheeks. She motioned me to take her place, and then added, "No, no, I will not leave him."

The Captain's eyes were closed, and he sighed wearily at intervals.   Presently he whispered slowly : —

> " There everlasting spring abides,"

then sighed, and seemed to sleep for a moment.

The matron felt his pulse and raised a warning hand.   The sick man's whisper went on : —

> " Bright fields beyond the swelling flood
> Stand — dressed — in living green."

The surgeon stood at the foot of the cot and shook his head.   The nurses gathered around with tearful eyes.   Presently in clear tones : —

> " Not Jordan's stream — nor death's cold flood
> Shall fright us — from — the shore,"

and in a moment more the Christian soldier had crossed the river and lain down to rest under the trees.

Each of the battles of those seven days brought a harvest of wounded to our hospital.   I used to veil myself closely as I walked to and from my hotel, that I might shut out the dreadful sights in the street, — the squads of prisoners, and, worst of all, the open wagons in which the dead were piled.   Once I *did* see one of these dreadful wagons! In it a stiff arm was raised, and shook as it was driven down the street, as though the dead owner appealed to Heaven for vengeance ; a horrible sight never to be forgotten.

After one of the bloody battles — I know not if

it was Gaines's Mill or Frazier's Farm or Malvern Hill — a splendid young officer, Colonel Brokenborough, was taken to our hospital, shot almost to pieces. He was borne up the stairs and placed in a cot — his broken limbs in supports swinging from the ceiling. The wife of General Mahone and I were permitted to assist in nursing him. A young soldier from the camp was detailed to help us, and a clergyman was in constant attendance, coming at night that we might rest. Our patient held a court in his corner of the hospital. Such a dear, gallant, cheery fellow, handsome, and with a grand air even as he lay prostrate! Nobody ever heard him complain. He would welcome us in the morning with the brightest smile. His aide said, " He watches the head of the stairs and calls up that look for your benefit." " Oh," he said one day, "you can't guess what's going to happen! Some ladies have been here and left all these roses, and cologne, and such; and somebody has sent — champagne! We are going to have a party!"

Ah, but we knew he was very ill! We were bidden to watch him every minute and not be deceived by his own spirits. Mrs. Mahone spent her life hunting for ice. My constant care was to keep his canteen — to which he clung with affection — filled with fresh water from a spring not far away, and I learned to give it to him so well that I allowed no one to lift his head for his drink during my hours.

One day, when we were alone, I was fanning him, and thought he was asleep. He said gravely, " Mrs. Pryor, beyond that curtain they hung up yesterday

poor young Mitchell is lying! They think I don't
know! But I heard when they brought him in, —
as I lie here, I listen to his breathing. I haven't
heard it now for some time. Would you mind seeing if he is all right?"

I passed behind the curtain. The young soldier
was dead. His wide-open eyes seemed to meet
mine in mute appeal. I had never seen or touched
a dead man, but I laid my hands upon his eyelids
and closed them. I was standing thus when his
nurse, a young volunteer like myself, came to me.

"I couldn't do that," she said; "I went for the
doctor. I'm so glad you could do it."

When I returned Colonel Brokenborough asked
no questions and I knew that his keen senses had
already instructed him.

To be cheerful and uncomplaining was the unwritten law of our hospital. No bad news was ever
mentioned, no foreboding or anxiety. Mrs. Mahone
was one day standing beside Colonel Brokenborough when a messenger from the front suddenly
announced that General Mahone had received a
flesh-wound. Commanding herself instantly, she
exclaimed merrily: "*Flesh*-wound! Now you all
know that is *just impossible.*" The General had no
flesh! He was as thin and attenuated as he was
brave.

As Colonel Brokenborough grew weaker I felt
self-reproach that no one had offered to write letters
for him. His friend the clergyman had said to me:
"That poor boy is engaged to a lovely young girl.
I wonder what is best? Would it grieve him to

speak of her? You ladies have so much tact; you might bear it in mind. An opportunity might offer for you to discover how he feels about it." The next time I was alone with him I ventured: "Now, Colonel, one mustn't forget absent friends, you know, even if fair ladies do bring perfumes and roses and what not. I have some ink and paper here. Shall I write a letter for you? Tell me what to say."

He turned his head and with a half-amused smile of perfect intelligence looked at me for a long time. Then an upward look of infinite tenderness; but the message was never sent — never needed from a true heart like his.

One night I was awakened from my first sleep by a knock at my door, and a summons to " come to Colonel Brokenborough." When I reached his bedside I found the surgeon, the clergyman, and the Colonel's aide. The patient was unconscious; the end was near. We sat in silence. Once, when he stirred, I slipped my hand under his head, and put his canteen once more to his lips. After a long time his breathing simply ceased, with no evidence of pain. We waited awhile, and then the young soldier who had been detailed to nurse him rose, crossed the room, and, stooping over, kissed me on my forehead, and went out to his duty in the ranks.

Two weeks later I was in my room, resting after a hard day, when a haggard officer, covered with mud and dust, entered. It was my husband.

"My men are all dead," he said, with anguish,

and, falling across the bed, he gave vent to the passionate grief of his heart.

Thousands of Confederate soldiers were killed, thousands wounded.

Richmond was saved!

General McClellan and General Lee both realized that their men needed rest. My husband was allowed a few days' respite from duty. Almost without pause he had fought the battles of Williamsburg, Seven Pines, Mechanicsville, Gaines's Mill, and Frazier's Farm. He had won his promotion early, but he had lost the loved commander who appreciated him, had seen old schoolmates and friends fall by his side, — the dear fellow, George Loyal Gordon, who had been his best man at our wedding, — old college comrades, valued old neighbors.

Opposed to him in battle, then and after, were men who in after years avowed themselves his warm friends, — General Hancock, General Slocum, General Butterfield, General Sickles, General Fitz-John Porter, General McClellan, and General Grant. They had fought loyally under opposing banners, and from time to time, as the war went on, one and another had been defeated; but over all, and through all, their allegiance had been given to a banner that has never surrendered, — the standard of the universal brotherhood of all true men.

CHAPTER XIV

THE privilege of nursing in the hospital had been bought at a dear price, for it was decided positively that I was to surrender, for the present, my dream of following the army. I was remanded to the mountains, and at Charlottesville I had news of the events that rapidly followed the Seven Days' Battles around Richmond.

McClellan had been relieved of his command, and the defenceless women and children of Northern Virginia were handed over to the tender mercies of General Pope. McClellan wrote, August 8 : " I will strike square in the teeth of all the infamous orders of Mr. John Pope, and forbid all pillaging and stealing, and take the highest Christian ground for the conduct of the war. I will not permit this army to degenerate into a mob of thieves, nor will I return these men of mine to their families as a set of wicked and demoralized robbers."

General Pope had announced his purpose (which he carried out) to subsist his army on our country, and to hang or shoot any non-combating citizens who might fall into his hands, in retaliation for the killing of his soldiers. This was one of " the infamous orders of Mr. John Pope " to which General

McClellan alluded; but infamy to some eyes is fame to others. Pope superseded McClellan; but he was himself superseded after his defeat at the hands of Lee, and McClellan reinstated.

My husband's brigade followed General Lee, fought the battle of Manassas, where he captured and paroled the hospital corps, went with him throughout the campaign, into Maryland and back, fought the battle of South Mountain and the bloody battle of Antietam (or Sharpsburg).

The histories of these battles have been given again and again by the military commanders who conducted them. At the close of the campaign General Lee reported that his men were in the finest possible condition — only there were too few of them. As the Federal armies were depleted, they could be reënforced by foreigners. As our men were lost, we had no fresh troops to take their places.

My husband commanded Anderson's division at Antietam, General Anderson having been wounded. This battle is quoted, along with the battle of Seven Pines, as one of the most hotly contested of the war. Sorely pressed at one time, General Pryor despatched an orderly to General Longstreet with a request for artillery. The latter tore the margin from a newspaper and wrote: "I am sending you the guns, dear General. This is a hard fight and we had better all die than lose it." At one time during the battle the combatants agreed upon a brief cessation, that the dead and wounded of both sides might be removed. While General Pryor waited, a Federal officer approached him.

"General," said he, "I have just detected one of my men in robbing the body of one of your soldiers. I have taken his booty from him, and now consign it to you."

Without examining the small bundle, — tied in a handkerchief, — my husband ordered it to be properly enclosed and sent to me. The handkerchief contained a gold watch, a pair of gold sleeve-links, a few pieces of silver, and a strip of paper on which was written, "Strike till the last armed foe expires," and signed "A Florida patriot." There seemed to be no clew by which I might hope to find an inheritor for these treasures. I could only take care of them.

I brought them forth one day to interest an aged relative, whose chair was placed in a sunny window. "I think, my dear," she said, "there are pin-scratched letters on the inside of these sleeve-buttons." Sure enough, there were three initials, rudely made, but perfectly plain.

Long afterward I met a Confederate officer from Florida who had fought at Antietam.

"Did you know any one from your state, Captain, who was killed at Sharpsburg?"

"Alas! yes," he replied, and mentioned a name corresponding exactly with the scratched initials.

The parcel, with a letter from me, was sent to an address he gave me, and in due time I received a most touching letter of thanks from the mother of the dead soldier.

General Lee went into winter quarters at Culpeper, and thither I repaired to visit a kind and hospitable family, who were good enough to invite me.   In their home I spent two weeks.   I had not imagined there were so many soldiers in the world as I saw then.   " You cannot take a step anywhere," said a lady, "without treading on a soldier !"   They were in the finest spirits, notwithstanding their long marches and short rations.   Thousands on thousands of Federal troops were in Virginia.   The highways of our chief rivers were closed, our railroads menaced.   Everything we needed was already scarce and held at high prices.   Nobody had comforts or luxuries ; nobody murmured because of such privations.

We made our host's drawing-room a camping ground, his fire our camp-fire.   Around it gathered a nightly crowd of gay young soldiers. They wished no serious talk, these young warriors ! They had a brief respite from fatigue and sorrow, and they intended to enjoy it.   They sentimentalized, however, over the tender and mournful song, " Lorena," which even then touched a chord in every heart, and which meant so much of devotion and heartbreak two years later.   For four years the daughters of the South waited for their lovers, and some, alas ! waited forever.

> " It matters little now, Lorena,
>   The past is the eternal past,
> Our heads will soon lie low, Lorena,
>   Life's tide is ebbing out so fast ;
> But there's a future — oh ! thank God —
>   Of life this is so small a part ;
> 'Tis dust to dust beneath the sod,
>   But *there*, up *there*, — 'tis *heart* to *heart*."

With pretty Nelly at the piano, her blue eyes raised to heaven, and Jack Fleming accompanying her on her guitar, his dark eyes raised to Nelly, the effect was overwhelming; and lest somebody should quite finish us by singing, "Flee as a bird to the mountain," we would hasten to demand the "Bonnie Blue Flag," or "Dixie," or the polite invitation to "Joe Hooker" to "come out the Wilderness," or, better still, a good story. The latter call would bring many we had heard before—there are so few good stories in the world—but we would welcome each one with applause, even if it were no better than the story of Captain —— (I can't remember the captain's name) and his black boy "Cæsar." I can only vouch for the story, which ran thus:—

The captain, going into a skirmish one day, left his tent and its contents in the care of the boy. "Mayn't I go he'p de cook?" said Cæsar, much desiring to place himself farther in the rear.

"Stay here, sir, and protect my property!" sternly commanded his master.

Cæsar, when left alone, grew unhappy, and when straggling shot fell like hail around the tent, he incontinently fled and hid in the bushes. When he returned, he found an angry captain indeed.

"You rascal! Didn't I leave you here to protect my property? It might have been all stolen."

"I knows it, sah, I knows it! An' I did purtect yo' property, sah! I sholy did! Dem ole cloes ain' wuth nothin'! I'se feared to bresh 'em less'n I git a hole in 'em; but *dis* property," laying his hand proudly on his breast, "*dis* property is wuth fifteen hundred dollars!"

Of course so good a story was soon capped by another. One of the boys who had been with my General at Williamsburg could tell it. A shell had entered the domain of pots and kettles and created what Domingo the cook termed a "clatteration." He at once started for the rear.

"What's de matter, Mingo?" asked a fellow-servant, "whar you gwine wid such a hurrification?"

"I gwine to git out o' trouble — dar whar I gwine. Dar's too much powder in dem big things. Dis chile ain't gwine bu'n hisself! An' dar's dem Minnie bullets, too, comin' frew de a'r, singin': '*Whar* — is — you? *Whar* — is — you?' I ain't gwine stop an' tell 'em whar I is! I'se a twenty-two-hundurd-dollar nigger, an' I'se gwine tek keer o' what b'longs to marster, I is."

Of course we heard again the story of Stonewall Jackson's body-servant, who always knew before anybody when a battle was imminent.

"The General tells you, I suppose," said one of the soldiers.

"Lawd, no, sir! De Gin'ral nuvver tell *me* nothin'! I observates de 'tention of de Gin'ral dis way: co'se he prays, jest like we all, mornin' an' night; but when he gits up two, three times in a night to pray, den I rubs my eye and gits up too, an' packs de haversack, — ca'se I done fine out dere's gwine to be de ole boy to pay right away."

Amusing as were the negro stories, there were plenty of others, revealing the peculiar characteristics of the common soldier.   The soldier from rural districts was a trial to his officers in the early days of the war.   Nothing could make him hurry.   "If he came to a stream, he would deliberately look around for two fence-rails and put them across, and the time consumed by a company in crossing in this way can be imagined.   If his feet hurt him, he would sit down on the roadside to tie rags around them." He never could be made to understand that freedom of speech with an officer, who had been perhaps a neighbor, was denied him; nor yet that he could not indulge in good-natured chaff or criticism.

"Are you sentinel here?" asked an officer, who found a sentry sitting down and cleaning his gun, having taken it entirely to pieces.

"Well, I am a sort of sentinel, I reckon."

"Well, *I* am a sort of officer of the day."

"Is *that* so?   Just hold on till I get my gun together, and I will give you a sort of a salute."[1]

When a picket guard at Harper's Ferry was being detailed for duty, one of these verdant volunteers loudly protested against that manner of carrying on war.

"What's the use of gwine out thar to keep everybody off?" he shouted.   "We've all kem here to hev a fight with them Yankees, an' ef you sen' fellers out thar to skeer 'em off, how in thunder are we gwine to hev a scrimmage?"

In the hardest times of starvation and weariness, according to our soldier boys, the situation would be relieved by the drollery of some good-natured, great-

---

[1] "Camp-fire and Battle-field," p. 456 *et seq.*

hearted countryman. Officers who had an easy place, and musicians, for a similar reason, were their special targets. Rather than be tormented, musicians would often leave the line of march and go through fields to avoid the running fire. " Ah, now ! give us a toot on yer old funnel," or, " Brace up thar with yer blowpipe ! "

These fellows who didn't fight were all classed under the general term of " bomb-proofs." One of these officers — a little man — having appeared in an enormous pair of cavalry boots, ran the gantlet of a neighboring brigade and heard a frank opinion of himself : —

" I say, Mister, better git out'r them smokestacks ! We know you're in thar 'cause we all kin see yer head stickin' out. You needn' say yer *ain't* in thar, — 'cause yer ears is workin' powerful."

The allusion to the celebrated long-eared animal was awful !

If a " bomb-proof " officer — a fellow who had a position in the rear — should happen to be smartly dressed when cantering along near a regiment, he would be apt to change his canter to a gallop as the men would shout and whoop : —

" Oh, *my !* Ain't he pooty ? Say, Mister ! whar'd ye git that biled shut ? Was ye ra-a-ly born so, or was ye put together by corntrack ? Sich a nice-lookin' rooster oughter git down an' scratch for a wurrum ! "

Even when a brigade would pass at double-quick, going into a battle in which the waiting soldier expected any moment to take part, the latter would call out : —

"What's your hurry, boys? Gwine to ketch a train?"

They made great fun, too, of their own fears, never considering them worthy of being treated seriously, or as in any way detrimental.

Under fire at Manassas, a raw recruit was doing pretty well, when a rabbit loped across the field. Dropping his gun as he was about to shoot, he yelled, with honest pathos : —

"Go it, little cotton-tail, go it! I'm jest as skeered as you be, an' ef I dar'd, I'd run too."

A number of militia having given way under fire, their commanding officer called out to one of the fugitives : —

"What are you running away for, you —— —— coward? You ought to be ashamed of yourself."

"I ain't runnin' away, Gin'ral! I'm just skeered! Them fellers over thar are shootin' bullets as big as watermillions! One of 'em went right peerst my head — right peerst ; — an' — an' I wants to go home."

"Well, why didn't you shoot back, sir? You are crying like a baby."

"I knows it, Gin'ral — I knows it. I wish I *was* a baby, and a gal-baby, too, and then I wouldn't hev been cornscripted."

The regiments of Georgia, North Carolina, and Virginia could never pass each other without some chaffing challenge.

"Hello, North Car'lina," said an officer to a lanky specimen in a shabby uniform.

"Hello, Virginia."

" Blockade on turpentine making ? You all hard up ? No sale for tar now ? "

" Well — yes ! " was the slow rejoinder. " We sell all our tar to Jeff Davis now."

" The thunder you do ! What does the President want with your tar ? "

" He puts it on the heels of Virginians to make 'em stick to the battle-field."

The staff officer rode on.

A good story had found its way into our lines from a Federal officer. He was commenting upon the fact that all Southern women were intense rebels — with one exception. He had been with others marching down a wooded lane which ended in a sharp curve. As they rounded it, they suddenly came upon a house, before which was a woman picking up chips. As she had evidently not seen them, the officer tip-toed up to her, put his arm around her waist, and kissed her — and stepped back to avoid the box on the ear he knew he deserved. The woman, however, straightened herself, looked at him seriously for a moment, and said slowly, " You'll find me right here every mornin' a-pickin' up chips."

It would seem that the telling of stories of a mildly humorous nature, with the characteristic of dialect, was a feature of the war-time, — the President of the United States affording a notable example. When the gravest matters were under consideration, all things were held in abeyance until the illustrative anecdote was duly presented. How Mr. Seward chafed under them we all know. The poor little stories that went the rounds among the rank and file at the camp-fires

in Virginia had their uses.   Whatever the weariness,
the discouragement, the failure of the wagons to come
up with provisions, by such simple means did the
brave boys lighten their own and each others' hearts.
Whenever they had cards they played; but before
going into battle the camp-ground would be strewn
with them, the soldier of the rank and file always
emptying his pockets of his cards!   His Testament
was pocketed in their stead.

In repeating these stories around our blazing log
fire, and in describing their marches and hard times,
the brave fellows made sport of all their discomforts
and of their shifts to supplement deficiencies.   They
told with merriment of the times they had proudly
drawn over their bruised feet boots found on the
march, and had suffered such agony from the swelling of the compressed members that they were fain
to implore a comrade to cut off the instrument of
torture; of the time Mr. Giddings and his pretty
daughters entertained them in Maryland, and of their
dreadful embarrassment at finding they had raven-
ously swept the table of every biscuit, every bit of
ham, every raw tomato — and had wanted, oh, so
much more!   And how some of them had been captured and soon released; but while prisoners and waiting for a train, how a Federal officer had talked most
kindly to them, inquiring for old West Point comrades of his who were on our side; and how they on
their part had asked after the welfare of Captain John
Lea of Petersburg, who had been captured at Williamsburg, — to be told by this Federal officer that
Captain Lea had been dreadfully wounded, and while

in the hospital had been nursed by a young lady with
whom he fell in love, and that the officer had been
present at their marriage in Williamsburg, and through
his intercession and that of other old West Point comrades Captain Lea had been released.   When the
time came for parting with the courteous officer our
boys had respectfully requested his name.   " My name
is Custer," he said.   " I do not belong to any regiment, but am on the staff of General McClellan."
He was none other than the famous George A.
Custer of the United States cavalry, destined to
win for himself immortal renown, and to meet gallantly an early death in the fight with the Indians
on the Little Big Horn River.

Many of these soldier boys — "boys" now no
longer, but " veterans "— were from Petersburg, and
had stood in line on the day when Alice and Tabb
and Marian and Molly and all the other girls had
waited with me to see them off.   It was delightful to
meet them and to hear news of the others.   Where
was Will Johnson?   Where was Berry Stainback?
Will had been captured " for no reason whatever
except that he and Berry had but one blanket between them, and Will had to get himself captured
when he found Berry had been, in order to continue
to share the blanket, which was in Berry's possession," a story which Will's friends could safely invent
for their amusement, as his known courage was beyond
all doubt.

General " Jeb " Stuart was a great hero with these
soldier boys, dashing as he did all over the country
with his eight thousand mounted men.   He was our

plumed knight — with his gold star and long feather. They never wearied of stories of his promptness, his celerity, his meteorlike dashes.

"They'll never catch him!" said one proudly. "They'll always reach the place where he recently was."

"He reminds me of the knights of the olden time," said a young lady.

"The mediæval knight, my dear young lady," said General Johnson, "would be of little use in this war. He would have stood no chance with one of Stuart's men."

"Fancy him," said another, "with his two hundred weight of iron on him, and as much on his big cart-horse. Imagine him, armed with a maul or a lance, a battle-axe, and six-foot pole, going into a fight at Manassas or Antietam."

"He would never get there," said the General. "A light cavalryman of the First Virginia would have ridden around King Arthur or Sir Launcelot half a dozen times while the knight was bracing himself up for action; and the Chicopee sabre would have searched out the joints under his chin, or his arm, or his sword-belt, and would have shucked him like an oyster before he could get his lance in rest."

And Jackson was another of their idols. Stories of his strategy, his courage, his faith in God, his successes, filled many an hour around the camp-fire in the hospitable Culpeper mansion.

But the chief idol of their hearts — of all our hearts — was our beloved commander, our Bayard *sans peur et sans reproche*, General Lee. The hand instinctively sought the cap at the mention of his name. Indignant comments were made upon the newspaper criticisms of his early misfortunes in the western part of Virginia in the autumn of 1861, and one occasion was remembered when, his own attention having been directed to a fierce newspaper attack, as unjust in its conclusions as it was untrue in its statements, he was asked why he silently suffered such unwarranted aspersions; and he had calmly replied that, while it was very hard to bear, it was perhaps quite natural that such hasty conclusions should be announced, and that it was better not to attempt a justification or defence, but to go steadily on in the discharge of duty to the best of our ability, leaving all else to the calmer judgment of the future and to a kind Providence.

Happy was the private soldier who had seen General Lee, thrice happy the one who had spoken to him. Of the latter, a plain countryman, having listened to the personal incidents of his fellows, as they related various occasions when they had been noticed by General Lee, was fired by a desire to emulate them, and confided that he, too, had once enjoyed a very interesting and gratifying interview with General Lee. Importuned to tell it, the soldier modestly hesitated, but urged by an evident incredulity on the part of his hearers, he took heart of grace and related as follows : —

" I was jest out of the horspittle an' was natchelly strollin' round when the scrimmage was goin' on, and I saw Gen'ral Lee on a little rise not fur off. I santered closer an' closer to him, and when I saw

him look at me I says, ' Pretty warm work over thar,
Gen'ral.'   He give me a keen look, an' says he,
quiet-like : ' Where do you belong ?   Where's your
regiment ? '   An' I says, ' I'm lookin' for my regiment now — Twelfth Virginia.'   ' I can help you,'
says he ; ' there is your regiment just going into the
fight.   Hurry up an' join it.'   An' I run off proud
as a pigeon."

" Didn't you think you might get shot ? " asked
his comrade.

" I suttenly did !   I always thinks that.   But
then, thinks I, Gen'ral Lee will be mighty sorry
'cause he knowed he sent me into danger when I
was feelin' mighty weak an' poly."

The incidents were many which the officers and
soldiers could remember, illustrating the dear commander's peculiar traits.   His aide, Colonel Taylor,
has written me of one most touching incident : —

" Tidings reached General Lee, soon after his
return to Virginia, of the serious illness of one of his
daughters — the darling of his flock.   For several
days apprehensions were entertained that the next
intelligence would be of her death.   One morning
the mail was received, and the private letters were
distributed as was the custom ; but no one knew
whether any home news had been received by the
General.   At the usual hour he summoned me to
his presence, to know if there were any matters of
army routine upon which his judgment and action
were desired.   The papers containing a few such
cases were presented to him ; he reviewed, and gave
his orders in regard to them.   I then left him, but

for some cause returned in a few moments, and with my accustomed freedom entered his tent without announcement or ceremony, when I was startled and shocked to see him overcome with grief, an open letter in his hand. That letter contained the sad intelligence of his daughter's death.

"Scarcely less to be admired than his sublime devotion to duty," continued Colonel Taylor, "was his remarkable self-control. General Lee was naturally of a positive temperament, and of strong passions; and it is a mistake to suppose him otherwise; but he held these in complete subjection to his will and conscience. He was not one of those invariably amiable men, whose temper is never ruffled; but when we consider the immense burden which rested upon him, and the numberless causes for annoyance with which he had to contend, the occasional cropping out of temper which we, who were constantly near him, witnessed, only showed how great was his habitual self-command.

"He had a great dislike to reviewing army communications; this was so thoroughly appreciated by me that I would never present a paper for his action unless it was of decided importance, and of a nature to demand his judgment and decision. On one occasion, when an audience had not been asked of him for several days, it became necessary to have one. The few papers requiring his action were submitted. He was not in a very pleasant mood; something irritated him, and he manifested his ill humor by a little nervous twist or jerk of the neck and head, peculiar to himself, accompanied by some harshness of manner.   This was perceived by me, and I hastily concluded that my efforts to save him annoyance were not appreciated.   In disposing of some case of a vexatious character, matters reached a climax; he became really worried, and, forgetting what was due to my superior, I petulantly threw the paper down at my side and gave evident signs of anger.   Then, in a perfectly calm and measured tone of voice, he said, 'Colonel Taylor, when I lose my temper, don't you let it make you angry.'

"Was there ever a more gentle and considerate, and yet so positive, reproof?   How magnanimous in the great soldier, and yet how crushing to the subordinate!   The rash and disrespectful conduct of the latter would have justified, if it did not demand, summary treatment at the hands of the former.   Instead of this, the first man of his day and generation, great and glorious in his humility, condescended to occupy the same plane with his youthful subaltern, and to reason with him as an equal, frankly acknowledging his own imperfections, but kindly reminding the inferior at the same time of his duty and his position."   Great indeed must be the man whom we can love all the better for his human weakness.

CHAPTER XV

G ENERAL PRYOR'S brigade had been composed of regiments from Alabama, Florida,
Mississippi, North Carolina, and Virginia.
Congress having recommended that regiments should
be enlisted under officers from their own states, — in
order to remedy, if possible, the disinclination to reën-
list for the war, — there was a general upheaval and
change throughout the entire army during the autumn
of 1862. On the 10th of November General Pryor
was ordered to report for duty to Major-General
G. W. Smith, commanding at Richmond, Virginia, the
Second, Fifth, and Eighth Florida Regiments of his
brigade being assigned to a Florida brigadier, the
Fourteenth Alabama and the Fifth North Carolina
to officers from their respective states.

On November 2 General Longstreet had written
to General Pryor: " I understand that General Perry
will have the Florida regiments. Please make some
suggestion as to what arrangement we may be able
to make for you."

Accordingly my husband consulted General Lee,
and received the following letter from him, dated
November 25, 1862 : —

" GENERAL : Your letter of the 23d inst. has just been received. I regret my inability to detach from this army the two regiments to operate on the Blackwater. As far as I am able to judge, troops are more wanted here than there, and it might be better to bring the troops which it is contemplated to unite with those in question to this army. I regretted at the time the breaking up of your former brigade, but you are aware that the circumstances which produced it were beyond my control. I hope it will not be long before you will be again in the field, that the country may derive the benefit of your zeal and activity."

On November 29, General Pryor was ordered by General G. W. Smith to report to Major-General French, and was personally introduced to the latter by the following letter : —

" RICHMOND, November 29, 1862.

" MY DEAR GENERAL : This will be handed you by my friend, Brigadier-General Pryor. General Pryor's brigade in General Lee's army was recently broken up in rearranging the brigades by states. It is intended by the government that he shall have a Virginia brigade as soon as one can be formed for him. In the meanwhile, it is General Lee's desire that General Pryor shall serve upon the Blackwater — his own section of the country — and he directs that the two regiments of cavalry on the Blackwater be placed under his command, etc. . . .

" General Pryor has already won for himself the reputation of being one of the best, most daring, and energetic officers in the army, highly distinguished in civil life, and one of the most influential men in the state, especially in his own section. He will coöperate with you thoroughly, and I am sure will render good service to the cause and be of great assistance to yourself.

" I am satisfied, from what General Lee writes me, that at present we can have no troops from his army. The impression is, that a great battle is impending in the vicinity of Fredericksburg. We must keep our house in order, and make the most of the means we have and can procure from other sources than General Lee's army.

"Very truly yours,

"G. W. Smith, *Major-General.*"

A rule enforced for the common good often falls heavily upon individuals. General Pryor grieved to lose his men, and they united in many petitions to be allowed to remain with him. He undertook the protection of the Blackwater region with an inadequate force, in the certain expectation that reënforcements would be sent to him.

The enemy destined to conquer us at last — the " ravenous, hunger-starved wolf " — already menaced us. General Longstreet had learned that corn and bacon were stored in the northeastern counties of North Carolina, and he had sent two companies of cavalry on a foraging expedition, to the region around Suffolk.

" The Confederate lines," says a historian, " extended only to the Blackwater River on the east, where a body of Confederate troops was stationed to keep the enemy in check." That body was commanded by General Pryor, now in front of a large Federal force, to keep it in check while the wagon-trains sent off corn and bacon for Lee's army. This was accomplished by sleepless vigilance on the part of the Confederate General. The Federal forces made frequent sallies from Suffolk, but were always driven back with heavy loss. It is amusing to read of the calmness with which his commanding officers ordered him to accomplish great things with his small force.

" I cannot," says General Colston, " forward your requisition for two regiments of infantry and one of cavalry : it is almost useless to make such requisitions, for they remain unanswered. You must use every possible means to deceive the enemy as to your strength, and you must *hold the line of the Blackwater to the last extremity.*"

General French writes : " If I had any way to increase your forces, I should do so, but I have to bow to higher authority and the necessities of the service. But you must annoy the villains all you can, and make them uncomfortable. Give them no rest. Ambush them at every turn."

General Pryor did not dream I would come to his camp at Blackwater. He supposed I would find quarters among my friends at home, but I had now no home. Our venerable father had sent his family to the interior after the battles around Richmond ; had given up his church in Petersburg, and, commending the women, old men, and children to the care of a successor, had entered the army as chaplain, " where," as he said, " I can follow my own church members and comfort them in sickness, if I can do no more."

As soon as the position of our brigade was made known to me, I drew forth the box containing the camp outfit, packed a trunk or two, and took the cars for the Blackwater. The terminus of the railroad was only a few miles from our camp. The Confederate train could go no farther because of the enemy. The day's journey was long, for the passenger car attached to the transportation train was dependent upon the movements of the latter. The few passengers who had set forth with me in the morning had left at various wayside stations, and I was now alone. I had no idea where we should sleep that night. I thought I would manage it somehow — somewhere.

We arrived at twilight at the end of our journey. When I left the car my little boys gathered around me. There was a small wooden building near, which served for waiting-room and post-office. The only dwelling in sight was another small house, surrounded by a few bare trees. My first impression was that I had never before seen such an expanse of gray sky. The face of the earth was a dead, bare level, as far as the eye could reach; and much, very much of it lay under water. I was in the region of swamps, stretching on and on until they culminated in the one great "Dismal Swamp" of the country. No sounds were to be heard, no hum of industry or lowing of cattle, but a mighty concert rose from thousands, nay, millions, of frogs.

"Now," thought I, "here is really a fine opportunity to be 'jolly'! Mark Tapley's swamps couldn't surpass these." But all the railroad folk were departing, and the postmaster was preparing to lock his door and leave also. I liked the looks of the little man, and ventured : —

"Can you tell me, sir, where I can get lodging

to-night?   I am the General's wife — Mrs. Pryor —
and to-morrow he will take care of me.   I know he
has no place for us in camp."

The little man considered, and looked us over —
a lady, three little boys, trunks, and a box.

"I can take thee in myself," he said.   "I am just
going home."

"Oh, thank you, thank you.   I shall need only
the smallest trunk to-night."

"I'm afraid I can hardly make thee comfortable,
as I live alone, but thee is welcome."

"Thee"!   Oh, joy!   I thought.   This is a blessed
little Quaker!   We'll not part again!   Here I rest.
We soon reached his door, and he called out for
"Charity!"

The call was answered in person by a black girl in
a short linsey-woolsey frock which revealed her ankles
and bare feet, her hair tied in innumerable little tails,
sticking all over her head like a porcupine's quills.
She was the most alert little creature I ever saw,
nimble-footed and quick.   "Charity," said my host,
"have a good fire made upstairs in the front room
at once.   Thee is welcome," he repeated, turning to
me, and I followed the sable maiden up the stair.

"And so your name is Charity?"

"Charity's meh name an' Charity's meh naycher,"
she informed me.   She soon brought in Dick with an
armful of wood, and a fine, welcome fire cheered us.

"You needn' be lookin' at de baid," said Charity.
"I'll soon sheet it.   He's got sto's o' quilts, but I
dunno as he'll s'render 'em."

It appeared that he would.   He brought them, an

armful, himself, and the bright patchwork on our two beds looked very inviting.

Charity leaned against the mantel, regarding me with leisurely scrutiny, her bare feet crossed one over the other. I felt it to be the part of prudence to placate her.

" We'll unlock the trunk," I said, — Dick had already fetched it, — " and I'll find a pretty ribbon for you."

" I knowed," said the girl, " you was some punkins soon's I sot eyes on you." Before I was summoned to the supper of biscuit, fried bacon, and coffee without cream, Charity had enlightened me about her employer; she made haste to tell me he was not her master. " I'se free, I is! Mo'n dat, he's a Quaker, an' ef you ever seen Quakers, you knows dey don' like no slaves 'roun'. Yas'm, I'se free — an' Dick, he's a po'-white boy. Me'n him does all de wuk cep'n in hawg-killin' time, an' den de fokes comes fum de quarters to he'p."

" Are you lonesome ? " I asked, making conversation.

" *Dat* I is. You see he los' his wife two mont' ago. Dese here quilts is hern. She made 'em."

" Dear me," I said, " I'm so sorry ! "

But Charity had broken down and was sobbing with her head against the mantel.

" Yas'm ! I cert'nly is lonesum ! She jes up an' die, an', an' de po' little baby daid too."

As I lay in bed I thought of the dear dead woman. I resolved to be nothing but a comfort to Charity and that little Quaker. I made plans for

the happiness of both.   With my heart full of sympathy, full of gratitude, full of hope, I slept sweetly
and long.

In the morning a message sent from the post-office
through an inquirer from the camp brought me my
General; brought, too, an invitation from my host to
make this house his headquarters, and during the day
he moved over bag and baggage.   A cook was detailed
from the camp, we were to furnish our own table;
and our kind host looked so deeply wounded when
we offered rent for our lodgings, that no more
was said on that subject.   I had brought nothing
with me except the plain contents of my camp chest.
The thick white china of the table was unattractive,
and I consulted Charity about the possibility of buying something better.   Our only market-town, Suffolk, was in the hands of the enemy.

"He's got painted cups an' saucers, but I dunno's
he'll s'render 'em," said Charity.

"Suppose you ask him!"

"I dun try 'im once.   I ax 'im dat time when his
mother-in-law cum to see 'im — an' he nuvver say
nuthin!   Den I let 'im rip!"

But after a few days "he" threw in my lap a
bunch of keys, saying simply, "Everything in the
house and on the plantation belongs to thee."
Some of them were enormous, like the key of the
Bastile, and all were rusted.   I selected a small one,
returning the rest, and in Charity's presence unlocked the old mahogany sideboard and counted to
her the cups, saucers, and plates, gilt-edged, and
decorated with a rosebud here and there.

"Good Gawd!" said Charity. "I *nuvver* thought he'd s'render the chany cups!"

"Not one is to be broken," I said, sternly. "If you break one, tell me at once and bring me the pieces, so I can send to Richmond and replace it."

I saw but little of my kind host. He lived at the post-office, remaining late every night to open the mail and have it ready for an early morning delivery to the camp, and returning home at twelve o'clock to sleep. Every night thereafter he found a bright fire, a clean-swept hearth, and on plates before the fire, biscuits, sausage or broiled ham, and a little pot of coffee. A table — with a lamp and the latest papers — was drawn up beside his armchair.

A few months after I left his house for Petersburg I received the following letter from him : —

"RESPECTED FRIEND: I have now married. I couldn't stand it.

"Thy friend,

"I. P."

Since then I have always counselled, as cure for an incorrigible bachelor, simply to take care of him beautifully for three months and then — leave him!

But to return : Charity's example was contagious. "I cert'nly was lonesum" on the Blackwater. The General and his staff were forever in the saddle. When he returned after his skirmishes and exploring expeditions, he was too tired to amuse me. I busied myself teaching the little boys and dispensing the provisions our men brought me. Bacon and biscuit,

HON. ROGER A. PRYOR.

From a photograph, about 1870.

without butter, fruit, or milk, was deadly diet for me, so I was allowed an occasional courier from the camp to take my money and scour the country for better fare. When he appeared, galloping down the lane, on his return, he looked like some extraordinary feathered creature with a horse's head, so completely were both covered with turkeys, ducks, geese, and chickens. Then would ensue a gift to the camp hospital of soups and stews and a fine supper for my General's staff, Major Shepard, Captain Whitner, Major Keiley, and Captain McCann, with as many choice spirits from the officers as we could entertain. Then was brewed, by the majors and captains aforesaid, a mighty bowl of egg-nog, sweet and very stiff, for there was no milk to temper its strength. I feared at first that my Quaker host might disapprove, but I never failed to find the foaming glass I placed beside his night lamp quite empty next morning.

I could manage to occupy myself during the day. I could make a study of Charity, in whom I soon perceived quite an interesting character, quick to learn, responsive, and most affectionate. She was literally my only female companion. I had no neighbors, nowhere to drive (the enemy was only fifteen miles off) except on the watery lanes, nothing to meet when driving except, perhaps, a slow-moving cart drawn by steeds like Sydney Smith's " Tug-and-Lug, Haul-and-Crawl," driven by a negro boy, who stood with feet planted on the shafts and who entertained his patient, long-suffering oxen by telling them of the torments awaiting them unless they would "go along." But the long and lonely evenings were hard to bear, when the general and his staff were abroad, roaming like watch-dogs around the frontier, deluding the enemy by a great show of bravado here and there. Nothing like the orchestra of frogs can be imagined. They serenaded the moon all night long; a magnificent diapason of mighty voices, high soprano, full baritone, and heavy bass. I could understand the desperate need of the lone woman who had once lived here. The patchwork quilts were eloquent witnesses.

As the time dragged on in this lonely place, I began to find that I wanted many articles classed in a woman's mind generally as "things."

There is not a more generous word in the English language than "things." It may mean, according to Stormonth, "A Swedish assize of justice, a Norwegian parliament, a meeting for palaver on public affairs, luggage, or clothes," — which proves how important is the making of new dictionaries as we travel along toward our highest civilization. For instance: when you say to your butler, "Be careful with the breakfast things," he understands you perfectly. He knows you mean the egg-shell cups, and blossomy plates. When you bid your maid bring your "things," she appears with your hat, gloves, cloak, and furs. "Her rooms are comfortable, but I don't like her things," you say when the *bric-à-brac* and curios are not to your taste. "I never speak of such things," you declare in haughty superiority when some guest has filled an hour with foolish or injurious gossip. "Such

things are beneath contempt," says the lawyer of
certain practices familiar in the courts.   And then
we have "poor thing," — not the traditional robin
who "hides his head under his wing, poor thing,"
but some fine lady, far from young and — unmarried!
And "a poor thing, sir, but mine own," — this time
not a fine lady by any means, only "an ill-favored
virgin."

And then, having vexed our souls all the week
over mundane "things," we are given, on Sunday,
glimpses of another world quite as full of them.

"Wean yourselves from earthly idols and fix
your hearts on heavenly things," says the bishop.
Things!   Heavenly things!   Stars, harps, crowns
of righteousness, high and lofty aspirations!

Not long after the battle of Fredericksburg a
participator described the panic, the horror, the
fleeing of the women and children from their homes.
"And then," he said, "there arose from that homeless, stricken crowd of women a cry of mortal agony,
'*My things! Oh, my things!*'"

"Things" to me meant only needful garments.
I could starve with perfect serenity.   I could live
without the latest novel, the late magazines, egg-
shell china, rich attire, jewels; but I had not had
a new bonnet for three years.   Shoes, and above
all shoestrings, were needed by my little boys,
needles, tapes, sewing thread and sewing silk, stays
and staylaces, gloves, combs.   Of course I needed
garments of muslin and linen.   Had I not rolled
bandages of mine?   I needed gowns.   A calico
dress now cost $40.   But these large "things"

were quite beyond all hope on the Blackwater. Smaller articles I might, perhaps, compass. The General's orders, however, strictly forbade the purchase by private individuals of articles smuggled through the lines. He once confiscated a sloop on the Blackwater laden with women's shoes, slippers, and Congress gaiters ! He would not allow me a shoe ; all were sent to Richmond to be sold for the benefit of the government. Communication with the enemy must be discouraged lest he discover our weakness.

I knew that most of the tight little carts peddling fish, potatoes, and eggs had double bottoms between which were all sorts of delightful things, but I never dared approach the pedler on the subject ; and as I was the commanding officer's wife, he dared not approach me.

One day I was in an ambulance, driving on one of the interminable lanes of the region, the only incident being the watery crossing over the " cosin," as the driver called the swamps that had been " Poquosin " in the Indian tongue. Behind me came a jolting two-wheeled cart, drawn by a mule and driven by a small negro boy, who stood in front with a foot planted firmly upon each of the shafts. Within, and completely filling the vehicle, which was nothing more than a box on wheels, sat a dignified-looking woman. The dame of the ambulance at once became fascinated by a small basket of sweet potatoes which the dame of the cart carried in her lap.

With a view to acquiring these treasures I essayed

a tentative conversation upon the weather, the prospects of a late spring, and finally the scarcity of provisions and consequent suffering of the soldiers.

After a keen glance of scrutiny the market woman exclaimed, " Well, I am doing all I can for them! I know you won't speak of it! Look here!"

Lifting the edge of her hooped petticoat, she revealed a roll of army cloth, several pairs of cavalry boots, a roll of crimson flannel, packages of gilt braid and sewing silk, cans of preserved meats, a bag of coffee! She was on her way to our own camp, right under the General's nose! Of course I should not betray her — I promised. I did more. Before we parted she had drawn forth a little memorandum book and had taken a list of my own necessities. She did not " run the blockade " herself. She had an agent — " a dear, good Suffolk man " — who would fill my order on his next trip.

It isn't worth while to tell men everything. They are not supposed to be interested in the needle-and-thread ways of women!

About three weeks after my interview with the blockade-runner, I was driving again in the ambulance. Suddenly Captain Whitner, who had galloped to overtake me, wheeled in front of the horses and stopped them.

" Good morning, Captain! Any news at camp I am permitted to learn?"

I perceived the corners of his mouth twitching, but he said gravely : —

" I am commissioned to tell you that you must

consider yourself under arrest. I am sent to discharge this painful duty and conduct you to camp."

"By whose order, pray?"

"Official orders from headquarters," and he presented a paper.

I knew he must be acting a part for his own amusement, and I asked no questions. I would not gratify him by seeming to be alarmed.

When I arrived at my husband's tent, I found him with Major Shepard, and a wretched-looking countryman standing near them. I comprehended the situation at a glance and resolved to play my part.

"This prisoner," said the General, "has been arrested for bringing in contraband goods in violation of express orders. He pleads that the goods were ordered by the General's wife for the use of the General's family. Have you anything to say to show cause why he should not be punished?"

"May it please the court," I said, turning to Major Shepard and Captain Whitner, "I call you to witness that I invited you last week to partake of a bowl of egg-nog, telling you it was made of contraband French brandy. When the commanding officer's attention was called to the fact, he said he could do nothing; he was obliged to submit because I was his superior officer, that I outranked him everywhere except on the march and the battle-field."

A burst of laughter interrupted me. The chairman called for order.

"I confess that I deputed this estimable gentleman to procure some sewing silk for the mending of the garments of my subordinate officer. I had hoped that through his valor the blockade would, ere this, have been raised. Finding myself mistaken —"

"The prisoner is discharged," said the General, — I uttered an exclamation of triumph, — "but," he added, "the goods are confiscated for the benefit of the Confederate government, and are already on the way to Richmond."

I was very sorry for the fright the poor man had suffered for my sake. I took him home with me beside the driver on the ambulance. Of course I paid him. I had one piece of family silver with me for which I had no use on the Blackwater, — a butter knife — and I gave it to him as a souvenir of his happy escape from danger.

How did I manage without my needles and thread?

Charity came to me early one morning with a brown paper parcel in her arms.

"Dat ole creeter," said Charity, "what come home wid you las' week, knock at de kitchen do' fo' day dis mornin'. He gimme dis, an' say you bleeged to git it fo' de Gen'al wake up; an' — an' — he say — but Lawd! 'tain' wuf while to tell you what he say! But he *do* say to tell you to gimme sumpin out'n de bundle. Gawd knows I ain' no cravin' po'-white-folks' nigger, but dat what he say."

I need not give an inventory of the contents of the bundle. They were perfectly satisfactory to me — and to Charity.

We had slender mails on the Blackwater, few

Q

papers, no books.   Occasionally a letter from Agnes
gave me news of the outside world.

"RICHMOND, January 7, 1863.

" MY DEARIE : Have you no pen, ink, and paper on the
Blackwater — the very name of which suggests ink ?   I get
no news of you at all.   How do you amuse yourself, and
have you anything to read ?   I am sending you to-day a
copy of Victor Hugo's last novel, " Les Misérables," re-
printed by a Charleston firm on the best paper they could
get, poor fellows, pretty bad I must acknowledge.   You'll
go wild over that book — I did — and everybody does.

" Major Shepard must order some copies for the brigade.
As he has plenty of meat and bread now, he can afford it.
I have cried my eyes out over Fantine and Cosette and
Jean Valjean.   The soldiers are all reading it.   They
calmly walk into the bookstores, poor dear fellows, and ask
for " Lee's Miserables faintin' !" — the first volume being
" Fantine."   I've worlds of news to tell you.   Alice
Gregory is engaged to Arthur Herbert, the handsomest
man I know.   Alice is looking lovely and so happy.
Helen came to see me in Petersburg, and is all the time
worried about Ben.   Did you know that Jim Field lost a
leg at Malvern Hills — or in the hospital afterwards ?   He
was such a lovely fellow — engaged to Sue Bland — I never
saw a handsomer pair.   Well, Sue thinks as much as I do
about good looks, and Jim wrote to release her.   She had
a good cry, and finally came down to Richmond, married
him, and took him home to nurse him.

" Do you realize the fact that we shall soon be without
a stitch of clothes ?   There is not a bonnet for sale in
Richmond.   Some of the girls smuggle them, which I for
one consider in the worst possible taste, to say the least.
We have no right at this time to dress better than our
neighbors, and besides, the soldiers need every cent of our

money. Do you remember in Washington my pearl-gray
silk bonnet, trimmed inside with lilies of the valley? I
have ripped it up, washed and ironed it, dyed the lilies blue
(they are bluebells now), and it is very becoming.   All
the girls intend to plait hats next summer when the wheat
ripens, for they have no blocks on which to press the coal-
scuttle bonnets, and after all when our blockade is raised
we may find they are not at all worn, while hats are hats
and never go out of fashion. The country girls made
them last summer and pressed the crowns over bowls and
tin pails.   I could make lovely paper flowers if I had
materials.

" It seems rather volatile to discuss such things while
our dear country is in such peril.   Heaven knows I would
costume myself in coffee-bags if that would help, but having no coffee, where could I get the bags? I'll e'en go
afield next summer, and while Boaz is at the front, Ruth
will steal his sheaves for her adornment.

" The papers announce that General French reports the
enemy forty-five thousand strong at Suffolk. How many
men has your General? Dear, dear!

" But we are fortifying around Richmond.   While I write
a great crowd of negroes is passing through the streets, singing as they march. They have been working on the fortifications north of the city, and are now going to work on
them south of us.   They don't seem to concern themselves
much about Mr. Lincoln's Emancipation Proclamation,
and they seem to have no desire to do any of the fighting.
" Your loving

" Agnes."

" P. S. — I attended Mrs. Davis's last reception.   There
was a crowd, all in evening dress. You see, as we don't
often wear our evening gowns, they are still quite passable.
I wore the gray silk with eleven flounces which was made

for Mrs. Douglas's last reception, and by the bye, who do you think was at the battle of Williamsburg, on General McClellan's staff? The Prince de Joinville who drank the Rose wine with you at the Baron de Limbourg's reception to the Japs. Doesn't it all seem so long ago — so far away? The Prince de Joinville escorted me to one of the President's levees — don't you remember? — and now I attend another President's levee and hear him calmly telling some people that rats, if fat, are as good as squirrels, and that we can never afford mule meat. It would be too expensive, but the time may come when rats will be in demand,

" Dearly,

" AGNES."

The Emancipation Proclamation did not create a ripple of excitement among the colored members of our households in Virginia. Of its effect elsewhere I could not judge. As to fighting, our own negroes never dreamed of such a thing. The colored troops of the North were not inferior, we were told, in discipline and courage to other soldiers; but the martial spirit among them had its exceptions. A Northern writer has recorded an interview with a negro who had run the blockade and entered the service of a Federal officer. He was met on board a steamer, after the battle of Fort Donelson, on his way to a new situation, and questioned in regard to his experience of war.[1]

" Were you in the fight? "

" Had a little taste of it, sah."

" Stood your ground, of course."

---

[1] " Camp-fire and Battle-ground," p. 238.

"No, sah! I run."

"Not at the first fire?"

"Yes, sah, an' would a' run sooner ef I knowed it was a-comin'!"

"Why, that wasn't very creditable to your courage, was it?"

"Dat ain't in my line, sah — cookin's my perfeshun."

"But have you no regard for your reputation?"

"Refutation's nothin' by de side o' life."

"But you don't consider your life worth more than other people's, do you?"

"Hit's wuth mo' to me, sah."

"Then you must value it very highly."

"Yas, sah, I does, — mo'n all dis wuld! Mo' dan a million o' dollars, sah. What would dat be wuth to a man wid de bref out o' 'im? Self-perserbashun is de fust law wid me, sah!"

"But why should you act upon a different rule from other men?"

"'Cause diffunt man set diffunt value 'pon his life. Mine ain't in de market."

"Well, if all soldiers were like you, traitors might have broken up the government without resistance."

"Dat's so! Dar wouldn't 'a' been no hep fer it. But I don' put my life in de scale against no gubberment on dis yearth. No gubberment gwine pay me ef I loss messef."

"Well, do you think you would have been much missed if you had been killed?"

"Maybe not, sah! A daid white man ain' much

use to dese yere sogers, let alone a daid niggah, but I'd 'a' missed mysef powerful, an' dat's de pint wid me."

Towards the last of January we had a season of warm, humid weather. Apparently the winter was over ; the grass was springing on the swamp, green and luxurious, and the willows swelling into bud. There were no singing birds on the Blackwater as early as January 28, but the frogs were mightily exercised upon the coming of spring, and their nightly concerts took on a jubilant note.

One day I had a few moments' conversation with my husband about army affairs, and he remarked that our Southern soldiers were always restless unless they were in action. " They never can stand still in battle," he said ; " they are willing to yell and charge the most desperate positions, but if they can't move forward, they must move backward. Stand still they cannot."

I thought I could perceive symptoms of restlessness on the part of their commander. Often in the middle of the night he would summon John, mount him, and send him to camp, a short distance away ; and presently I would hear the tramp, tramp of the General's staff officers, coming to hold a council of war in his bedroom. On the 28th of January he confided to me that on the next day he would make a sally in the direction of the enemy. " He is getting entirely too impudent," said he ; " I'm not strong enough to drive him out of the country, but he must keep his place."

I had just received a present of coffee. This was at

once roasted and ground. On the day of the
march, fires were kindled under the great pots used
at the "hog-killing time" (an era in the household) and many gallons of coffee were prepared.
This was sweetened, and when our men paused near
the house to form the line of march, the servants
and little boys passed down the line with buckets of
the steaming coffee, cups, dippers, and gourds.
Every soldier had a good draught of comfort and
cheer. The weather had suddenly changed. The
great snow-storm that fell in a few days was gathering, the skies were lowering, and the horizon was
dark and threatening.

After the men had marched away, I drove to the
hospital tent and put myself at the disposal of the
surgeon. We inspected the store of bandages and
lint, and I was intrusted with the preparation of
more.

"I ain' got no use for dis stuff," said my one
female friend and companion, Charity, whom I pressed
into service to help me pick lint. " 'Pears like 'tain't
good for nuthin' but to line a bird's nes'."

"It will be soft for the wound of a soldier," I
said, "after he has fought the Yankees."

"I'll pick den; I'll tar up my onlies' apun ef he'll
kill one."

"Oh, Charity!"

"Yas'm, I will dat! Huccome we all don' drive
'm out o' Suffolk? Der's lodes an lodes o' shoes
an' stockin's, an' sugar an' cawfy in Suffolk! An'
dese nasty Abolition Yankees got 'em all!"

"Those are not proper words for you to use," I

said. "What have you against the Northern people? They never did you harm."

"Dey ain't, ain't dey?" she replied, with feeling. "Huccome I'se got to go barfooted? Hit's scan'-lous for a free gal to go barfooted, like she was so no 'count she couldn't git a par o' shoes fer her-se'f."

"I'll ask the General to order a pair for you."

"Humph!" said Charity, scornfully; "you can't do nothin' wid dat Gen'al. Ain' I hear you baig an' baig 'im for a par o' slippers dat time he fris-tricated de boatload full? I ain' seen you git de slippers."

Charity was not the only one of the Nation's Wards who held the enemy in contempt. The special terms in which she designated them were in common use at the time. She had often heard them from the General's servant, John, who shared the opinions of the common soldier. Some of the ex-pressions of the great men I knew in Washington were quite as offensive and not a bit less inelegant, although framed in better English. I never ap-proved of "calling names," I had seen what comes of it; and I reproved John for teaching them to my little boys.

"No'm," said John, "I won't say nothin'; I'll just say the Yankees are mighty mean folks."

My first news from the General was cheering, but he would not return for a day or two. He must fly about the frontier a little in various direc-tions to let the enemy know he was holding his own. His official report was as follows : —

" To Brigadier-General Colston, Petersburg, Va.

"Carrsville, Isle of Wight, January 30, 1863.

" General : This morning at 4 o'clock the enemy under Major-General Peck attacked me at Kelly's store, eight miles from Suffolk. After three hours' severe fighting we repulsed them at all points and held the field. Their force is represented by prisoners to be between ten and fifteen thousand. My loss in killed and wounded will not exceed fifty — no prisoners. I regret that Col. Poage is among the killed. We inflicted a heavy loss on the enemy.

" Respectfully,

" Roger A. Pryor, *Brigadier-General Commanding.*"

On February 2 the General thus addressed his troops : " The Brigadier-General congratulates the troops of this command on the results of the recent combat.

" The enemy endeavored under cover of night to steal an inglorious victory by surprise, but he found us prepared at every point, and despite his superior numbers, greater than your own, in the proportion of five to one, he was signally repulsed and compelled to leave us in possession of the field.

" After silencing his guns and dispersing his infantry, you remained on the field from night until one o'clock, awaiting the renewal of the attack, but he did not again venture to encounter your terrible fire.

" When the disparity of force between the parties is considered, with the proximity of the enemy to his stronghold, and his facilities of reënforcements by railway, the result of the action of the 30th will be accepted as a splendid illustration of your courage and good conduct."

One of the " enemy's " papers declared that our force was "three regiments of infantry, fourteen pieces of artillery, and about nine hundred cavalry."

The temptation to "lie under a mistake " was great in those days of possible disaffection, when soldiers had to believe in their cause in order to defend it. One of the newspaper correspondents of the enemy explained why we were not again attacked after the first fight. He said : " Some may inquire why we did not march forthwith to Carrsville and attack the rebels again. The reasons are obvious. Had he went [sic] to Carrsville Pryor would have had the advantage to cut off our retreat. The natives know every bypath and blind road through the woods and are ever ready to help the rebels to our detriment. Pryor can always cross the Blackwater on his floating bridge. It is prudent to allow an enemy to get well away from his stronghold the better to capture his guns and destroy his ammunition," etc.

Another paper declares he was heavily reënforced at Carrsville.

Another records : " The rebels have been very bold in this neighborhood. Pryor has been in the habit of crossing the Blackwater River whenever he wanted to. Our attacking him this time must have been a real surprise to him. We took a large number of prisoners ! "

He continued the indulgence of this habit until spring, receiving from his countrymen unstinted praise for his protection of that part of our state. While he could not utterly rout the invading army, he " held them very uneasy."

I was made rich by enthusiastic congratulations from our capital and from Petersburg. Agnes wrote from Richmond : —

" Have you seen the *Enquirer?* Of course this is very grand for you because this is your own little fight — all by yourself. In Richmond everybody says the General is to be promoted Major-General. When he is, I shall attach myself permanently to his staff. The life of inglorious idleness here is perfectly awful. If you suppose I don't long for a rich experience, you are mistaken. Give me the *whole* of it — victory, defeat, glory and misfortune, praise and even censure (so it be *en plein air*) — anything, everything, except stolid, purposeless, hopeless uselessness.

" The worst effect of this inaction is felt in this city, where we can manufacture nothing for the soldiers, and only consume in idleness what they need. A sort of court is still kept up here — but the wives of our great generals are conspicuous for their absence. Mrs. Lee is never seen at receptions. She and her daughters spend their time knitting and sewing for the soldiers, just as her great-grandmother, Martha Washington, did in '76; and General Lee writes that these things are needed. People here, having abundant time to find fault, do not hesitate to say that our court ladies assume too much state for revolutionary times. They had better be careful! We won't guillotine them — at least not on the block (there are other guillotines), but it would be lovelier if they could realize their fine opportunities. Think of Florence Nightingale! Mrs. Davis is very chary of the time she allots us. If King Solomon were to call with the Queen of Sheba on his arm the fraction of a moment after the closing minute of her reception, he would not be admitted! I can just see you saying, in that superior manner you see fit to assume with me : —

"'But, Agnes dear! that is good form, you know, and belongs to the etiquette of polite life.'

"Of course I know it! Did I say that Mrs. Davis should admit King Solomon? *I* wouldn't! I only tell you what other folks think and say — but *ajew*, until I hear some more news and gossip.

"Dearly again,

"AGNES."

CHAPTER XVI

MY friend Agnes could soon record graver things than idleness or gossip. On April 4, 1863, she wrote from Richmond: —

"MY DEAR: I hope you appreciate the fact that you are herewith honored with a letter written in royal-red ink upon sumptuous gilt-edged paper. There is not, at the present writing, one inch of paper for sale in the capital of the Confederacy, at all within the humble means of the wife of a Confederate officer. Well is it for her — and I hope for you — that her youthful admirers were few, and so her gorgeous cream-and-gold album was only half filled with tender effusions. Out come the blank leaves, to be divided between her friend and her Colonel. Don't be alarmed at the color of the writing. I have not yet dipped my goose-quill (there are no steel pens) in the 'ruddy drops that visit my sad heart,' nor yet into good orthodox red ink. There are fine oaks in the country, and that noble tree bears a gall-nut filled with crimson sap. One lies on my table, and into its sanguinary heart I plunge my pen.

"Something very sad has just happened in Richmond — something that makes me ashamed of all my jeremiads over the loss of the petty comforts and conveniences of life — hats, bonnets, gowns, stationery, books, magazines, dainty food. Since the weather has been so pleasant, I have been in the habit of walking in the Capitol Square before break-

fast every morning. Somehow nothing so sets me up after
a restless night as a glimpse of the dandelions waking up
from their dewy bed and the songs of the birds in the Park.
Yesterday, upon arriving, I found within the gates a crowd
of women and boys — several hundreds of them, standing
quietly together. I sat on a bench near, and one of the
number left the rest and took the seat beside me. She was
a pale, emaciated girl, not more than eighteen, with a sunbonnet on her head, and dressed in a clean calico gown.
'I could stand no longer,' she explained. As I made room
for her, I observed that she had delicate features and large
eyes. Her hair and dress were neat. As she raised her
hand to remove her sunbonnet and use it for a fan, her
loose calico sleeve slipped up, and revealed the mere skeleton
of an arm. She perceived my expression as I looked at it,
and hastily pulled down her sleeve with a short laugh.
'This is all that's left of me!' she said. 'It seems real
funny, don't it?' Evidently she had been a pretty girl —
a dressmaker's apprentice, I judged from her chafed fore-
finger and a certain skill in the lines of her gown. I was
encouraged to ask: 'What is it? Is there some celebra-
tion?'

"'There *is*,' said the girl, solemnly; 'we celebrate our
right to live. We are starving. As soon as enough of us
get together we are going to the bakeries and each of us
will take a loaf of bread. That is little enough for the
government to give us after it has taken all our men.'

" Just then a fat old black Mammy waddled up the walk
to overtake a beautiful child who was running before her.
'Come dis a way, honey,' she called, 'don't go nigh dem
people,' adding, in a lower tone, 'I's feared you'll ketch
somethin' fum dem po'-white folks. I *wonder* dey lets 'em
into de Park.'

The girl turned to me with a wan smile, and as she rose
to join the long line that had now formed and was moving,

she said simply, ' Good-by ! I'm going to get something to eat ! '

" ' And I devoutly hope you'll get it — and plenty of it,' I told her. The crowd now rapidly increased, and numbered, I am sure, more than a thousand women and children. It grew and grew until it reached the dignity of a mob — a bread riot. They impressed all the light carts they met, and marched along silently and in order. They marched through Cary Street and Main, visiting the stores of the speculators and emptying them of their contents. Governor Letcher sent the mayor to read the Riot Act, and as this had no effect he threatened to fire on the crowd. The city battalion then came up. The women fell back with frightened eyes, but did not obey the order to disperse. The President then appeared, ascended a dray, and addressed them. It is said he was received at first with hisses from the boys, but after he had spoken some little time with great kindness and sympathy, the women quietly moved on, taking their food with them. General Elzey and General Winder wished to call troops from the camps to ' suppress the women,' but Mr. Seddon, wise man, declined to issue the order. While I write women and children are still standing in the streets, demanding food, and the government is issuing to them rations of rice.

" This is a frightful state of things. I am telling you of it because *not one word* has been said in the newspapers about it. All will be changed, Judge Campbell tells me, if we can win a battle or two (but, oh, at what a price !), and regain the control of our railroads. Your General has been magnificent. He has fed Lee's army all winter — I wish he could feed our starving women and children.

" Dearly,   " Agnes."

My good Agnes reckoned without her host when she supposed General Pryor would be rewarded for his splendid service on the Blackwater. He had never ceased all winter to remind the Secretary of War of his promise to give him a permanent command. He now felt that he had earned it. He had fought many battles, acquitting himself with distinction in all, — Williamsburg, Seven Pines, Mechanicsville, Gaines's Mill, Frazier's Farm, the Second Manassas, and Sharpsburg, besides the fight on the Blackwater.

He now wrote, April 6, 1863, an almost passionate appeal to the President himself, imploring that he be sent into active service, and not be " denied participation in the struggles that are soon to determine the destinies of my country. If I know myself," he added, " it is not the vanity of command that moves me to this appeal. A single and sincere wish to contribute somewhat to the success of our cause impels me to entreat that I may be assigned to duty. That my position is not the consequence of any default of mine you will be satisfied by the enclosed letter from General Lee." The letter was followed by new promises. It was supplemented by General Pryor's fellow-officers, who not only urged that the country should not lose his services, but designated certain regiments which might easily be assigned to him. The President wrote courteous letters in reply, always repeating assurances of esteem, etc. The *Richmond Examiner* and other papers now began to notice the matter and present General Pryor as arrayed with the party against the administration. This, being untrue, he contradicted. On March 17, 1863, the President wrote to him the following : —

" GENERAL ROGER A. PRYOR;

" GENERAL : Your gratifying letter on the 6th inst. referring to an article in the *Examiner* newspaper which seems to associate you with the opposition to the administration, has been received.

" I did not see the article in question, but I am glad it has led to an expression so agreeable. The good opinion of one so competent to judge of public affairs, and who has known me so long and closely, is a great support in the midst of many and arduous trials.

" Very respectfully and truly yours,
" JEFFERSON DAVIS."

Among the letters sent to Mr. Davis in General Pryor's behalf was one from General Lee and one from General Jackson, both of which unhappily remained in the President's possession, no copies having been kept by General Pryor.

As time went on, my husband waited with such patience as he could command. Finally he resigned his commission as brigadier-general, and also his seat in Congress, and entered General Fitz Lee's cavalry as a private soldier. His resignation was held a long time by the President "in the hope it would be reconsidered," and repeatedly General Pryor was "assured of the President's esteem," etc. General Jackson, General Longstreet, General A. P. Hill, General D. H. Hill, General Wilcox, General George Pickett, General Beauregard, were all his friends. Some of them had, like General Johnston and General McClellan, similar experience. It was a bitter hour for me when my General followed me to the Amelia Springs with news that he had entered the

R

cavalry as a private.   "Stay with me and the children," I implored.

"No," he said; "I had something to do with bringing on this war.   I must give myself to Virginia.   She needs the help of all her sons.   If there are too many brigadier-generals in the service, — it may be so, — certain it is there are not enough private soldiers."

The Divinity that "rules our ends, rough hew them as we may," was guiding him.   I look back with gratitude to these circumstances, — then so hard to bear, — circumstances to which, I am persuaded, I owe my husband's life.

General Fitz Lee welcomed him in hearty fashion :

"HEADQUARTERS, August 26, 1863.

"Honorable, General, or Mr?   How shall I address you?   Damn it, there's no difference !   Come up to see me.   Whilst I regret the causes that induced you to resign your position, I am glad, really, that the country has not lost your active services, and that your choice to serve her has been cast in one of my regiments.

"Very respectfully,

"FITZ LEE."

As a common soldier in the cavalry service, General Pryor was assigned the duties of his position, from not one of which did he ever excuse himself.

On May 3 General Lee had offered thanks to Almighty God for a great victory at Chancellorsville.

On May 4, the date of Agnes's letter, news came that General Jackson had been seriously wounded

and his arm amputated.   On May 10 the General
died, and we were all plunged into the deepest grief.
By every man, woman, and child in the Confederacy
this good man and great general was mourned
as never man was mourned before.   From the
moment of his death the tide of fortune seemed to
turn.   Henceforth there would be only disaster and
defeat.   In losing General Jackson our dear commander lost his right arm.   But this only inspired
him to greater and more aggressive action.

He decided to take his army into Pennsylvania,
and after entering that state, on June 27, he issued
his famous order, reminding one of General Washington's similar order from Pennsylvania, 1777 : —

" GENERAL ORDER NO. 73.   FROM THE HEADQUARTERS,
ARMY OF NORTHERN VIRGINIA

" The commanding general has observed the conduct of
the troops upon the march, and confidently anticipates results commensurate with the high spirit they have manifested. . . . Their conduct has, with few exceptions, been
in keeping with their character as soldiers, and entitles them
to approbation and praise.

" There have, however, been instances of forgetfulness,
on the part of some, that they have in keeping the yet un-
sullied reputation of the army, and that the duties exacted
of us by civilization and Christianity are not less obligatory
in the country of the enemy than in our own.

" The commanding general considers that no greater
disgrace could befall the army, and through it our whole
people, than the perpetration of the barbarous outrages
upon the innocent and defenceless, and the wanton destruction of private property, which have marked the course of

the enemy in our country. Such proceedings not only disgrace the perpetrators and all connected with them, but are subversive of the discipline and efficiency of the army, and destructive of the ends of our present movements. It must be remembered that we make war only on armed men, that we cannot take vengeance for the wrongs our people have suffered without lowering ourselves in the eyes of all whose abhorrence has been excited by the atrocities of our enemy, and offending against Him to whom vengeance belongeth, without whose favor and support must all prove vain."

Washington, Lee, and McClellan were not alone in their ideas of civilized and Christian warfare.

Eighty-four years before this time there was a war in this same country. It was a rebellion, too, and a nobleman led the troops of Great Britain through the country to subdue the rebellion. The people through whose land he marched were bitterly hostile. They shot his foraging parties, sentinels, and stragglers; they fired upon him from every wood.

On January 28, 1781, this order was issued from camp near Beatty's Ford : —

" Lord Cornwallis has so often experienced the zeal and good will of the army that he has not the smallest doubt that the officers and soldiers will most cheerfully submit to the ill conveniences that must naturally attend war, so remote from water, carriage, and the magazines of the army. The supply of rum for a time will be absolutely impossible, and that of meal very uncertain. It is needless to point out to the officers the necessity of preserving the strictest discipline, and of preventing the oppressed people from suffering violence by the hands from whom they are taught to look for protection."

Again : —

"Headquarters, Causler's Plantation,
"February 27, 1781.

" Lord Cornwallis is highly displeased that several houses
have been set on fire to-day during the march — a disgrace
to the army — and he will punish to the utmost severity any
person or persons who shall be found guilty of committing
so disgraceful an outrage.   His Lordship requests the commanding officers of the corps will endeavor to find the persons who set fire to the houses this day. . . .   Any officer
who looks on with indifference and does not do his utmost
to prevent shameful marauding will be considered in a more
criminal light than the persons who commit these scandalous
crimes."

Again : —

"Headquarters, Freelands, February 28, 1781.

" A watch found by the regiment of Bose.   The owner
may have it from the adjutant of that regiment upon proving property."

Another : —

"Smith's Plantation, March 1, 1781.

" Brigade Orders. — A woman having been robbed of
a watch, a black silk handkerchief, a gallon of brandy, and
a shirt, and as by description, by a soldier of the guards, the
camp and every man's kit is to be immediately searched for
the same, by the officer of the brigade."

And so it is that every circumstance of life is
an opportunity for a noble spirit.   When we " let
slip the dogs of war," some men find excuse for
license and cruelty, others for the exercise of self-
restraint and compassion.   Admiral Porter tells a
story which may illustrate the strange " point of

view " in the minds of some brave men upon the legitimate conduct of war.

" The exploits of the army in foraging," said the Admiral, "afforded matter for much amusement among the officers at Vicksburg. At Bruensburg, General Grant made his headquarters in the spring of 1863. Bruensburg and the surrounding country was the great depot for live stock, grain, etc., and the soldiers' lines seemed to have fallen in pleasant places. *Foraging was not prohibited;* in fact the soldiers were cautioned to save the government rations for an emergency, so that the squealing of pigs, the bleating of calves and sheep, and the cackling of poultry were common sounds in camp."

As an illustration of the wholesale robbery of the peaceful citizens Admiral Porter tells of an appeal made to General Grant by an old man, long past the age to bear arms, who pushed aside the flaps of the General's tent and thrust in his head. In his hand he held a rope to which was attached a miserable mule, minus one eye. He told the General, in the poor-white's vernacular, of his nice little farm, well stocked "with the finest lot of chickens, turkeys, pigs, an' sheep as ever you seen," and that the Yankee soldiers had stolen everything except the " ole muel and one goose."

" Here, Rawlins, attend to this man," said the General, and walked away.

" What do you expect me to do ? " inquired General Rawlins. " How are you going to find out who did all you complain of ? "

" Well, I *know* who did it," said the old fellow;

"it's one of Gin'ral A. J. Smith's rigiments.   I
know the sargint what led 'em on.   He belongs to
the Thirteenth Iowy, an' he kin skin a hog quicker'n
greased lightnin'!"

Just then General Smith walked in the tent, and
the complaint was laid before him.

"They weren't my men, sir," said General Smith.
"I know my boys too well.   They would never
have left that mule and goose!   No, sir, my boys
don't do things that way ; and I advise you, old
man, to go back and keep your eye on your goose
and mule."

The old man turned to gaze on his beloved mule.
It was gone!   A soldier stood at the end of the
rope!

General Smith glanced proudly around.   "Ah,
Rawlins," he said, "those must have been my men
after all.   If I could only hear they had eaten the
goose, I should be sure of it."

The story does not follow the aged man to his
desolate cabin ; but it followed the Admiral as an
amusing story for many an evening around the
punch-bowl.

Among the men arrayed against the South in
battle were many worthy descendants of the men
who achieved their independence in 1775–1781,
and who then fought shoulder to shoulder with
the South.

"They were a brave, self-reliant, patriotic race,
and in all the characteristics of manliness, persever-
ance, fortitude, and courage, were the equals of
any race that ever lived."   It was from these men,

native-born Americans of the North and West, that
many a persecuted woman in Georgia, South Carolina, and North Carolina received help and restitu-
tion of property. But war brutalizes mean men.
The few cannot control the many.

War, wicked, cruel war, knows no mercy, no justice. War is the dreadful crime of the world.
Against war prayer should ascend day and night
until it shall cease forever. It is not right that it
should be classed with " pestilence and famine" in
our prayers. It should have an hour — a daily
hour — to itself, when old men and women, young
men and maidens, and little children should implore
God to make wars to cease from the fair world He
has created.

The refugees who came to us from exposed districts within the enemy's lines thrilled our souls with
horror. We heard these stories from the valley of
Virginia and from Norfolk. Liberty of speech in
child or woman was sternly punished. At Norfolk
a clergyman, the Rev. Dr. Armstrong, had been put
in the chain gang and compelled to work on the
streets because of disrespectful allusion to the presence of Federal troops. We trembled at these
recitals; but we never dreamed the war would
come to us. At twilight, when the air was clear
and still, we could hear the booming of the heavy
guns of the ironclads on James River; but
McClellan had been unable to take Richmond, and
nobody would want little Petersburg.

In July, General Lee fought and lost the great
battle of Gettysburg, which plunged our state into

mourning and lamentation. Never can the world read with dry eyes of the charge of Pickett's brigade and the manner in which it was met. " Decry war as we may and ought," says Rhodes in his "History," "'breathes there the man with soul so dead' who would not thrill with emotion to claim for his countrymen the men who made that charge and the men who met it? General Lee bore the disaster magnificently. An officer, attempting to place on other shoulders some portion of the blame, General Lee said solemnly, '*All this has been* MY *fault* — it is *I* that have lost this fight, and you must all help me out of it in the best way you can.'"

The Federal loss in this battle, killed, wounded, and captured, was 23,003, the Confederate 20,451 — making a total of 43,454 good and true men lost, in one battle, to their country. The emblem of mourning hung at many a door among our friends in Richmond and Petersburg. Close upon this disaster came news of the fall of Vicksburg.

On July 3d my General (this was before he resigned his commission) was in Richmond serving on a court-martial. In the evening he called upon Mr. and Mrs. Davis, and was told the President was not receiving, but that Mrs. Davis would be glad to see him. The weather was intensely hot, and my husband felt he must not inflict a long visit; but when he rose to leave, Mrs. Davis begged him to remain, and seemed averse from being left alone. After a few minutes the President came in, weary, silent, and depressed. The news from Gettysburg sufficiently accounted for his melancholy aspect.

Presently a dear little boy entered in his night-robe, and kneeling beside his father's knee repeated his evening prayer of thankfulness, and of supplication for God's blessing on the country. The President laid his hand on the boy's head and fervently responded, "Amen." The scene recurred vividly, in the light of future events, to my husband's memory. With the coming day came the news of the surrender of Vicksburg, — news of which Mr. Davis had been forewarned the evening before, — and already the Angel of Death was hovering near, to enfold the beautiful boy and bear him away from a world of trouble.

I had taken my young family to a watering place in the county of Amelia, and there a few homeless women like myself were spending the months of July and August. Everything was so sad there was no heart in any one for gayety of any kind; but one evening the proprietor proposed that the ball room be lighted and a solitary fiddler, " Bozeman," — who was also the barber, — be installed in the musicians' seat and show us what he could do. Young feet cannot resist a good waltz or polka, and the floor was soon filled with care-forgetting maidens — there were no men except the proprietor and the fiddler. Presently a telegram was received by the former. We all huddled together under the chandelier to read it. Vicksburg had fallen! The gallant General Pemberton had been starved into submission. Surely and swiftly the coil was tightening around us. Surely and swiftly should we, too, be starved into submission.

CHAPTER XVII

A HOMELESS WANDERER

HAVING no longer a home of my own, it was decided that I should go to my people in Charlotte County. One of my sons, Theo, and two of my little daughters were already there, and there I expected to remain until the end of the war.

But repeated attempts to reach my country home resulted in failure. Marauding parties and guerillas were flying all over the country. There had been alarm at a bridge over the Staunton near the Oaks, and the old men and boys had driven away the enemy. I positively *could* not venture alone.

So it was decided that I should return to my husband's old district, to Petersburg, and there find board in some private family.

I reached Petersburg in the autumn and wandered about for days seeking refuge in some household. Many of my old friends had left town. Strangers and refugees had rented the houses of some of these, while others were filled with the homeless among their own kindred. There was no room anywhere for me, and my small purse was growing so slender that I became anxious. Finally my brother-in-law offered me an overseer's house on one of his "quarters."

The small dwelling he placed at my disposal was to be considered temporary only ; some one of his town houses would soon be vacant. When I drove out to the little house, I found it hardly better than a hovel. We entered a rude, unplastered kitchen, the planks of the floor loose and wide apart, the earth beneath plainly visible. There were no windows in this smoke-blackened kitchen. A door opened into a tiny room with a fireplace, window, and out-door of its own ; and a short flight of stairs led to an unplastered attic, so that the little apartment was entered by two doors and a staircase. It was already cold, but we had to beat a hasty retreat and sit outside while a colored boy made a " smudge " in the house, to dislodge the wasps that had tenanted it for many months. My brother had lent me bedding for the overseer's pine bedstead and the low trundle-bed underneath. The latter, when drawn out at night, left no room for us to stand. When that was done, we had to go to bed. For furniture we had only two or three wooden chairs and a small table. There were no curtains, neither carpet nor rugs, no china. There was wood at the woodpile, and a little store of meal and rice, with a small bit of bacon in the overseer's grimy closet. This was to be my winter home.

Petersburg was already virtually in a state of siege. Not a tithe of the food needed for its army of refugees could be brought to the city. Our highway, the river, was filled, except for a short distance, with Federal gunboats. The markets had long been closed. The stores of provisions had been exhausted, so that a grocery could offer little except a barrel or two of molasses made from the domestic sorghum sugar-cane — an acrid and unwholesome sweet used instead of sugar for drink with water or milk, and for eating with bread. The little boys at once began to keep house. They valiantly attacked the woodpile, and found favor in the eyes of Mary and the man, whom I never knew as other than " Mary's husband." He and Mary were left in charge of the quarter and had a cabin near us.

I had no books, no newspapers, no means of communicating with the outside world; but I had one neighbor, Mrs. Laighton, a daughter of Winston Henry, granddaughter of Patrick Henry. She lived near me with her husband — a Northern man. Both were very cultivated, very poor, very kind. Mrs. Laighton, as Lucy Henry, — a brilliant young girl, — had been one of the habitués of the Oaks. We had much in common, and her kind heart went out in love and pity for me.

She taught me many expedients: that to float tea on the top of a cup of hot water would make it " go farther " than when steeped in the usual way; also that the herb, " life everlasting," which grew in the fields would make excellent yeast, having somewhat the property of hops; and that the best substitute for coffee was not the dried cubes of sweet potato, but parched corn or parched meal, making a nourishing drink, not unlike the "postum" of to-day. And Mrs. Laighton kept me a " living soul " in other and higher ways. She reckoned intellectual ability the greatest of God's gifts, raising us so far above the petty need of material things that we could live in spite of their loss.   Her talk was a tonic to me.   It stimulated me to play my part with courage, seeing I had been deemed worthy, by the God who made me, to suffer in this sublime struggle for liberty.   She was as truly gifted as was ever her illustrious grandfather.   To hear her was to believe, so persuasive and convincing was her eloquence.

I had not my good Eliza Page this winter.   She had fallen ill.   I had a stout little black girl, Julia, as my only servant; but Mary had a friend, a "corn-field hand," "Anarchy," who managed to help me at odd hours.   Mrs. Laighton sent me every morning a print of butter as large as a silver dollar, with two or three perfect biscuits, and sometimes a bowl of persimmons or stewed dried peaches. She had a cow, and churned every day, making her biscuits of the buttermilk, which was much too precious to drink.

A great snow-storm overtook us a day or two before Christmas.   My little boys kindled a roaring fire in the cold, open kitchen, roasted chestnuts, and set traps for the rabbits and "snowbirds" which never entered them.   They made no murmur at the bare Christmas; they were loyal little fellows to their mother.   My day had been spent in mending their garments, — making them was a privilege denied me, for I had no materials.   I was not "all unhappy!"   The rosy cheeks at my fireside consoled me for my privations, and something within me proudly rebelled against weakness or complaining.

The flakes were falling thickly at midnight, when I suddenly became very ill. I sent out for Mary's husband and bade him gallop in to Petersburg, three miles distant, and fetch me Dr. Withers. I was dreadfully ill when he arrived — and as he stood at the foot of my bed I said to him : "It doesn't matter much for me, Doctor! But my husband will be grateful if you keep me alive."

When I awoke from a long sleep, he was still standing at the foot of my bed where I had left him — it seemed to me ages ago! I put out my hand and it touched a little warm bundle beside me. God had given me a dear child!

The doctor spoke to me gravely and most kindly. "I must leave you now," he said, "and, alas! I cannot come again. There are so many, so many sick. Call all your courage to your aid. Remember the pioneer women, and all they were able to survive. This woman," indicating Anarchy, "is a field-hand, but she is a mother, and she has agreed to help you during the Christmas holidays — her own time. And now, God bless you, and good-by!"

I soon slept again — and when I awoke the very Angel of Strength and Peace had descended and abode with me. I resolved to prove to myself that if I was called to be a great woman, I *could* be a great woman. Looking at me from my bedside were my two little boys. They had been taken the night before across the snow-laden fields to my brother's house, but had risen at daybreak and had "come home to take care" of me!

My little maid Julia left me Christmas morning. She said it was too lonesome, and her "mistis" always let her choose her own places. I engaged "Anarchy" at twenty-five dollars a week for all her nights. But her hands, knotted by work in the fields, were too rough to touch my babe. I was propped upon pillows and dressed her myself, sometimes fainting when the exertion was over.

I was still in my bed three weeks afterward, when one of my boys ran in, exclaiming in a frightened voice, " Oh, mamma, an old gray soldier is coming in!"

He stood — this old gray soldier — and looked at me, leaning on his sabre.

" Is this the reward my country gives me? " he said; and not until he spoke did I recognize my husband. Turning on his heel, he went out, and I heard him call: —

" John! John! Take those horses into town and sell them! Do not return until you do so — sell them for anything! Get a cart and bring butter, eggs, and everything you can find for Mrs. Pryor's comfort."

He had been with Fitz Lee on that dreadful tramp through the snow after Averill. He had suffered cold and hunger, had slept on the ground without shelter, sharing his blanket with John. He had used his own horses, and now if the government needed him the government might mount him. He had no furlough, and soon reported for duty; but not before he had moved us, early in January, into town — one of my brother-in-law's houses hav-

ing been vacated at the beginning of the year. John
knew his master too well to construe him literally,
and had reserved the fine gray, Jubal Early, for his
use.   That I might not again fall into the sad
plight in which he had found me, he purchased
three hundred dollars in gold, and instructed me to
prepare a girdle to be worn all the time around my
waist, concealed by my gown.   The coins were
quilted in ; each had a separate section to itself, so
that with scissors I might extract one at a time without disturbing the rest.

From the beginning of the war to its last year Petersburg had remained in a state of comparative repose,
broken only by the arrival and departure of the troops
passing from the South to the Army of Northern
Virginia.   These, as we have said, were always welcomed, if they passed through by day, with gifts of
flowers, fruit, and more substantial refreshment.

To continue this greeting, Petersburg women
denied themselves every luxury.   The tramp of
soldiers was a familiar sound in our streets, but no
hostile footsteps had ever resounded there, no hostile
gun had yet been fired within its limits.   It is true
the low muttering of distant artillery as it came up
the James and the Appomattox from the field of
Big Bethel had caught the ears of the citizens, and
they had listened with heightened interest in its
louder booming as it told of Seven Pines, and the
seven days' struggle around Richmond, just twenty
miles away.   But when the baffled army of Mc-
Clellan retired in the direction of Washington, and
General Lee moved away beyond the Potomac, the

s

old men, women, and children (for there were no men left capable of bearing arms) settled down to their daily avocations — and daily prayers for the dear boys at the front.

Families that had fled from Petersburg at the time of McClellan's advance upon Richmond had now returned. My next-door neighbors were Mr. Thomas Branch and the Rev. Churchill Gibson. From one of my windows I could look into a large garden, where the workmen were busy planting seeds and setting long rows of onions, cabbage plants, tomato plants, and sticks for the green peas just peeping out of the brown earth. Across the street lived the widow of the Hon. Richard Kidder Meade, with her accomplished daughters, Mary, Marion, and Julia. These were delightful neighbors. Lower down lived the Bollings, — parents of Tabb Bolling, the superb, already affianced to General Rooney Lee. Then Mr. and Mrs. William Banister, with another houseful of lovely young women, " Mollie " and " Gussie " Banister ; and their cousin, Alice Gregory, waiting until the cruel war should be over to reward handsome Colonel Arthur Herbert. Alice's own home was just outside our fortifications, and was, I believe, burned when Petersburg was assaulted. Beautiful Patty Hardee was another of these girls. Helen made the ninth of the band of Muses. All were accomplished in music. Marion's latest fancy was significant, — Gottschalk's " Last Hope ! " Sweet Alice took our hearts with her touching hymns, giving a new meaning to the simplest words.

Gussie Banister, the youngest of all, sang "Lo-rena" and "Juanita"; and Mattie Paul, who often came over from Richmond, infused an intenser tone of sadness with Beethoven's andantes and Chopin's "Funeral March." None of the gayety of Richmond, of which we read in our letters, was apparent in Petersburg. Too many of her sons had been slain or were in present peril.

"What friends you girls are!" I said, when I met them, walking together, like a boarding school.

"We are all going to be old maids together," said one, "and so we are getting acquainted with each other."

"Speak for yourself, John," said Helen, who had become the fortunate possessor of "The Courtship of Miles Standish" and was lending "Longfellow's last" around to the rest. "I spoke for *my*self, you remember," she added, laughing.

"Well! it will be no disgrace to be an old maid," said another. "We can always swear our going-to-be-husband was killed in the war." And then a wistful look passed over the young faces as each one remembered some absent lover.

The camp-fire of my own family brigade was now lighted in the kitchen, where the hero, John, who had been left to take care of me, popped corn for my little boys and held them with stories of Fitz Lee's pursuit of Averill.

"Tell us, John," implored his audience, "tell us every bit of it. Begin at Winchester."

"No," said John. "You'll tell your ma, and then she won't sleep a wink to-night."

" She doesn't sleep anyway, John! When we wake up, she's always sitting by the window, looking out at the stars."

" Co'se, if that's the case, here goes. Gen'al Lee had five thousand troopers, an' they marched from Winchester to Salem. We hadn't a tent, an' no rations wuth talkin' about, an' it rained an' hailed an' sleeted most every step o' the way. Your pa never took off his boots for two solid weeks, an' they were full of water all the time, an' the icicles hung from his long hair. We drew up in line at the White Sulphur Springs an' *dar'd* Averill to fight us — but he slunk away in the night. I cert'inly was sorry for Marse Roger at the White Sulphur. He went up into the po'ch of one of the little cottages an' sat down thinkin' an' thinkin'. ' Are you sick, Marse Roger ? ' I asked him. ' No, John,' he said, ' only a little homesick, to think of the happy times we used to spend here — and our fathers and mothers before us!' ' But we done drive 'im away!' I say to him, an' he got up and said, ' Do you think so, John?' Anyway, Averill didn't git a chance to sleep in one of them cottages, nor yet to burn it! Ther' was a hospital thar' then."

" Where did *you* sleep ? " the boys asked.

" Who, me? I slep' every night o' my life under the same blanket with your pa, I did. I don' care how tired he was, he never slep' so sound he couldn't hear the snorin'. ' Git up, John,' he would say, ' tell that man snorin' that he's burnin'.' " John laughed at the reminiscence. " I've scared many a good soldier that way, an' made him turn over —

when the fightin' an' shootin' couldn't move him."

"But you *did* retreat after all, didn't you, John?"

"Retreat! Retreat nothin'! Gen'al Lee got so he didn' care to ketch that scalawag Yankee. He warn' wuth ketchin'. We got pris'ners enough now an' to spar. Gen'al Lee come home cos he didn' have no use for Averill. He drove him away, though. He sholy did!"

John was installed as cook and commissary-general. He had no material except flour, rice, peas, and dried apples, such grease or "shortening" as he could extract from bones he purchased of the quartermaster, and sorghum molasses. He made yeast of "life everlasting" I brought from the country, — and he gave us waffles and pancakes. John's pancakes, compared with the ordinary article, were as the fleecy cloud to the dull, heavy clod beneath. Butter could be had at eight dollars a pound; meat was four and five dollars a pound — prices we learned very soon afterward to regard as extremely cheap; bargains, indeed, of the first water. From Agnes's letters I have reason to suppose that Petersburg suffered more from scarcity than did Richmond. There, dinners were given by the members of the Cabinet, and wine was served as of old. In Petersburg we had already entered upon our long season of want. The town was drained by its generous gifts to the army; regiments were constantly passing, and none ever departed without the offer of refreshment.

We heard no complaints from our soldier boys,

still in their winter quarters. But a letter to the army from General Lee filled our hearts with anxiety.

"HEADQUARTERS ARMY OF NORTHERN VIRGINIA,
"January 22, 1864.

"GENERAL ORDERS No. 7. — The commanding general considers it due to the army to state that the temporary reduction of rations has been caused by circumstances beyond the control of those charged with its support. Its welfare and comfort are the objects of his constant and earnest solicitude and no effort has been spared to provide for its wants. It is hoped that the exertions now being made will render the necessity but of short duration, but the history of the army has shown that the country can require no sacrifice too great for its patriotic devotion.

"Soldiers! you tread, with no unequal steps, the road by which your fathers marched through suffering, privation, and blood to independence.

"Continue to emulate in the future, as you have in the past, their valor in arms, their patient endurance of hardships, their high resolve to be free, which no trial could shake, no bribe seduce, no danger appall; and be assured that the just God who crowned their efforts with success will, in His own good time, send down His blessings upon yours.

"[Signed] R. E. LEE, *General.*"

Calm, strong, fatherly words! They deserve to be printed in letters of gold. They still have power to thrill the souls of the children of the fathers who marched through suffering, privation, and blood to independence, — children who wait, still wait, for the fulfilment of his promise that God will in His own good time send down His blessing upon them.

On January the 30th Agnes wrote from Richmond : —

"How can you be even dreaming of new cups and saucers ?   Mend your old ones, my dear, with white lead. That is what we are doing here; and when the cup is very much broken, the triangular, rectangular, and other 'angular' lines of white give it quite a Japanesque effect. There is not a bit of china for sale in the capital of the Confederacy.   A forlorn little chipped set — twelve odd pieces — sold last week at auction for $200 — and as to hats and bonnets !   We are washing the old ones and plaiting straw for the new.   I'll send you a package of straw I gleaned and dyed for you last summer.   Did I tell you about that straw ?   I asked my host at the farmhouse to give me a few sheaves, but he shook his head and opined it would be ' sinful in these hard times to take good vittles and convert it into hats.'   I could not see clearly that straw came under the generic term ' vittles ' — unless indeed the straw fed the animal that fed the soldier.   However, I meekly borrowed a sunbonnet and gleaned my straw. Half of it I popped into the kettle of boiling black dye behind the kitchen, — when the lady of the manor was looking another way, — and we will mix the black and white for the boys' hats.   But mark the quick and sure grinding of the mills of the gods.   After the wheat was all stacked there came a mighty rain with fog and warm mist.   One day my host brought in what seemed to be a feathery bouquet of delicate green.   It was a bunch of wheat, every grain of which had sprouted.   He had lost his crop !

"President and Mrs. Davis gave a large reception last week, and all the ladies looked positively gorgeous.   Mrs. Davis is in mourning for her father.   We should not expect suppers in these times, but we do have them !

Champagne is $350 a dozen, but we sometimes have champagne! The confectioners charge $15 for a cake, but we have cake. My flounced gray silk is behaving admirably, but I am afraid my Washington friends remember it as an old acquaintance. I never go out without meeting them. I have seen Dr. Garnett and Judge Scarborough and Mr. Dimitri on the street, and often meet Mr. Hunter, running about, in his enthusiasm, like a boy. But what do you think? I never could bear that Lord Lyons, with his red face and small eyes like ferrets'; and now we have reason to suppose that England would have recognized us but for his animosity against us. He says 'the Confederacy is on its last legs.' We have heard from dear old Dudley Mann; but of course *he* can do nothing for us in England, and he had as well come home and go with me to receptions. Mrs. Davis receives every Tuesday, and Mr. Mann is a better squire of dames than he is a diplomat."

My Petersburg beauties were all wearing hats of their own manufacture, the favorite style being the Alpine with a pointed crown. For trimming, very soft and lovely flowers were made of feathers, the delicate white feather with a tuft of fleecy marabout at its stem. The marabout tuft would be carefully drawn off, to be made into swan's-down trimming. A wire was prepared and covered with green paper for a stem, a little ball of wax fastened on the end, and covered with a tiny tuft of the down for a centre, and around this the feathers were stuck — with incurving petals for apple blossoms and half-open roses, — and reversed for camellias. Neatly trimmed and suitably tinted, these flowers were hand-

some enough for anybody, and were in great demand.
Cocks' plumes were also used on hats, iridescent,
and needing no coloring.   With the downy breast
of a goose which came into my possession I essayed
the making of a powder-puff for my baby, but alas !
the oil in the cuticle proved a perennial spring which
could not be dried up by soda or sunning, and finally
I saw my powder-puff disappearing in a hole, drawn
downward by a vigorous and hungry rat.

The young girls who visited me never complained
of their privations in the matter of food, but they
sorely grieved over their shabby wardrobes.

" I really think," said one, " if we can only get
along until we can wear white waists, we shall do very
well.   Every time a white waist is washed it's made
new — but these old flannel sacks — ugh ! "

One day Mary Meade made me a visit.   Always
beautiful, her face wore on this afternoon a seraphic,
beatific expression.

" Tell me, dear," I said, " all about it."   I supposed she had heard her lover had been promoted
or was coming home on a furlough.

She held up her two hands.   " *It's just these
gloves !* " said Mary.   " I can't help it.   They
make me perfectly happy !   They have just come
through the blockade."

The butcher shops were closed, and many of the
dry-goods stores ; but somebody had ordered a large
quantity of narrow crimson woollen braid, and had
failed to accept it.   We seized upon it.   Every one
of us had garments embroidered with it — in scrolls,
Maltese crosses, undulating lines, leaves ; all of

which goes to prove that the desire for ornament is an instinct of our nature, outliving the grosser affections for the good things of the table. The consciousness of being well dressed, we have been told, will afford a peace of mind far exceeding anything to be derived from the comforts of religion.

It had not been many years since every Virginia farm owned a house for a great cumbrous loom, with beams supported against the ceiling. The door of the loom-house was again opened, and the weaver installed upon her high bench. Cotton cloth was woven and dyed yellow with butternut, black with walnut-bark, gray with willow. A mordant to "set the dye" was unattainable — but at last rusty iron, nails, old horseshoes, old clamps and hinges, were found to be effective. Every atom of black silk was a treasure. It was shredded to mix with the cotton before carding. Even now the cells of my brain waken at the sight of a bundle of old black silk, and my fingers would fain respond.

Pins became scarce. People walked about with downcast eyes; they were looking for pins! Thorns were gathered and dried to use as pins. Dentists' gold soon disappeared. The generation succeeding the war period had not good teeth. Anæsthetics — morphine, chloroform, opium — were contraband of war. This was our great grief. Our soldier boys, who had done nothing to bring the war upon the country, must suffer every pang that followed the disasters of battle. The United States gave artificial limbs to its maimed soldiers. Ours had only their crutches, and these of rude home manufacture.

The blockade-running, for which our women were so much blamed, was often undertaken to bring morphine and medicine to our hospitals. The fashions of the day included a small round cushion worn at the back of a lady's belt, to lift the heavy hoop and many petticoats then in vogue. It was called "a bishop," and was made of silk. These were brought home from "a visit to friends at the North" filled with quinine and morphine. They were examined at the frontier by a long pin stuck through them. If the pin met no resistance, they were allowed to pass.

The famine moved on apace, but its twin sister, fever, never visited us. Never had Petersburg been so healthy. No garbage was decaying in the streets. Every particle of animal or vegetable food was consumed, and the streets were clean. Flocks of pigeons would follow the children who were eating bread or crackers. Finally the pigeons vanished having been themselves eaten. Rats and mice disappeared. The poor cats staggered about the streets, and began to die of hunger. At times meal was the only article attainable except by the rich. An ounce of meat daily was considered an abundant ration for each member of the family. To keep food of any kind was impossible — cows, pigs, bacon, flour, everything, was stolen, and even sitting hens were taken from the nest.

In the presence of such facts as these General Lee was able to report that nearly every regiment in his army had reënlisted — and for the war! And very soon he also reported that the army was out of meat and had but one day's rations of bread. One of our papers copied the following from the *Mobile Advertiser* : —

" In General Lee's tent meat is eaten but twice a week, the General not allowing it oftener, because he believes indulgence in meat to be criminal in the present straitened condition of the country. His ordinary dinner consists of a head of cabbage boiled in salt water, and a pone of corn bread. Having invited a number of gentlemen to dine with him, General Lee, in a fit of extravagance, ordered a sumptuous repast of bacon and cabbage. The dinner was served, and behold, a great pile of cabbage and a bit of bacon, or ' middling,' about four inches long and two inches across. The guests, with commendable politeness, unanimously declined the bacon, and it remained in the dish untouched. Next day General Lee, remembering the delicate titbit which had been so providentially preserved, ordered his servant to bring that ' middling.' The man hesitated, scratched his head, and finally owned up : —

" ' Marse Robert — de fac' is — dat ar middlin' was borrowed middlin'. We-all didn' have no middlin'. I done paid it back to de place whar I got it fum.'

" General Lee heaved a sigh of deepest disappointment, and pitched into the cabbage."

No man had ever lived in more comfort, nor was more surrounded by the accessories and appointments of luxury and refinement. His aide, Colonel Walter Taylor, has written me : —

" During the time that General Lee was in service he manifested that complete self-abnegation and dislike of parade and ceremony which became characteristic of him. Accompanied originally by a staff of but two persons, and, after the death of Colonel Washington, with but one aide-de-camp, with no escort or body-guard, no couriers or guides, he made the campaign under altogether unostentatious and really uncomfortable circumstances. One solitary tent constituted his headquarters camp; this served for the General and his aide; and when visitors were entertained, as actually occurred, the General shared his blanket with his aide, turning over those of the latter to his guest. His dinner service was of tin, — tin plates, tin cups, tin bowls, everything of tin, — and consequently indestructible; and to the annoyance and disgust of the subordinates who sighed for porcelain could not or would not be lost; indeed, with the help of occasional additions, this tin furniture continued to do service for several campaigns; and it was only in the last year of the war, while the army was around Petersburg, that a set of china was surreptitiously introduced into the baggage of the headquarters of the army. This displaced for a time the chaste and elaborate *plate;* but on resuming 'light marching order' at the time of the evacuation of Richmond and Petersburg, the china, which had been borrowed by the staff, was returned; the tins were again produced, and did good service until the surrender of the army, when they passed into the hands of individuals who now preserve them as mementos of the greatest commander in the great war."

CHAPTER XVIII

THE SIEGE OF PETERSBURG

JUNE 9 will always be a sacred day to the citizens of Petersburg. Every man capable of bearing arms had enlisted early in the service of the Southern Confederacy. They felt that much was expected of them. Petersburg had behaved gallantly in 1776, and had been the "Cockade City" in 1812. For the first three years of the war, as we have seen, no gun was fired near her gates. Only old men, women, and children were left in the town. The maidens bore their denied lives with cheerfulness, sustained and encouraged by the steadfast and serene bearing of their elders. Everybody worked for the soldiers and assembled every afternoon to pray for them. The city was almost as quiet as Blandford, her sister city of the dead, where the old Blands, Bollings, and Poythresses slept in perfect peace.

True, Petersburg, like Richmond, had her day of feverish excitement, known in Confederate history as "*Pawnee* Sunday," when both cities had been menaced by an ironclad. Early in the morning a telegraph operator had relieved a dull hour by interviewing his colleague at City Point, "Any danger from the *Pawnee*?" receiving as answer, "The

Pawnee is coming up the Appomattox." The town was wild. Everything valuable was hidden away, and the militia was drawn up, the lads of twelve and fourteen loading their hunting pieces and rallying to the town hall. Time having been allowed for any reasonable, well-conducted man-of-war to steam twelve miles, the telegraph operator, sorely pressed by questions, again interrogated his City Point friend. "What's become of the *Pawnee?* She isn't here yet." The irate answer spun over the line: "You — fool! I said the *Pawnee* is *not* coming up the river." Everything fell flat at once. There was an avowed sense of disappointment at the loss of an opportunity which might not come again. The dear women — the best I have ever known in any land — resumed their gentle ministrations, working much for the hospitals, and supplementing with culinary skill many deficiencies in material. But the men chafed. The veterans had felt the blood leap in their veins with the fire of youth; the boys longed for the fray; the physician, tied to his humdrum routine, yearned for the larger sphere in the field. "The dearest sacrifice a man can make to his country is his ambition."

The *Pawnee* incident was a fortunate one for the city, for it awakened the authorities to the necessity of preparing against surprise. The old, exempt citizens were formed into companies for home de- fence, and a breastwork was prepared commanding a road, "particularly interesting," says one of the survivors, "because it opened to deserving Peters- burgers the beatific vision of Sussex hams and South-

ampton whiskey ; " for at that moment the dreaded
foe was the wolf already at the door, rather than the
possible thunderbolt.

When General Butler, in June, 1864, commenced
his advance against Richmond, which was intended
as a coöperative movement with General Grant to
accomplish what was done the following spring, he
sent General Kautz on June 9 to make a cavalry
attack on Petersburg, twenty miles below Richmond.
The city, as I have said, was almost defenceless.
There had been much strategy, — marching and
countermarching, — too long a story to tell here;
but one thing at least was accomplished, as one of
the Confederate colonels pithily remarked, "Whatever blunders were made, the citizens and militia
had been trotted out in the direction of the enemy
at least." Kautz's superb cavalry appeared suddenly,
was met by the old men and boys of Petersburg, and
was repulsed. Colonel Fletcher Archer commanded
the militiamen. Forewarned only a few minutes before the charge, he hastily formed his men into line.
He says : "And what a line ! In number scarcely
more than sufficient to constitute a single company,
in dress nothing to distinguish them from citizens
pursuing the ordinary avocations of life, in age many
of them silvered over with the frosts of advancing
years, while others could scarcely boast of the down
upon the cheek of youth ; in arms and accoutrements such as an impoverished government could
afford them. But there was that in their situation
which lifted them above the ordinary rules of criticism. They stood there, not as mercenaries who,

having enlisted on account of profit, required the strong arm of military law to keep them to their post, nor as devotees of ambition craving a place in the delusive pages of history, but they stood as a band of patriots whose homes were imperilled and whose loved ones were in danger of falling into the hands of an untried foe. As they stood in line before me I could see them glancing back at their own dwellings under the sun of a lovely June morning. When I addressed them in a few words of encouragement, they listened with gravity and a full appreciation of their situation. There was no excitement, no shout, only calm resolution."

Thus their commander. What did the men themselves feel? One of them wrote: "We had not long to wait. A cloud of dust in our front told of the hurried advance of cavalry, and the next moment the glitter of spur and scabbard revealed a long line of horsemen half a mile in front of us. Oh, how we missed our cannon! Our venerable muskets were not worth a tinker's imprecation at longer range than a hundred yards, and we were compelled perforce to watch the preparations for our slaughter, much after the fashion that a rational turtle may be presumed to contemplate the preliminaries of an aldermanic dinner."

These were the men who saved the city. It was in honor of them that the women and children marched through dust and heat on June 9, 1866, to lay garlands of flowers upon their humble graves, and by their pious action to inaugurate the beautiful custom, which is now observed all over the country,

T

of honoring the dead who fell in the Civil War.   No
lovelier day ever dawned than June 9, 1864.   The
magnolia grandiflora was in full flower, bee-haunted
honey-locusts perfumed the warm air, almost extin-
guishing the peachy odor of the microphylla roses,
graceful garlands of jessamine hung over the trel-
lised front porches.   Almost the first intimation
that the town received of its great peril was the
impetuous dash through the streets of the Confederate artillery.   The morning was so sweet and bright
that the women and little children were abroad in
the streets, on their way to market, or on errands
to the shops, or to visit with fruit and flowers the
old and sick among their friends.   Lossie Hill, the
daintiest of dainty maidens, was picking her leisurely
way in the dusty street, going to spend the morning
with old Mrs. Mertens, when she heard the frantic
shout: "Get out of the way!   Damn the women!
Run over them if they won't get out of the way."
This was the morning greeting of the politest of
gentlemen, — Captain Graham, — whose guns were
thundering down the street to the rescue of the
slender line at the front.   As fast as the dread news
reached the men exempt from duty, who were engaged in their various professions and vocations,
every one dropped his business and rushed to the
firing line.   The oldest men were as ardent as the
youngest.   One man, a druggist, began, while pulling on his accoutrements, to give directions to a
venerable clerk whom he expected to dispense drugs
in his absence.   "Now," said the old man, "if you
want anything done at home you must talk to some-

body else! I am going to the front! I'm just like General Lee. I should be glad if these fellows would go back to their homes and let us alone, but if they won't they must be made to, that's all." With their arms around their father, pretty Molly and Gussie Banister implored him not to go forth. He was president of the bank, he was frail and not young. "The duty of every man lies yonder," said he, pointing to the puffs of smoke at the gates of the town, and shouldering his musket he marched away.

Mr. William C. Banister was a cultivated, Christian gentleman, one of Petersburg's most esteemed and beloved citizens. His widow and sweet daughters received him — dead — on the evening of the battle. Molly Banister, one of the dear girls who blessed my life in those anxious days, has told the story of her martyred father's patriotic fervor: —

"My father had been on duty out on the lines on previous occasions, always against the entreaty of the members of his family. We thought his infirmity, deafness, ought to excuse him. Besides this, he was a bank officer and over military age. When the court-house bell, on the morning of the 9th of June, sounded the alarm, he was at his place of business, in the old Exchange Bank, and we hoped he would not hear it. He got information, however, of the condition of things, came at once home, and informed us of his purpose to go out to the lines. My mother and I besought him not to go, urging that he could not hear the orders.

"'If I can't hear,' he said, 'I can fight — I can fire a gun. This is no time for any one to stand back.

Every man that can shoulder a musket must fight. The enemy are now right upon us.'

"Bidding us good-by he left the house. On the street, near our gate, was a man, just from the lines. Addressing him, my father said, pointing to the lines : —

"'My friend, you are needed in this direction.'

"'I am absent on leave,' said the man.

"'No leave,' replied my father, 'should keep you on such an occasion as this. Every man should fight now!'

"I have been informed that as he came up from the bank he urged in the same way all whom he met, capable, as he thought, of bearing arms."

Patty Hardee's father, another man past age for military service, was one of the first to report for duty, and among the first to be borne, dead, to his daughter.

Robert Martin, also exempt, and the father of an adoring family, immediately joined the ranks. Almost totally deaf, he could hear no orders, and continued to load his gun after the order to cease firing was given and the company had begun to move off. A comrade ran up, put his lips to his ear, and remonstrated. "Stop firing!" exclaimed the veteran with disgust. "Orders? I haven't any orders to stop firing," and he continued to advance. As Nelson at Copenhagen, who, when told that he had been signalled to stop fighting, turned his blind eye to the station, exclaiming, "*I* see no signal!"

These are but a few of the many incidents which illustrate the courage of these stout-hearted veterans

and the spirit behind their small force which inspired that courage and compelled success.   They
fought — one hundred and twenty-five men, badly
armed and untrained — behind their frail defence;
one hundred and twenty-five against twenty-three
hundred of the enemy, holding them at bay for two
hours!   General Butler was greatly chagrined at
the failure of this move upon Petersburg.   He sent
a characteristic letter of reproof to his general officer
north of the Appomattox.   After detailing all the
mistakes that had led to the humiliating repulse, he
adds testily: "You have endeavored to state in
your report what my orders to General Kautz
were.   That was no part of your report.   I know
what my orders were without any information from
that source," adding, "certain it is that forty-five
hundred of my best troops have been kept at bay
by some fifteen hundred men, six hundred only of
which were Confederate troops and the rest old
men and boys, the cradle and the grave being
robbed of about equal proportions to compose the
force opposed to you."

"The cradle and the grave!"   Alas, yes!
There was no triumph on the evening of that day.
Half the gallant company was gone.   There was
wailing within the city gates that night.   "The
hand of the reaper" had taken "the ears that were
hoary," and the daughters wept for the good, gray
head gone forward to the "eternal camping ground"
after a long life of peace.   For these gallant gentlemen the white rose which shaded my door yielded
all its pure blossoms.   Well was it for the sake of

my own devotion that this was an ever blooming rose! I had watered and nourished it with care, unconscious of its high vocation, to bud and blossom and lie on the noble heart of more than one soldier. My own husband was in the fight, and sent the first news of the repulse of the enemy and the safety of his boyhood's home.

Immediately after the battle on the line, June 9, we observed unusual activity in our streets. Great army wagons passed continually, pausing often at a well before my door to water their horses. Clouds of dust filled the city. Evidently something unusual was going on. "We are only re-enforcing our defences," we said, and comforted ourselves in the thought.

One day my father came in unexpectedly. The army corps to which he was attached had camped near Petersburg!

"I've just met General Lee in the street," he said.

I uttered an exclamation of alarm. "Oh, *is* he going to fight here?"

"My dear," said my father, sternly, "you surprise me! The safest place for you is in the rear of General Lee's army, and that happens to be just where you are! The lines are established just here, and filled with Lee's veterans."

This was startling news, but more was to follow. One Sunday afternoon, — the next, I think, — the Presbyterian minister had gathered his flock of women and children for service in the church opposite my home, and had just uttered the first sentence of his opening prayer, " Almighty Father, we are assembled to worship Thee in the presence of our enemies," when an awful, serpentlike hiss filled the church, and a shell burst through the wall.

In a moment the church was empty, and Dr. Miller, the pastor, was telling me that his congregation had dismissed itself without a benediction!

" And the shell?" I inquired.

" It lies upon the table in the church," said the doctor; " nobody dares remove it."

This was the first shell that entered our part of the town. From that moment we were shelled at intervals, and very severely. There were no soldiers in the city. Women were killed on the lower streets, and an exodus from the shelled districts commenced at once.

As soon as the enemy brought up their siege guns of heavy artillery, they opened on the city with shell without the slightest notice, or without giving opportunity for the removal of non-combatants, the sick, the wounded, or the women and children. The fire was at first directed toward the Old Market, presumably because of the railroad depot situated there, about which soldiers might be supposed to collect. But the guns soon enlarged their operations, sweeping all the streets in the business part of the city, and then invading the residential region. The steeples of the churches seemed to afford targets for their fire, all of them coming in finally for a share of the compliment.

To persons unfamiliar with the infernal noise made by the screaming, ricocheting, and bursting of shells, it is impossible to describe the terror and demoralization which ensued. Some families who could not leave the besieged city dug holes in the ground, five or six feet deep, covered with heavy timbers banked over with earth, the entrance facing opposite the batteries from which the shells were fired. They made these bomb-proofs safe, at least, and thither the family repaired when heavy shelling commenced. General Lee seemed to recognize that no part of the city was safe, for he immediately ordered the removal of all the hospitals, under the care of Petersburg's esteemed physician, Dr. John Herbert Claiborne. There were three thousand sick and wounded, many of them too ill to be moved. A long, never-ending line of wagons, carts, everything that could run on wheels, passed my door, until there were no more to pass. We soon learned the peculiar, deep boom of the one great gun which bore directly upon us. The boys named it " Long Tom." Sometimes for several weeks " Long Tom " rested or slept — and would then make up for lost time. And yet we yielded to no panic. The children seemed to understand that it would be cowardly to complain. One little girl cried out with fright at an explosion; but her aunt, Mrs. Gibson, took her in her arms, and said : " My dear, you cannot make it harder for other people ! If you feel very much afraid, come to me, and I will clasp you close, but you mustn't cry."

Charles Campbell, the historian, lived near us, at the Anderson Seminary. He cleared out the large coal cellar, which was fortunately dry, spread rugs on the floor, and furnished it with lounges and chairs. There we took refuge when the firing was unbearable. Some of our neighbors piled bags of sand around their houses, and thus made them bomb-proof.

The Rev. Dr. Hoge, who had come South from the Brick Church, New York, of which he had been pastor, was lying ill and dying a few miles from Petersburg, and my friend Mrs. Bland invited me to accompany her to visit him. She had borrowed an ambulance from General Bushrod Johnston.

We made our call upon our sick friend, and were on our return when we were suddenly startled by heavy firing. The ambulance driver was much excited, and began to pour forth in broken English a torrent of abuse of the Confederacy. As we were near home, we kept silence, thinking that, if he grew more offensive, we could leave him and walk. Mrs. Bland undertook to reason with him.

"What is your grievance?" she inquired. "Perhaps we might see the colonel and arrange a better place for you — some transfer, perhaps."

"Nevare! nevare!" said our man, "I transfare to my own koontree! I make what you call — 'desairt.' Mon Dieu! dey now tell me I fight for neeger! Frenshman nevare fight for neeger."

All this time the guns were booming away, and clouds of smoke were drifting toward us. We were glad to arrive at my door.

It was closed. There was not a soul in the house. One of the chimneys had been knocked down, and the bricks lay in a heap on the grass. I thought of

Mr. Campbell's bomb-proof cellar; there we found my children, and there we remained until the paroxysmal shelling ceased.

One night, after a long, hot day, we were so tired we slept soundly. I was awakened by Eliza Page, standing trembling beside me. She pulled me out of bed and hurriedly turned to throw blankets around the children. The furies were let loose! The house was literally shaking with the concussion from the heavy guns. We were in the street, on our way to our bomb-proof cellar, when a shell burst not more than fifty feet before us. Fire and fragments rose like a fountain in the air and fell in a shower around us. Not one of my little family was hurt.

Another time a shell fell in our own yard and buried itself in the earth. My baby was not far away, in her nurse's arms. The little creature was fascinated by the shells. The first word she ever uttered was an attempt to imitate them. "Yonder comes that bird with the broken wing," the servants would say. The shells made a fluttering sound as they traversed the air, descending with a frightful hiss, to explode or be buried in the earth. When they exploded in midair by day, a puff of smoke, white as an angel's wing, would drift away, and the particles would patter down like hail. At night, the track of the shell and its explosion were precisely similar in sound, although not in degree, to our Fourth of July rockets, except that they were fired, not upward, but in a slanting direction. I never felt afraid of them! I was brought up to believe in predestination. Courage, after all, is much

a matter of nerves.   My neighbors, Mr. and Mrs.
Gibson and Mrs. Meade, agreed with me, and we
calmly elected to remain in town.   There was no
place of safety accessible to us.   Mr. Branch
removed his family, and, as far as I knew, none
other of my friends remained throughout the
summer.

Not far from the door ran a sunken street, with a
hill, through which it was cut, rising each side of it.
Into this hill the negroes burrowed, hollowing out a
small space, where they sat all day on mats, knitting,
and selling small cakes made of sorghum and flour,
and little round meat pies.   I might have been
tempted to invest in the latter except for a slight
circumstance.   I saw a dead mule lying on the
common, and out of its side had been cut a very
neat, square chunk of flesh !

With all our starvation we never ate rats, mice, or
mule-meat.   We managed to exist on peas, bread,
and sorghum.   We could buy a little milk, and we
mixed it with a drink made from roasted and ground
corn.   The latter, in the grain, was scarce.   Mr.
Campbell's children picked up the grains wherever
the army horses were fed.

My little boys never complained, but Theo, who
had insisted upon returning to me from his uncle's
safe home in the country, said one day : " Mamma,
I have a queer feeling in my stomach ! Oh, no ! it
doesn't ache the least bit, but it feels like a nut-
meg grater."

Poor little laddie ! His machinery needed oiling.
And pretty soon his small brother fell ill with fever.

My blessed Dr. Withers obtained a permit for me
to get a pint of soup every day from the hospital,
and one day there was a joyful discovery.   In the
soup was a drumstick of chicken !

"I cert'nly hope I'll not get well," the little man
shocked me by saying.

"Oh, is it as bad as that?" I sighed.

"Why," he replied, "my soup will be stopped if
I get better!"

Just at this juncture, when things were as bad
as could be, my husband brought home to tea the
Hon. Pierre Soulé, General D. H. Hill, and General Longstreet.   I had bread and a little tea, the
latter served in a yellow pitcher without a handle.
Mrs. Campbell, hearing of my necessity, sent me a
small piece of bacon.

When we assembled around the table, I lifted my
hot pitcher by means of a napkin, and offered my
tea, pure and simple, allowing the guests to use their
discretion in regard to a spoonful or two of very
dark brown sugar.

"This is a great luxury, Madam," said Mr. Soulé,
with one of his gracious bows, "a good cup of tea."

We talked that night of all that was going wrong
with our country, of the good men who were constantly relieved of their commands, of all the mistakes we were making.

"Mistakes!" said General Hill, bringing his
clinched fist down upon the table, "I could forgive
mistakes! I cannot forgive lies! I could get along
if we could *only, only* ever learn the truth, the real
truth."   But he was very personal and used much
stronger words than these.

They talked and talked, these veterans and the charming, accomplished diplomat, until one of them inquired the hour. I raised a curtain.

"Gentlemen," I said, "the sun is rising. You must now breakfast with us." They declined. They had supped!

I had the misfortune early in June to fall ill, with one of the sudden, violent fevers which cannot be arrested, but must "run its course" for a certain number of days. I was delirious from this fever, and wild with the idea that a battle was raging within hearing. I fancied I could hear the ring of the musket as it was loaded! Possibly my quickened senses had really heard, for a fierce battle was going on at Port Walthall, a station on the Richmond and Petersburg railroad, six miles distant. General Butler had landed at Bermuda Hundred and had been sent by General Grant to lead a column against Richmond on the south side of the James and to coöperate with forces from the Wilderness. Butler had reached Swift Creek, there to be met by General Johnston, and repulsed as far as Walthall Junction on the railroad. The following day there was a hotly contested battle at close quarters, continued on the next, when our men, although greatly outnumbered by Butler's forces, drove these back to their base on the James River. All this time my excited visions were of battle and soldiers, culminating at last by the presence of one soldier, leaning wearily on his sabre in my own room. I did not recognize the soldier, but memory still holds his attitude of grief as he looked

at me, and the sound of his voice as he answered
my question, " Where have you been all this time ? "
with, " In more peril than in all my life before."

But the fever crisis was passing even then, and
I was soon well enough to learn more.   This was
another of the well-planned schemes for taking Richmond, another of the failures which drew from
Lincoln the gravely humorous reply, when application was made to him for a pass to go to
Richmond : —

" I don't know about that ; I have given passes
to about two hundred and fifty thousand men to go
there during the last two or three years, and not one
of them has got there yet."

Dr. Claiborne went out to this Walthall battle-field
to help the wounded, taking with him surgeons and
ambulances.   A dreadful sight awaited him.   Bodies
of dead men, Federal and Confederate, lay piled together in heaps.   On removing some of these to
discover if any one of them might be still alive, a
paper dropped from the pocket of a young lieutenant, written in German to a lady in Bremen.
Upon reading it, Dr. Claiborne found it was addressed to his betrothed.   He told her that his term
of service having expired, he would soon leave for
New York City, and he gave her the street and number where she should meet him on her arrival in this
country.   This was his last fight, into which he went
no doubt voluntarily, as he was about to leave the
army.   Doubtless the blue-eyed *Mädchen* looked
long for him on the banks of the Weser ! The doctor indorsed the sad news on the letter, and sent it

through the lines. Perhaps it reached her, or perhaps she is telling her story this day to other blue eyes on the Weser, eyes that look up and wonder she could ever have been young, lovely, and the promised bride of a gallant Union officer.

The Confederate government utterly neglected the praise and distinction so freely awarded by other nations in time of war, for deeds of gallantry and valor. Says Major Stiles: " Not only did I never see or hear of a promotion on the field, but I do not believe such a thing ever occurred in any army of the Confederacy from the beginning to the end of the war. Indeed, I am confident it never did ; for, incredible as it may appear, even Lee himself did not have the power to make such promotion. I never saw or heard of a medal or a ribbon being pinned on a man's jacket, or even so much as a man's name being read out publicly in orders of gallantry in battle." [1]

Hanging in my husband's library, among other war relics, is a heavy silver medal, representing in high relief a soldier charging a cannon. On the obverse side is a laurel wreath, space for a name, and the words, " Distinguished for courage : U. S. Colored Troops." No such medal was ever given by our government to its hardly used, poorly paid private soldiers. Some of them fought through the war. They starved and froze in the trenches during that last dreadful winter, but no precious star or ribbon was awarded, to be hung with the sabre or musket and venerated by generations yet to come.

[1] " Four Years with Marse Robert," p. 341.

Among my few preserved papers I have two in faded ink. One is signed Bushrod Johnston, the other D. H. Hill. The latter says: "The victory at Walthall Junction was greatly due to General Roger A. Pryor. But for him it is probable we might have been surprised and defeated." The other from General Johnston runs at length: "At the most critical juncture General Roger A. Pryor rendered me most valuable service, displaying great zeal, energy, and gallantry in reconnoitring the positions of the enemy, arranging my line of battle, and rendering successful the operations and movements of the conflict." At General Johnston's request my husband served with him during the midsummer. Such letters I have in lieu of medal or ribbon, — a part only of much of similar nature ; but less was given to many a man who as fitly deserved recognition.

My General, who had been in active service in all the events around Petersburg, was now requested by General Lee to take with him a small squad of men, and learn something of the movements of the enemy.

"Grant knows all about me," he said, "and I know too little about Grant. You were a school-boy here, General, and have hunted in all the by-paths around Petersburg. Knowing the country better than any of us, you are the best man for this important duty."

Accordingly, armed with a pass from General Lee, my husband set forth on his perilous scouting expedition, sometimes being absent a week at a time. One morning, very early, he entered my room.

"I am dead for want of sleep," he said. "I was

obliged to take some prisoners. They are coming in under guard, and you must give them a good breakfast." As he walked out of the room to find a quiet corner, he called back, " Be sure, now! Feed my prisoners, if all the rest of us lose our breakfast."

He had suggested the only way in which he could be obeyed.

Five forlorn blue-coated soldiers soon appeared, and lay down under the trees. Presently they were all asleep. I called my little family together. We had only a small pail of meal. Would they be willing to give it to these poor prisoners?

They were willing, never fear; but I had trouble with John. He grew very sullen when I ordered him to bake the bread for Yankee prisoners in five small loaves. I promised to send out for more provisions later, and finally he yielded, but with an ill grace. When the hot loaves were on the table, flanked by sweetened corn-coffee, I deputed Paterson Gibson, my neighbor's kindly young son, to waken my guests. This was no easy matter.

" Come, now, Yank," said Pat, " get up and eat your breakfast. Come now! Cheer up! We'll send you home pretty soon."

We left them alone at their repast. It occurred to me they might try to escape, and I heartily wished they would. But after an hour they were marched away, we knew not whither.

On July 30th occurred the dreadful explosion of the mine which the enemy had tunnelled under our line of fortifications.

A little after four in the morning the city was

u

roused by the most awful thunder — like nothing I can imagine, except, perhaps, the sudden eruption of a volcano. This was the explosion of a mine tunnelled by General Grant under our works. Instantly the unhappy residents of the town poured into the street and out on the road, anywhere to escape what we supposed to be an earthquake. No words can adequately describe this horror! We lost a part of our line. Colonel Paul, a member of Beauregard's staff, was sent to inform General Lee of the disaster, and bore back his orders that the line must be at once recaptured. As the colonel passed his father's house, he ran in and found the old gentleman's hand on the bell-rope to summon his household to family prayers.

" Stay, my son, and join us at prayers," said the old man. " Get some breakfast with your mother and me." The colonel could not pause. He must leave this peaceful home, and bear his part in protecting it.

When the veterans meet to-day for their camp-fire talk, it is of the " battle of the Crater," the shocking incidents of which cannot be told to gentle ears, that they speak most frequently. The fountain of fire that shot up to heaven bore with it the dismembered bodies of man made in God's own image. Then infuriated men, black and white, leaped into the chasm and mingled in an orgy of carnage. No one has ever built on that field. Nature smooths its scars with her gentle hand, but no dwelling of man will ever rest there while this tragedy is remembered.

On May 3d, 1887, Federal and Confederate vet-

erans met on this spot and clasped hands together.
Since then the Confederates have met there again
and again. Each one has some story to tell of
heroism, of devotion, and the stories are not always
tragic. Some of them have been gleaned from the
experiences of the boys in blue.

Lieutenant Bowley of the Northern army delivered an address before the California commandery
of the Loyal Legion of the United States, and
quotes from the address of a negro preacher to his
fellows just before the explosion of the crater. He
was sergeant of a company of negroes, and thus
exhorted them : —

"Now, men, dis is gwine to be a gret fight, de
gretest we seen yit; gret things is 'pending on dis
fight; if we takes Petersburg, mos' likely we'll take
Richmond an' 'stroy Lee's army an' close de wah.
Eb'ry man had orter liff up his soul in pra'r for a
strong heart. Oh! 'member de pore colored people
ober dere in bondage. Oh! 'member dat Gin'ral
Grant an' Gin'ral Burnside an' Gin'ral Meade an'
all de gret gin'rals is right ober yander a watchin' ye;
an' 'member *I'se* a watchin' ye an 'any skulker is a
gwine ter git a prod ob dis ba'net — you heah me!"

Words than which, except for the closing sentence,
I know none more pathetic.

CHAPTER XIX

BEHIND LEE'S LINES

THE month of August in the besieged city passed like a dream of terror. The weather was intensely hot and dry, varied by storms of thunder and lightning — when the very heavens seemed in league with the thunderbolts of the enemy. Our region was not shelled continuously. One shot from "our own gun," as we learned to call it, would be fired as if to let us know our places ; this challenge would be answered from one of our batteries, and the two would thunder away for five or six hours. We always sought shelter in Mr. Campbell's bomb-proof cellar at such times, and the negroes would run to their own "bum-proofs," as they termed the cells hollowed under the hill.

Agnes wrote from Richmond, August 26, 1864 : —

"You dear, obstinate little woman! What did I tell you? I implored you to get away while you could, and now you are waiting placidly for General Grant to blow you up. That awful crater! Do the officers around you consider it honorable warfare to dig and mine under a man and blow him up while he is asleep — before he has time to get his musket? I always thought an open field and a fair fight, with the enemy in front at equal chances,

was the American idea of honest, manly warfare.   To
my mind this is the most awful thing that could be imagined.   There is a strong feeling among the people I meet
that the hour has come when we should consider the lives
of the few men left to us.   Why let the enemy wipe us
off the face of the earth?   Should this feeling grow, nothing but a great victory can stop it.   Don't you remember
what Mr. Hunter said to us in Washington?   'You may
sooner check with your bare hand the torrent of Niagara
than stop this tidal wave of secession.'   *I* am for a tidal
wave of peace — and I am not alone.   Meanwhile we
are slowly starving to death.   Here, in Richmond, if we
can afford to give $11 for a pound of bacon, $10 for a
small dish of green corn, and $10 for a watermelon, we
can have a dinner of three courses for four persons.   Hampton's cavalry passed through town last week, amid great
excitement.   Every man as he trotted by was cutting and
eating a watermelon, and throwing the rinds on the heads
of the little negro boys who followed in crowds on either
side of the street.   You wouldn't have dreamed of war —
such shouting and laughing from everybody.   The con-
trasts we constantly see look like insanity in our people.
The President likes to call attention to the fact that we
have no beggars on our streets, as evidence that things are
not yet desperate with us.   He forgets our bread riot which
occurred such a little while ago.   That pale, thin woman
with the wan smile haunts me.   Ah! these are the people
who suffer the consequence of all that talk about slavery in
the territories you and I used to hear in the House and
Senate Chamber.   Somebody, somewhere, is mightily to
blame for all this business, but it isn't you nor I, nor yet
the women who did not really deserve to have Governor
Letcher send the mayor to read the Riot Act to them.
They were only hungry, and so a thousand of them loaded
some carts with bread for their children.   You are not to

suppose I am heartless because I run on in this irrelevant fashion. The truth is, I am so shocked and disturbed I am hysterical. It is all so awful.

"Your scared-to-death

"AGNES."

My husband sent me a note by his courier, one hot August day, to tell me that his old aide, Captain Whitner, having been wounded, was now discharged from the hospital, but was much too weak for service in the trenches, so he had obtained for the captain leave of absence for two weeks, and had sent him to me to be built up. On the moment the sick man appeared in an ambulance. I was glad to see him, but a gaunt spectre arose before my imagination and sternly suggested: "Built up, forsooth! And pray, what are you to build him up with? You can no more make a man without food than the Israelites could make bricks without straw."

However, the captain had brought a ration of bacon and meal, with promise of more to come. I bethought me of the flourishing garden of my neighbor, whose onions and beets were daily gathered for her own family. I wrote a very pathetic appeal for my wounded Confederate soldier, now threatened with scurvy for want of fresh food, and I fully expected she would be moved by my eloquence and her own patriotism to grant me a daily portion from her garden. She answered that she would agree to send me a dish of vegetables fourteen days for fourteen dollars. Gold was then selling at the rate of twenty-five dollars in our paper currency for one dollar in gold, so the dish was not a very costly one.

But when it appeared it was a very small dish indeed, — two beets or four onions.   Homœopathic as were the remedial agents, they helped to cure the captain.

One morning, late in August, Eliza came early to my bedside.   I started up in alarm.

" Shelling again ? " I asked her.

" Worse," said Eliza.

" Tell me, tell me quick — is the General — "

" No, no, honey," said my kind nurse, laying a detaining hand upon me.   " You cert'nly sleep sound !   Didn't you hear a stir downstairs in the night ?   Well, about midnight somebody hallooed to the kitchen, and John ran out.   There stood a man on horseback and a dead soldier lying before him on the saddle.   He said to John, ' Boy, I know General Pryor would not refuse to take in my dead brother.'

" John ran up to my room and asked me what he must do.   ' Take him in,' I told him.   ' Marse Roger will never forgive you if you turn him away.' "

" You were perfectly right," I said, beginning to dress myself.   " Where is he ? "

" In the parlor," said Eliza.   " He had a man-servant with him.   John brought in his own cot, and he is lying on it.   His brother is in there, and his man, both of them."

The children were hushed by their nurse's story, and gathered under the shade in the yard.   When breakfast was served, I sent John to invite my guest in.   He returned with answer that " the captain don' feel like eatin' nothin'."

" Captain ? " I asked.

"No'm, he ain't a captain, but his dead brother was. He was Captain Spann of South Carolina or Georgia, I forget which. His man came into the kitchen for hot water to shave his dead master, but I didn't ask many questions 'cause I saw he was troubled."

I went out to my ever blooming rose and found it full of cool, dewy blossoms. I cut an armful, and knocked at the parlor door myself. It was opened by a haggard, weary-looking soldier, who burst into tears at seeing me. I took his hand and essayed to lead him forth, but he brokenly begged I would place the roses upon his brother's breast. "Will you, for the sake of his poor wife and mother?"

Very calm was the face of the dead officer. His servant and his brother had shaven and cared for him. His dark hair was brushed from a noble brow, and I could see that his features were regular and refined.

I persuaded the lonely watcher to go with John to an upper room, to bathe and rest a few minutes; but he soon descended and joined us at our frugal breakfast, and then Mr. Gibson, my good rector, came in to help and advise, and in the evening my husband returned, much gratified that we had received and comforted the poor fellow.

As August drew to a close, I began to perceive that I could no longer endure the recurrence of such scenes; and I learned with great relief that my brother-in-law had moved his family to North Carolina and had placed Cottage Farm, three miles distant from the besieged city, at my disposal. Accordingly, I wrote to General Bushrod Johnston, requesting an army wagon to be sent me early the next morning, and all night was spent in packing and preparing to leave. I had collected needful furniture when I moved into town eight months before.

The wagon did not come at the specified hour. All day we waited, all the next night (without our beds), and the next day. As I looked out of the window in the twilight, hoping and watching, the cannonading commenced with vigor, and a line of shells rose in the air, describing luminous curves and breaking into showers of fragments. Our gun will be next, I thought, and for the first time my strength forsook me, and I wept over the hopeless doom which seemed to await us. Just then I heard the wheels below my window, and there was my wagon with four horses.

We were all bestowed, bag and baggage, in a few minutes, and were soon safely beyond shell fire. I did not know until then how great had been the strain of keeping up under fire for three months. I literally "went all to pieces," trembling as though I had a chill. When we arrived at Cottage Farm, my driver allowed John, Eliza, and my little boys to unload in the road before the lawn, and then calmly turned his horses' heads and drove away.

It was nine o'clock, we had no lights, we had no strength to lift our packages into the house. John advised that he should remain on guard during the night, and that some blankets should be spread for us in the cottage, and we proceeded to carry out this plan. In a few minutes, however, half a dozen soldiers came up, and one of their officers pleasantly greeted us as "welcome neighbors," for their company was encamped near us. They had seen our plight and had come to "set things to rights," also to assure us of protection.

About twelve o'clock we found ourselves comfortable. Our beds were put up, our boxes were all under cover. John's commissariat yielded some biscuits, there was a well of pure water near the door. We were safe. We could sleep. No shell could reach us!

The cool freshness of a lovely September morning filled our hearts with life and hope. A large circle of flowers, chrysanthemums, dahlias, and late-blooming roses surrounded the carriage drive to the door, a green lawn stretched to the limits of a large yard in the rear, and beyond this a garden with a few potatoes to dig, and an apple tree in fruit which the soldiers had respected. John and the little boys were in fine spirits. They laid plans for a cow, chickens, ducks, and pigeons. The cow was purchased at once from a neighboring farmer, was named Rose, and was installed in a shelter attached to the kitchen, where John could protect her from marauders.

"'Cause," said John, "I knows soldiers! They get up before day and milk your cow under your very eyebrows. Ain't you hear about Gen'al Lee in Pennsylvania? The old Dutch farmers gave him Hail Columbia because his soldiers milked their cows. Gen'al Lee could keep 'em from stealin' horses, but the queen o' England herself couldn't stop a soldier when he hankers after milk. An' he don't need no pail, neither; he can milk in his canteen an' never spill a drop."

My brother had left two old family servants, "Uncle Frank" and his wife "Aunt Jinny," as caretakers of the premises; and to their dignified bearing, supplemented by the presence of a company of honorable soldiers, we were indebted for the unrifled apple tree and the tiny potatoes, like marbles, left after the autumn digging. "Aunt Jinny" also had a few fowls. An egg for my baby was now possible.

Her faithful Christian character had won for her a high place in the esteem of the family. Uncle Frank's manners were perfect,—polished, suave, and conciliatory; but when judge and jury sat upon the case of a culprit arraigned by him, his testimony was apt to be challenged by his prisoner.

"You knows, Marse Robert, you can't b'lieve ole Uncle Frank!"

"Frank always knows what he is talking about! He is only more polite than the rest of you."

"Well, Marse Robert, Gawd knows I hates to fling dut at Uncle Frank, but he's a liar. He sholy is! An' jist 'cause he's a *sweet* liar he gets we all in trouble."

My father, the chaplain, soon joined us, his corps having camped within riding distance. There was an office in the yard, and there my father took up his abode. His life was an active one among the soldiers, and he was often absent for days at a time; but I felt the protection of his occasional presence.

My husband was now employed, day and night, often in peril, gleaning from every possible source information for General Lee.

One day Theo and Roger ran in with stirring news. They had seen General Lee dismount at Mr. Turnbull's, a short distance on the road beyond us, and had learned from Mr. Turnbull himself that his house had been given to General Lee for his headquarters, also that the General did not require Mr. and Mrs. Turnbull to leave, and that they were delighted to have the General.

The whole face of the earth seemed to change immediately. Army wagons crawled unceasingly along the highroad, just in front of our gate. All was stir and life in the rear, where there was another country road, and a short road connecting the two passed immediately by the well near our house. This, too, was constantly travelled; the whir of the well-wheel never seemed to pause, day or night. We soon had pleasant visitors, General A. P. Hill, Colonel William Pegram, General Walker, General Wilcox, and others. General Wilcox, an old friend and comrade, craved permission to make his headquarters on the green lawn in the rear of the house, and my husband rejoiced at his presence and protection for our little family.

In less than twenty-four hours I found myself in the centre of a camp. The white tents of General Wilcox's staff officers were stretched close to the door.

GENERAL ROBERT E. LEE ON "TRAVELLER."

From a photograph by Miley, Lexington, Va.

When we left Washington, our library and pictures had been sent to Petersburg, and had remained there in a warehouse ever since.   My father eagerly advised us to set up the library and hang the pictures in our new home at Cottage Farm.

" But suppose General Lee moves away," I suggested.

" My dear, he will not move away !   He is here to protect Petersburg and Richmond.   He will never surrender either place — and, as I have tried to impress upon you, the safest place for you on this continent is in the rear of Lee's army."

So timber was brought for shelving the dining room, and three thousand or more books were arranged on the shelves.   The parlor and the two bedrooms (we had no more in the little cottage) were hung with the pictures bought by my husband when he was Minister to Greece.   My favorite — the Raffaello Morghen proof impression of the " Madonna della Seggiola " — hung over the mantel in the parlor, and to it I lifted weary eyes many a time during the remaining days of the war.   Sundry delicate carvings were also in the boxes, with my music.   My sister had not taken her piano with her to North Carolina.   There were a baby-house and toys in another box, and in a French trunk with many compartments some evening dresses, at which I did not even glance, well knowing I should not need them.   The trunk containing them was stored in the cellar.

We were happier than we had been for a long time. Things seemed to promise a little respite.   To be sure, Grant's army was in front of us; but if we could only avoid a collision for a month or two, the troops on both sides would go into winter quarters, and everybody would have the rest so much needed to fit them for the spring campaign.

"We are here for eight years, — not a day less," said my father, and he fully believed it.

That being the case, it behooved me to look after the little boys' education. School books were found for them. I knew "little Latin and less Greek," but I gravely heard them recite lessons in the former; and they never discovered the midnight darkness of my mind as to mathematics.

I knew nothing of the strong line of fortifications which General Grant was building at the back of the farm, fortifications strengthened by forts at short intervals. Our own line — visible from the garden — had fewer forts, two of which, Fort Gregg and Battery 45, protected our immediate neighborhood. These forts occasionally answered a challenge, but there was no attempt at a sally on either side.

The most painful circumstance connected with our position was the picket firing at night, incessant, like the dropping of hail, and harrowing from the apprehension that many a man fell from the fire of a picket. But, perhaps to reassure me, Captain Lindsay and Captain Glover of General Wilcox's staff declared that "pickets have a good time. They fire, yes, for that is their business; but while they load for the next volley, one will call out, 'Hello, Reb,' be answered, 'Hello, Yank,' and little parcels of coffee are thrown across in exchange for a plug of tobacco." After accepting this fiction I could sleep better.

Nothing could better illustrate the fact that this war was not a war of the men at the guns, than one of General John B. Gordon's anecdotes.[1]

A short distance from Blandford was the strong work on the Federal line called Fort Steadman. It was determined to take this by assault. There were obstructions in front of our lines which had to be removed. The lines were so close this could only be done under cover of darkness. Then there were obstructions to be removed from the front of Fort Steadman, and an immediate rush to be made before the gunners could fire.

This delicate and hazardous duty was successfully performed by General Gordon, near the close of the war, and was the last time the stars and bars were carried to aggressive assault.

About four o'clock in the morning our axemen were quietly at work on our obstacle when the unavoidable noise attracted the notice of a Federal picket. In the black darkness he called out: —

"Hello there, Johnny Reb! What are you making all that fuss about over there?"

Our men were leaning forward for the start, and General Gordon was for a moment disconcerted; but a rifleman answered in a cheerful voice: —

"Oh, never mind us, Yank! Lie down and go to sleep! We are just gathering a little corn; you know rations are mighty short over here!"

There was a patch of corn between the lines, some

[1] "Camp-fire and Battle-field," p. 489.

still hanging on the stalks. After a few moments there came back the kindly reply of the Yankee picket : —

"All right, Johnny, go ahead and get your corn. I won't shoot at you."

General Gordon was about to give the command to go forward, when the rifleman showed some compunctions of conscience for having used deception which might result in the picket's death, by calling out loudly : —

"Look out for yourself now, Yank! We're going to shell the woods."

Such exhibitions of true kindness and comradeship were not uncommon during the war.

On a hill a short distance off was the farmhouse of "old Billy Green," as he was known to his neighbors. He had a good wife, kind to me and to everybody, and a fine-looking, amiable daughter, Nannie Green. These were my only female acquaintances. Nannie soon became an out-and-out belle — the only young lady in the neighborhood. Tender songs were paraphrased in her honor; Ben Bolt's Sweet Alice became "Sweet Nannie," and "Sweet Annie of the Vale" easily became "Sweet Nannie of the Hill." I was very stern with the young officers around me, about Nannie Green. She was a modest, dignified girl, and I did not intend to have her spoiled, nor her father ridiculed.

I found some cut-glass champagne glasses in one of my boxes. Every night a request would come from Captain Lindsay, or Captain Glover, or some

other of my staff tenants, for a champagne glass.
At last I asked: —

"Why do you limit yourselves to one glass?"

"Oh, we don't drink from it. We have no wine,
you know."

It appeared upon investigation that they cut pro-
file pictures of Nannie Green out of paper, laid this
cut paper on another, weighting it down with bullets,
and turned the glass over it. As they sat around
the table smoking, each one would lift a little edge
of the glass and blow the smoke under it, shutting
down quickly. When the smoking was over, and
glass and paper were lifted, there was a pure white
silhouette of Nannie's face on an amber-colored
background, cameo-like in effect. The face would
be delicately shaded, soulful eyes added, and —
voilà!

"Why was I not to know this?" I asked sternly.

"Because we feared you would lend us no more
glasses."

"So it appears you all have a young lady's picture
without her consent?"

"Why not?" they pleaded. "Isn't she perfectly
welcome to ours?"

"Do you expect her to exchange, for something
she doesn't want, something which you *do* want?"

"Well, we think she might," said one, ruefully.
"If her shadow can comfort a poor fellow's cold and
lonely evening, she might spare it. She can't
possibly miss it."

I never refused to lend them the glasses.

x

CHAPTER XX

MY husband's duties kept him from home several days at a time during the early autumn, but now that the lines were drawn so closely together, he could usually return to us after reporting to General Lee at night. I had ceased to feel anxious when he rode away in the morning on his gray horse, Jubal Early. Jubal had brought him safely through many a difficulty. Once he found himself suddenly confronted by a small company of Federals aligned for drill. He saluted, as if he were an officer on inspection, rode gravely past the line, and then Jubal's fleet feet dashed quite out of range before the volley which followed the discovery of his ruse.

One frosty morning I was writing letters, — to Agnes, to my mother, to my little girls in Charlotte, expressing the gratitude of my heart for the new blessings of the hour, — when General Wilcox entered, and took his accustomed stand before the fire.

"Madam," he commenced, "is the General at home?"

"No, General, he did not return last night."

"You are not uneasy?"

"Not a bit. He sometimes stops at Mrs. Friend's when he is belated. She's his cousin, you know."

"Of course!" laughed the General. "All the pretty women in Virginia are cousins to the Virginia officers. Couldn't you naturalize a few unfortunates who were not born in Virginia?"

I was sealing and stamping my letters, and looked up without immediately answering his badinage. To my surprise his face was pale and his lip quivering.

"You have to know it," said he. "The General will not return. The Yankees caught him this morning."

"Oh, impossible!" I exclaimed. "Jubal never fails."

"Look out of the window," said the general.

There stood Jubal! A groom was removing his saddle. General Wilcox most kindly hastened to reassure me. "It will be all right," he declared. "A little rest for the General, and we will soon exchange him."

I was completely stunned. I had never expected this. My head reeled. My heart sickened within me.

As I sat thus, shivering beside the fire, I heard the clank of spurs, and looked up. An officer was at the door.

"Madam," he said, "General Lee sends you his affectionate sympathies."

Through the open window I saw the General on his horse, Traveller, standing at the well. He waited until his messenger returned, and then rode slowly toward the lines.

I had small hope of the speedy exchange promised me by General Wilcox. From day to day he
reported the efforts made for my husband's release
and their failure. General Lee authorized a letter
to General Meade, detailing the circumstances of his
capture and requesting his release. General Meade
promptly refused to release him.

We naturally looked to the enemy for all information, and although my husband had written me
a pencilled note at City Point on the inside of a
Confederate envelope, and had implored his guard
(a Federal officer) to have it inserted in a New York
paper, I did not receive it until thirty-one years
afterward. We soon had news, however, through
a despatch from the North Army Corps to the *New
York Herald*. The paper of November 30, 1864,
contained the following : —

"Yesterday a rebel officer made his appearance in
front of our lines, waving a paper for exchange. The
officer in charge of the picket, suddenly remembering
that Captain Burridge, of the Thirty-sixth Massachusetts, was taken prisoner some time since by the
enemy while on a similar errand, 'gobbled' the rebel,
who proved to be the famous Roger A. Pryor, ex-
member of Congress and ex-brigadier-general of Jeff
Davis's army. He protested vehemently against
what he styled a flagrant breach of faith on our part.
He was assured he was taken in retaliation for like
conduct on the part of his friends, and sent to General Meade's headquarters for further disposition."

Press despatch to *Herald*, November 30, from
Washington, "Roger A. Pryor has been brought

to Washington, and committed to the old Capitol Prison."

Herald, December 1, 1864, " Pryor was ferried over to Fort Lafayette, where he is now confined."

Then later I received a personal through *The News* : " To Mrs. R. A. Pryor. Your husband is in Fort Lafayette, where a friend and relative is permitted to visit him. — [Signed] MARY RHODES."

Not until December, 1864, could Colonel Ould arrange to have a letter from me sent through the lines. All letters from and to prisoners were examined by Federal officials.

On the 20th of December I received a brief note from Fort Lafayette : " My philosophy begins to fail somewhat. In vain I seek some argument of consolation. I see no chance of release. The conditions of my imprisonment cut me off from every resource of happiness."

I learned afterward that he was ill, and under the care of a physician all winter, but he tried to write as encouragingly as possible. In February, however, he failed in health and spirits, but bore up bravely : —

" I am as contented as is compatible with my condition. My mind is ill at ease from my solicitude for my family and my country. Every disaster pierces my soul like an arrow ; and I am afflicted with the thought that I am denied the privilege of contributing even my mite to the deliverance of ——. How I envy my old comrades their hardships and privations. I have little hope of an early exchange, and you may be assured my mistrust is not without reason. *Except some special instance be employed to procure my release, my detention here will be indefinite.* I cannot be more explicit. While this is my conviction, I wish it distinctly understood that I would not have my government compromise any scruple for the sake of my liberation. I am prepared for any contingency — am fortified against any reverse of fortune."

The problem now confronting me was this: How could I maintain my children and myself? My husband's rations were discontinued. My only supply of food was from my father's ration as chaplain. I had a part of a barrel of flour which a relative had sent me from a county now cut off from us. Quite a number of my old Washington servants had followed me, to escape the shelling, but they could not, of course, look to me for their support. I frankly told John and Eliza my condition, but they elected to remain. One day John presented himself with a heart-broken countenance and a drooping attitude of deep dejection. He had a sad story to tell. The agent of the estate to which he belonged was in town, and John had been commissioned to inform me that all the slaves belonging to the estate were to be immediately transferred to a Louisiana plantation for safety. Those of us who had hired these servants by the year were to be indemnified for our loss.

"How do you feel about it, John?" I asked.

The poor fellow broke down. "It will kill me," he declared. "I'll soon die on that plantation."

All his affectionate, faithful service, all his hard-

ships for our sakes, the Averill raid, rushed upon
my memory. I bade him put me in communication
with the agent. I found that I could save the boy
only by buying him. A large sum of gold was named
as the price. I unbuckled my girdle and counted
my handful of gold — one hundred and six dollars.
These I offered to the agent (who was a noted negro
trader), and although it was far short of his figures,
he made out my bill of sale receipted.

When John appeared with smiling face he informed me with his thanks that he belonged to me.

"You are a free man, John," I said. "I will make
out your papers and I can very easily arrange for
you to pass the lines."

"I know that," he said. "Marse Roger has
often told me I was a free man. I never will leave
you till I die. Papers indeed! Papers nothing! I
belong to you — that's where I belong."

All that dreadful winter he was faithful to his
promise, cheerfully bearing, without wages, all the
privations of the time. Sometimes, when the last
atom of food was gone, he would ask for money,
sally forth with a horse and light cart, and bring in
peas and dried apples. Once a week we were allowed
to purchase the head of a bullock, horns and all,
from the commissary; and a small ration of rice was
allowed us by the government. A one-armed boy,
Alick, who had been reared in my father's family,
now wandered in to find his old master, and installed
himself as my father's servant.

The question that pressed upon me day and night
was: How, where, can I earn some money? to be

answered by the frightful truth that there could be no opening for me anywhere, because I could not leave my children.

One wakeful night, while I was revolving these things, a sudden thought darted, unbidden, into my sorely oppressed mind : —

"Why not open the trunk from Washington? Something may be found there which can be sold."

At an early hour next morning John and Alick brought the trunk from the cellar.   Aunt Jinny, Eliza, and the children gathered around.   It proved to be full of my old Washington finery.   There were a half-dozen or more white muslin gowns, flounced and trimmed with Valenciennes lace, many yards ; there was a rich bayadere silk gown trimmed fully with guipure lace ; a green silk dress with gold embroidery ; a blue and silver brocade, — these last evening gowns.   There was a paper box containing the shaded roses I had worn to Lady Napier's ball, the ball at which Mrs. Douglas and I had dressed alike in gowns of tulle.   Another box held the garniture of green leaves and gold grapes which had belonged to the green silk ; and still another the blue and silver feathers for the brocade.   An opera cloak trimmed with fur ; a long purple velvet cloak ; a purple velvet "coalscuttle" bonnet, trimmed with white roses ; a point lace handkerchief ; Valenciennes lace ; Brussels lace ; and at the bottom of the trunk a package of *ciel* blue zephyr, awakening reminiscences of a passion which I had cherished for knitting shawls and "mariposas" of zephyr, — such was the collection I had discovered.

The velvet cloak had come to grief.   Somebody had put the handsome books President Pierce had given me into this box, for special safe-keeping; and all these years the cloak had cushioned the books so that they made no inroads upon the other articles, and had given up its own life in their protection.   Not an inch of the garment was ever fit for use.   It was generously printed all over with the large cords and tassels of its own trimming.

These were my materials.   I must make them serve for the support of my family.

I ripped all the lace from the evening gowns, and made it into collars and undersleeves.   John found an extinct dry-goods store where clean paper boxes could be had.

My first instalment of lace collars was sent to Price's store in Richmond and promptly sold.   Mr. Price wrote me that all of my articles would find purchasers.   There were ladies in Richmond who could afford to buy, and the Confederate court offered opportunities for display.

Admiral Porter records the capture of a blockade-runner whose valuable goods included many commissions for " ladies at court.   In the cabin of the vessel," says the admiral, " was a pile of band-boxes in which were charming little bonnets marked with the owners' names.   It would have given me much pleasure to have forwarded them to their destination " (the admiral had ever a weakness for Southern ladies) " but the laws forbade our giving aid and comfort to the enemy, so all the French bonnets, cloaks, shoes, and other feminine *bric-à-*

brac had to go to New York for condemnation by the Admiralty Court, and were sold at public auction.

"These bonnets, laces, and other vanities rather clashed with the idea I had formed of the Southern ladies, as I heard that all they owned went to the hospitals, and that they never spent a cent on their personal adornment; but human nature," sagely opines the admiral, "is the same the world over, and ladies will indulge in their little vanities in spite of war and desolation."[1]   To these vanities I now found myself indebted.

The zeal with which I worked knew no pause. I needed no rest.   General Wilcox, who was in the saddle until a late hour every night, said to me, "Your candle is the last light I see at night — the first in the morning."

"I should never sleep," I told him.

One day I consulted Eliza about the manufacture of a Confederate candle.   We knew how to make it — by drawing a cotton rope many times through melted wax, and then winding it around a bottle. We could get wax, but our position was an exposed one.   Soldiers' tents were close around us, and we scrupulously avoided any revelation of our needs, lest they should deny themselves for our sakes. Eliza thought we might avail ourselves of the absence of the officers, and finish our work before they returned.   We made our candle; but that night, as I sat sewing beside its dim, glow-worm light, I heard a step in the hall, and a hand, hastily thrust out, placed a brown paper parcel on the

[1] Porter's "Anecdotes and Incidents of the Civil War," p. 274.

piano near the door.   It was a soldier's ration of candles !

After I had converted all my laces into collars, cuffs, and sleeves, and had sold my silk gowns, opera cloak, and point lace handkerchiefs, I devoted myself to trimming the edges of the artificial flowers, and separating the long wreaths and garlands into clusters for hats and *bouquets de corsage.*

Eliza and the children delighted in this phase of my work, and begged to assist, — all except Aunt Jinny.

" Honey," she said, " don't you think, in these times of trouble, you might do better than tempt them po' young lambs in Richmond to worship the golden calf and bow down to mammon ?   We prays not to be led into temptation, and you sho'ly is leadin' 'em into vanity."

" Maybe so, Aunt Jinny, but I must sell all I can.   We have to be clothed, you know, war or no war."

" Yes, my chile, that's so ; but we're told to con-sider the lilies.   Gawd Almighty tells us we must clothe ourselves in the garment of righteousness, and He — "

" You always 'pear to be mighty intimate with God A'mighty," interrupted Eliza, in great wrath. " Now you just go 'long home an' leave my mistis to her work.   How would *you* look with nothin' on but a garment of righteousness ? "

When I had stripped the pretty muslin gowns of their trimmings, what could be done with the gowns themselves ?   Finally I resolved to embroider them with the blue zephyr. I rolled the edges of the flounces, and edged them delicately with a spiral line of blue. I traced with blue a dainty vine of forget-me-nots on bodice and sleeves, with a result that was simply ravishing !

My first purchase was a barrel of flour, for which I paid thirteen hundred dollars. John made hot biscuits three times a day thereafter. As the winter wore on, and the starvation became stern in the army, a soldier would occasionally bring to the kitchen his ration of a small square of beef to be cooked, or *eight grains of coffee* to trade with John for a few biscuits. I sternly forbade the trade, and ordered John to grind the coffee in the owner's presence, mix it with our toasted corn, and give him the biscuits, with a good, strengthening drink. Often a brown hand would place a tiny bundle on the piano, as the donor passed through the hall, and my heart would ache to find it contained a soldier's ration of coffee. My dear father had friends among his old parishioners who never allowed him to do without his coffee — a necessity for a man who never, under any circumstances, fortified his strength with ardent spirits. He was almost fanatical on the total abstinence subject.

Of course I could not command shoes for my boys. I made them of carpet lined with flannel for my baby. I could in one day make a pair which she wore out in three ! A piece of bronze morocco fell into my hands, of which I made a pair of boots for my little daughter, Mary, and out of an old leather pocket-book and two or three leather bags which Alick found in his prowling over the fields, a soldier-shoemaker contrived shoes for each of the boys.

My own prime necessity was for the steel we women wear in front of our stays. I suffered so much for want of this accustomed support, that Captain Lindsay had a pair made for me by the government gunsmith.

The time came when the salable contents of the Washington trunk were all gone. I then cut up my husband's dress-coat, and designed well-fitting ladies' gloves, with gauntlets made of the watered silk lining. Of an interlining of gray flannel I made gray gloves, and this glove manufacture yielded me hundreds of dollars. Thirteen small fragments of flannel were left after the gloves were finished. Of these, pieced together, I made a pair of drawers for my Willy — my youngest boy.

The lines around us were now so closely drawn that my father returned home after short absences of a day or two. But we were made anxious, during a heavy snow early in December, by a more prolonged absence. Finally he appeared, on foot, hatless, and exhausted. He had been captured by a party of cavalrymen. He had told them of his non-combatant position, but when he asked for release, they shook their heads. At night they all prepared to bivouac upon the ground, assigned to him a sheltered spot, gave him a good supper and blankets, and left him to his repose. As the night wore on and all grew still, he raised his head cautiously to reconnoitre, and to his surprise found himself at some distance from the guard — but his horse tied to a tree within the circle around the fire. My father took the hint, and quietly walked away unchallenged. "Which proves, my dear," he said, "that a clergyman is not worth as much as a good horse in time of war."

CHAPTER XXI

I RESOLVED to give my family a Christmas dinner. John invented a method of making a perfectly satisfactory pie out of sorghum molasses, thickened with a little flour, mixed with walnut meats, and baked in a "raised" crust. He prepared a number of these. I bought a piece of corned beef for fifty dollars. This was boiled with peas. But just as we were about to gather around the table, we saw a forlorn company of soldiers passing the door. They had gone out on some raid a week before. The snow was falling fast, the soldiers walked wearily, with dejected countenances. "Boys," I said, "are you willing to send the dish of beef and peas out to them?" They agreed, if only they might carry it; and the brave little fellows liked the pleasure they gave more than they would have enjoyed the dinner. They were full of it for days afterward.

We had grown very fond of some of the men around us, and my boys were so rich in their companionship, that they never complained of their privations. They were good, wholesome comrades, interested in our books and in the boys' studies. Captain Lindsay and Captain Glover of General

Wilcox's staff were great comforts.   General A. P.
Hill and Colonel William Pegram came often to see
us.   General Lee often passed the door on his way
to the lines, and paused to inquire concerning our
welfare.   I established a little circulating library for
dear Colonel Pegram and our own officers.   The
books were always faithfully returned, with warm
thanks for the comfort they gave.

The month of January brought us sleet and storm.
Our famine grew sterner every day.   Poor little
Rose, my cow, could yield only one cupful of milk,
so small was her ration; but we never thought of
turning the faithful animal into beef.   The officers
in my yard spared her something every day from the
food of their horses.

The days were so dark and cheerless, the news
from the armies at a distance so discouraging, it was
hard to preserve a cheerful demeanor for the sake
of the family.   And now began the alarming tidings,
every morning, of the desertions during the night.
General Wilcox wondered how long his brigade would
hold together at the rate of fifty desertions every
twenty-four hours.

The common soldier had enlisted, not to establish
the right of secession, not for love of the slave, — he
had no slaves, — but simply to resist the invasion of
the South by the North, simply to prevent subjugation.   The soldier of the rank and file was not
always intellectual or cultivated.   He cared little for
politics, less for slavery.   He did care, however,
for his own soil, his own little farm, his own humble
home; and he was willing to fight to drive the invader

from it.   Lincoln's Emancipation Proclamation did not stimulate him in the least.   The negro, free or slave, was of no consequence to him.   His quarrel was a sectional one, and he fought for his section.

In any war, the masses rarely trouble themselves about the merits of the quarrel.   Their pugnacity and courage are aroused and stimulated by the enthusiasm of their comrades, or by their own personal wrongs and perils.

Now, in January, 1865, the common soldier perceived that the cause was lost.   He could read its doom in the famine around him, in the faces of his officers, in tidings from abroad.   His wife and children were suffering.   His duty was now to them; so he stole away in the darkness, and, in infinite danger and difficulty, found his way back to his own fireside.   He deserted, but not to the enemy.

But what can we say of the soldier who remained unflinchingly at his post *knowing* the cause was lost for which he was called to meet death?   Heroism can attain no loftier height than this.

Sir Charles Napier,[1] in his campaign against the robber tribes of Upper Scinde, found that the hillsmen had a custom of binding, with a scarlet thread, the wrist of a leader who fell after some distinguished act of courage.   They thus honored the hand that had wielded a valiant sword.

A party of eleven English soldiers were once separated from their fellows, and mistook a signal for an order to charge.   The brave fellows answered with a cheer.   On a summit in front of them was a

1 "Robertson's Life and Letters," edited by S. A. Brooke, p. 804.

Y

breastwork manned by seventy of the foe.   On they went, charging up the fearful path, eleven against seventy.   There could be but one result.   When their comrades arrived to aid them, every one of the British soldiers was dead — and around *both* wrists of every one was twined the red thread!

And so I am sure that to every man who fell in that last hopeless fight, our brave foes will award the red badge of honor — as our own hearts will ever strive to deserve it for their sakes.

The horror of military execution was now upon us.   Nothing so distressed my father and myself.   Finally General Lee offered the men who had deserted a last opportunity to wipe out their disgrace and escape the punishment of their crimes.   He granted, by authority of the government, amnesty to those who would report to the nearest officer on duty within twenty days, thus giving them the privilege of reëntering the service in companies where they would not be known.

"Let us," said the general, "oppose constancy to adversity, fortitude to suffering, and courage to danger, with the firm assurance that He who gave freedom to our fathers will bless the efforts of their children to preserve it."

Alas! few availed themselves of this solemn appeal to their manhood.

Meanwhile we received occasional letters from our prisoner in Fort Lafayette.   He was confined in a casemate with about twenty men.   A small grate for burning coal sufficed for the preparation of their rations, which were issued to them raw.   They lay

upon straw mats on the floor. Once daily they
could walk upon the ramparts, and my husband's
eyes turned sadly to the dim outlines of the beautiful city where he had often been an honored guest.
The veil which hid from him so much of the grief
and struggle of the future hid also the reward.
Little did he dream he should administer justice on
the supreme bench of the mist-veiled city.

His letters bore but one theme, his earnest prayer
for exchange, so that he might do his part in our
defence.

One night all these things weighed more heavily
than usual upon me, — the picket firing, the famine,
the military executions, the dear one "sick and in
prison." I sighed audibly, and my son, Theodorick, who slept near me, asked the cause, adding,
"Why can you not sleep, dear mother?"

"Suppose," I replied, "you repeat something for
me."

He at once commenced, "Tell me not in mournful numbers" — and repeated the "Psalm of Life." I
did not sleep; those brave words were not strong
enough for the situation.

He paused, and presently his young voice broke
the stillness : —

"Bless the Lord, O my soul, and all that is
within me, bless His holy name" — going on to
the end of the beautiful psalm of adoration and faith
which nineteen centuries have decreed to be in very
truth a Psalm of Life.

I felt great responsibility in keeping with me my
sons, now ten and twelve years old. At a farmhouse

about fifteen miles in the country a member of the family was living, and availing myself of a passing wagon, I sent the boys to share his plenty and comfort. A few days afterwards they returned — a dusty, footsore pair of urchins. They had run away and come home! Moreover, they had found an old horse left on the roadside to die, — which Roger refused to leave, — had shared their luncheon with him, given him water, assisted him to his feet, and by slow stages led him home!

"Oh! *how* shall we feed him?" I exclaimed, in despair.

"I'll help," said Captain Lindsay; "he shall be immediately introduced to my mare, and she shall share her oats with him;" and a very sober minded, steady horse he proved to be, quite good enough to be stolen, as he finally was, by the enemy.

My friend, General Wilcox, put my own friendship to a severe test one morning. Standing by the mantel in his accustomed attitude, he informed me that he had received many kind attentions from the ladies of Petersburg (I was aware of an affair of the heart in which a pretty widow was concerned), and he proposed to give a *déjeuner à la fourchette*, and invite them out to his tent. Would I chaperon the occasion, and might my parlor be used as a reception room?

"Of course, General!" I replied. "They will be welcome to me, and to the parlor. The '*fourchette*' will be forthcoming without fail, but where, oh, where can we find the '*déjeuner*'?"

"I have thought of all that," said the General.

"I will send half a dozen fellows out with guns to bring in birds. I'll get John to make some cakes and biscuits, we'll brew a bowl of punch. *Voilà!* What more do you want?"

"That will be fine," I assured him, and accordingly his invitations were sent, handsomely written, to about thirty people. A load of evergreens was delivered at the tent, and all hands set to work to weave garlands. Every candle in camp was "pressed." John made a fine success of his sponge cakes, and also fruit and nut cake — the fruit, disguised dried apples, the nuts, walnuts.

The day before the event the General leaned, a dejected figure, against the mantel.

"Those — blamed — soldiers have returned. They didn't bag a bird."

"I feared that! Virginia partridges are hunted with dogs. Besides, where can you find game within twenty miles of an army?"

"Well, it will take six months' pay, but we must buy oysters. I don't know what else we can do."

"General," I said, "suppose you have a breakfast like one Mrs. ——, from North Carolina, gave here when she stayed with me last month. She had little *ménus* neatly written, including various dishes. The dishes, however, were imaginary. They did not appear! The guests left with the impression that these things had been provided, but that accidents which were to be counted on in time of war had spoiled them. Now, John could easily announce a fall of soot from the chimney, — like Caleb Balderstone! Aunt Jinny would make an

admirable ' Mysie.'   Have you never heard her
' skirl'?   We might imagine partridges, turkey, and
ham, and then imagine the accidents.   What could
be simpler?"

The General's breakfast was a great success.   The
weather was fine.   One of his staff, who was not
invited, confided to me his fear that there would be
nothing left!   And, indeed, the guests brought noble
appetites.   The General took in the pretty widow.
General A. P. Hill honored me.   A gay procession
of open wagons filled with merry guests left the door
at sunset, and sang " The Bonnie Blue Flag " as they
wended their way home.   General Lee from his headquarters could hear the song, and doubtless it cheered
his sympathetic heart, albeit he knew a battle was near
at hand.   He could not know that in that battle
General Hill and Colonel Pegram would fall with
all their wounds in front, among the first of those
martyrs whose lives were sacrificed after the leaders
knew there was no more life in the cause for which
they died.

Our friends in town sent many invitations to us
dwellers in tents.   Of course, I accepted none of
them.   I had no heart for gayety, and not one
moment's time to spare from my sewing.   It is
passing strange — this disposition to revel in times
of danger and suffering.   Florence was never so gay
as during the Plague!   The men of our army who
had been absent three years were now near their
homes, and they abandoned themselves to the opportunities of the hour.   Some of them were engaged to the beautiful young women of Petersburg.

"This is no time for marriage," said General Lee, "no time while the country is in such peril;" and yet he granted a furlough now and then to some soldier who was unwilling to wait.

There were parties, "starvation parties," as they were called on account of the absence of refreshments impossible to be obtained. Not even the lump of sugar allowed by Lady Morgan at her *conversazioni* was possible here; but notwithstanding this serious disadvantage, ball followed ball in quick succession. "The soldier danced with the lady of his love at night, and on the morrow danced the dance of death in the deadly trench on the line." There the ranks closed up; and in the ball room they closed up also. There was always a comrade left for the partner of the belle; and not one whit less valiant was the soldier for his brief respite. He could go from the dance to his place in the trenches with a light jest, however heavy his heart might be. And when the beloved commander ordered him forth, he could step out with martial tread and cheer and song — to the march or into battle. I think all who remember the dark days of the winter of 1864–1865 will bear witness to the unwritten law enforcing cheerfulness. It was tacitly understood that we must make no moan, yield to no outward expression of despondency or despair.

On January 30 General Wilcox came in, bringing great news. Three commissioners authorized to meet representatives of the Federal government had arrived in Petersburg *en route* for Fortress Monroe. They were Vice-President Stephens,

Senator R. M. T. Hunter, and James A. Campbell, former Assistant Justice of the Supreme Court of the United States, and now Assistant Secretary of War of the Confederate States.

"I thought," said the General, "you might come out and listen to the cheering. It is echoed by the enemy. There seems to be no doubt of the feeling on both sides."

I begged the General to lend me an ambulance, and drove out to the front. The troops of Fort Gregg and Battery 45 — just in the rear of my garden — had come out and were cheering vociferously. There seemed to be a truce for the moment. We could distinctly hear the answering cheers from the opposing fortifications.

My ambulance drew up to the side of the road, and presently an open carriage appeared, with the mayor and the three commissioners. They paused for a few minutes before crossing the line. With my heart beating painfully, I left my ambulance and walked to the carriage. There Mr. Hunter greeted me kindly and introduced me to his companions. Trembling with emotion, I said : —

"My errand is to you, dear Mr. Hunter. You are going to see President Lincoln or his representative. I entreat you, I implore you, to remember your friend General Pryor. He is breaking his heart in prison. Beg his release from Mr. Lincoln."

"I will — we will," they promised. The carriage proceeded, and as it crossed the line a mighty cheer went up from the hundreds of soldiers, Confederate and Union, who were standing on duty and looking on.

In an instant we were enemies again, and I was hastening out of the range of shot and shell.

On February 5 the commissioners returned from their bootless errand. Mr. Hunter wrote me that they had "remembered Pryor as was promised, but his release would not be considered."

An extract from Order No. 2, February 11, 1865, from General Lee, explains the manner in which our proposals had been received : —

"The choice between war and abject submission is before us.

"To such a proposal, brave men, with arms in their hands, can have but one answer.

"They cannot barter manhood for peace, nor the right of self-government for life or property.

"Taking new resolution from the fate which our enemies intend for us, let every man devote all his energies to the common defence."

I am afraid we were too faint from want of food to be as courageous as our noble commander expected. Flour was now selling for $1500 a barrel; bacon, $20 a pound; beef, $15 ditto : butter could be had at $20 a pound. One chicken could be bought for $50. Shad sold for $50 a pair (before the war the price was not more than ten or fifteen cents). One hundred dollars was asked for one dollar in gold, making the price I had given to save John from a negro trader $10,600 ! — news which he heard with such concern that I hastened to tell him I had never regretted it.

John bethought himself of the fishes in the pond and streams, but not a fish-hook was for sale in Richmond or Petersburg. He contrived, out of a cunning arrangement of pins, to make hooks, and sallied forth with my boys. But the water was too cold, or the fish had been driven down-stream by the firing. The usual resource of the sportsman with an empty creel — a visit to the fishmonger — was quite out of the question. There was no fish-monger any more.

Under these circumstances you may imagine my sensations at receiving the following note: —

"MY DEAR MRS. PRYOR: General Lee has been honored by a visit from the Hon. Thomas Connolly, Irish M.P. from Donegal.

"He ventures to request you will have the kindness to give Mr. Connolly a room in your cottage, if this can be done without inconvenience to yourself."

Certainly I could give Mr. Connolly a room; but just as certainly I could not feed him! The messenger who brought the note hastily reassured me. He had been instructed to say that Mr. Connolly would mess with General Lee. I turned Mr. Connolly's room over to John, who soon became devoted to his service. The M.P. proved a most agreeable guest, a fine-looking Irish gentleman with an irresistibly humorous, cheery fund of talk. He often dropped in at our biscuit toasting, and assured us that we were better provided than the commander-in-chief.

"You should have seen ' Uncle Robert's ' dinner to-day, Madam! He had two biscuits, and he gave me one."

Another time Mr. Connolly was in high feather.

"We had a glorious dinner to-day! Somebody sent ' Uncle Robert ' a box of sardines."

General Lee, however, was not forgotten. On fine mornings quite a procession of little negroes, in every phase of raggedness, used to pass my door, each one bearing a present from the farmers' wives of buttermilk in a tin pail, for General Lee. The army was threatened with scurvy, and buttermilk, hominy, and every vegetable that could be obtained was sent to the hospital.

Mr. Connolly interested himself in my boys' Latin studies.

"I am going home," he said, "and tell the Engglish women what I have seen here: two boys reading Cæsar while the shells are thundering, and their mother looking on without fear."

"I am too busy keeping the wolf from my door," I told him, "to concern myself with the thunderbolts."

The wolf was no longer at the door! He had entered and had taken up his abode at the fireside. Besides what I could earn with my needle, I had only my father's army ration to rely upon. My faithful John foraged right and left, and I had reason to doubt the wisdom of inquiring too closely as to the source of an occasional half-dozen eggs or small bag of corn. This last he would pound on a wooden block for hominy. Meal was no longer

procurable.   As I have said, we might occasionally
purchase for five dollars the head of a bullock from
the commissary, every other part of the animal
being available for army rations.   By self-denial on
our own part, we fondly hoped we could support
our army and at last win our cause.   We were not,
at the time, fully aware of the true state of things.
Our men were so depleted from starvation that the
most trifling wound would end fatally.   Gangrene
would supervene, and then nothing could be done to
prevent death.   Long before this time, at Vicksburg,
Admiral Porter found that many a dead soldier's
haversack yielded nothing but a handful of parched
corn.   *We* were now enduring a sterner siege.

Before daylight, on the 2d of March, General Lee
sent for General Gordon, who was with his command
at a distant part of the line.[1]   Upon arriving, General
Gordon was much affected by seeing General Lee
standing at the mantel in his room, his head bowed
on his folded arms.   The room was dimly lighted
by a single lamp, and a smouldering fire was dying
on the hearth.   The night was cold and General
Lee's room chill and cheerless.

"I have sent for you, General Gordon," said
General Lee, with a dejected voice and manner, "to
make known to you the condition of our affairs and
consult with you as to what we had best do.   I have
here reports sent in from my officers to-night.   I
find I have under my command, of all arms, hardly
forty-five thousand men.   These men are starving.
They are already so weakened as to be hardly effi-

---

[1] "Camp-fire and Battle-field," p. 185.

cient. Many of them have become desperate, reckless, and disorderly as they have never been before.
It is difficult to control men who are suffering for
food. They are breaking open mills, barns, and
stores in search of it. Almost crazed from hunger,
they are deserting in large numbers and going home.
My horses are in equally bad condition. The supply
of horses in the country is exhausted. It has come
to be just as bad for me to have a horse killed as a
man. I cannot remount a cavalryman whose horse
dies. General Grant can mount ten thousand men
in ten days and move around your flank. If he
were to send me word to-morrow that I might move
out unmolested, I have not enough horses to move
my artillery. He is not likely to send me any such
message, although he sent me word yesterday that
he knew what I had for breakfast every morning.
I sent him word I did not think that this could be
so, for if he did he would surely send me something better.

"But now let us look at the figures. As I said,
I have forty-five thousand starving men. Hancock
has eighteen thousand at Winchester. To oppose
him I have not a single vidette. Sheridan, with his
terrible cavalry, has marched unmolested and unop-
posed along the James, cutting the railroads and the
canal. Thomas is coming from Knoxville with thirty
thousand well-equipped troops, and I have, to oppose
him, not more than three thousand in all. Sherman
is in North Carolina with sixty-five thousand men.
. . . So I have forty-five thousand poor fellows in
bad condition opposed to one hundred and sixty

thousand strong and confident men. These forces, added to General Grant's, make over a quarter of a million. To prevent them all from uniting to my destruction, and adding Johnston's and Beauregard's men, I can oppose only sixty thousand men. They are growing weaker every day. Their sufferings are terrible and exhausting. My horses are broken down and impotent. General Grant may press around our flank any day and cut off our supplies."

As a result of this conference General Lee went to Richmond to make one more effort to induce our government to treat for peace. It was on his return from an utterly fruitless errand that he said : —

" I am a soldier ! It is my duty to obey orders ; " and the final disastrous battles were fought.

It touches me to know now that it was after this that my beloved commander found heart to turn aside and bring me comfort. No one knew better than he all I had endeavored and endured, and my heart blesses his memory for its own sake. At this tremendous moment, when he had returned from his fruitless mission to Richmond, when the attack on Fort Steadman was impending, when his slender line was confronted by Grant's ever increasing host, stretching twenty miles, when the men were so starved, so emaciated, that the smallest wound meant death, when his own personal privations were beyond imagination, General Lee could spend half an hour for my consolation and encouragement.

Cottage Farm being on the road between headquarters and Fort Gregg — the fortification which held General Grant in check at that point — I saw

General Lee almost daily going to this work, or to
" Battery 45." On Sundays he regularly passed
on his famous horse, Traveller, on his way to a
little wooden chapel, going often through sleet and
rain, bending his head to shield his face from the
storm.

I was, as was my custom, sewing in my little
parlor one morning, about the middle of March,
when an orderly entered, saying : —

" General Lee wishes to make his respects to
Mrs. Pryor." The General was immediately
behind him. His face was lighted with the antici-
pation of telling me his good news. With the
high-bred courtesy and kindness which always distinguished his manner, he asked kindly after my
welfare, and, taking my little girl in his arms, began
gently to break his news to me : —

" How long, Madam, was General Pryor with me
before he had a furlough ? "

" He never had one, I think," I answered.

" Well, did I not take good care of him until we
camped here so close to you ? "

" Certainly," I said, puzzled to know the drift of
these preliminaries.

" I sent him home to you, I remember," he continued, " for a day or two, and you let the Yankees
catch him. Now he is coming back to be with you
again on parole until he is exchanged. You must
take better care of him in future."

I was too much overcome to do more than stam-
mer a few words of thanks.

Presently he added, " What are you going to

say when I tell the General that in all this winter you have never once been to see me?"

"Oh, General Lee," I answered, "I had too much mercy to join in your buttermilk persecution!"

"Persecution!" he said; "such things keep us alive! Last night, when I reached my headquarters, I found a card on my table with a hyacinth pinned to it, and these words: 'for General Lee, with a kiss!' Now," he added, tapping his breast, "I have here my hyacinth and my card — *and I mean to find my kiss!*"

He was amused by the earnest eyes of my little girl, as she gazed into his face.

"They have a wonderful liking for soldiers," he said. "I knew one little girl to give up all her pretty curls willingly, that she might look like Custis! 'They *might* cut my hair like Custis's,' she said. Custis! whose shaven head does not improve him in any eyes but hers."

His manner was the perfection of repose and simplicity. As he talked with me I remembered that I had heard of this singular calmness. Even at Gettysburg, and at the explosion of the crater, he had evinced no agitation or dismay. I did not know then, as I do now, that nothing had ever approached the anguish of this moment, when he had come to say an encouraging and cheering word to me, after abandoning all hope of the success of the cause.

After talking awhile and sending a kind message to my husband, to greet him on his return, he rose, walked to the window, and looked over the fields —

the fields through which, not many days afterward, he dug his last trenches!

I was moved to say, "You only, General, can tell me if it is worth my while to put the ploughshare into those fields."

"Plant your seeds, Madam," he replied; sadly adding, after a moment, "the doing it will be some reward."

I was answered. I thought then he had little hope. I now know he had none.

He had already, as we have seen, remonstrated against further resistance — against the useless shedding of blood. His protest had been unheeded. It remained for him now to gather his forces for endurance to the end.

Twenty days afterward his headquarters were in ashes; he had led his famished army across the Appomattox; and, telling them they had done their duty, and had nothing to regret, he had bidden them farewell forever.

z

CHAPTER XXII

THE EVACUATION OF PETERSBURG

THE happy day was not distant when the husband and father of our little family was to be restored to his own home and his own people. I never inquired the source from which John drew his materials for a festival; but, a day or two before my husband was to arrive, he appeared with a small duck! This he roasted to perfection, to served cold, as the hour for the dinner could not be determined in advance.

We were all expectation and excitement when a lady drove up rapidly and asked for shelter, as she had been "driven in from the lines." Shelter I could give by spreading quilts on the parlor floor — but, alas, my duck! Must my precious duck be sacrificed upon the altar of hospitality? I unlocked the little tin safe to assure myself that I could manage to keep it hidden, and behold, it was gone! Not until next day, when it was placed before my husband with a triumphant flourish (our unwelcome guest had departed), did I discover that John had stolen it! "Why, there's the duck!" I exclaimed.

"Course here's the duck," said John, respectfully. "Ducks got plenty of sense. They knows as well as folks when to hide."

We found our released prisoner pale and thin, but devoutly thankful to be at home. Mr. Connolly and the officers around us called in the evening, keenly anxious to hear his story, and heartily expressing their joy at his release. My friends in Washington had wished to send me some presents, but my husband declined them, accepting only two cans of pineapple. Mr. Connolly sent out for the "boys in the yard" and assisted me in dividing the fruit into portions, so each one should have a bit. It was served on all the saucers and butter-plates we could find, and Mr. Connolly himself handed the tray around, exclaiming, "Oh, lads! It is just the *best* thing you ever tasted!" Then each soldier brought forth his brier-root and gathered around the traveller for his story. His story was a thrilling one — of his capture, his incarceration, his comrades; finally, of the unexpected result of the efforts of his ante-bellum friends, Washington McLean and John W. Forney, for his release. It was ascertained by these friends in Washington that he was detained as hostage for the safety of some Union officer whom the Confederate government had threatened to put to death.

Mr. McLean and Colonel Forney first approached General Grant. The General positively refused to grant their request. Then Mr. McLean visited Mr. Stanton. He found Mr. Stanton in the library of his own home, with his daughter in his arms, and the following conversation ensued: —

"This is a charming fireside picture, Mr. Secretary! I warrant that little lady cares nothing for war or the Secretary of War! She has her father, and that fills all her ambition."

"You never said a truer word, did he, pet?" pressing the curly head close to his bosom.

"Well, then, Stanton, you will understand my errand. There are curly heads down there in old Virginia, weeping out their bright eyes for a father loved just as this pretty baby loves you."

"Yes, yes! Probably so," said Stanton.

"Now — there's Pryor —"

But before another word could be said the Secretary of War pushed the child from his knee and thundered: —

"He shall be hanged! Damn him!"

But he had reckoned without his host when he supposed that Washington McLean would not appeal from that verdict. Armed with a letter of introduction from Horace Greeley, Mr. McLean visited Mr. Lincoln. The President remembered General Pryor's uniformly generous treatment of prisoners who had, at various times, fallen into his custody, especially his capture at Manassas of the whole camp of Federal wounded, surgeons and ambulance corps, and his prompt parole of the same. Mr. Lincoln listened attentively, and, after ascertaining all the facts, issued an order directing Colonel Burke, the commander at Fort Lafayette, to "deliver Roger A. Pryor into the custody of Washington McLean."

Armed with this order, Mr. McLean visited Fort Lafayette, where he found his friend in close confinement in the casemate with other prisoners.

At that time John Y. Beall, a Confederate officer, was confined with General Pryor, under sentence of death as a spy.   Mr. McLean became interested in his fate, and suggested that if General Pryor would make a personal appeal in his behalf to President Lincoln, his execution might probably be prevented. To that end, Mr. McLean telegraphed a request to Mr. Lincoln, that he accord General Pryor an inter- view, to which a favorable response was promptly returned.   The next evening, General Pryor, with Mr. McLean and Mr. Forney, called at the White House, and was graciously received by the President. General Pryor at once opened his intercession in be- half of Captain Beall; but, although Mr. Lincoln evinced the sincerest compassion for the young man, and an extreme aversion to his death, he felt constrained to yield to the assurance of General Dix, in a telegram just received, that the execution was indispensable to the security of the Northern cities — it being believed, though erroneously, that Cap- tain Beall was implicated in the burning of the New York hotels.   Mr. Lincoln then turned the conver- sation to the recent conference at Hampton Roads, the miscarriage of which he deplored with the pro- foundest sorrow.   He said that had the Confederate government agreed to the reëstablishment of the Union and the abolition of slavery, the people of the South might have been compensated for the loss of their negroes and would have been protected by a universal amnesty, but that Mr. Jefferson Davis made the recognition of the Confederacy a condition *sine qua non* of any negotiations.   Thus, he declared, would Mr. Davis be responsible for every drop of blood that should be shed in the further prosecution of the war, a futile and wicked effusion of blood, since it was then obvious to every sane man that the Southern armies must be speedily crushed.   On this topic he dwelt so warmly and at such length that General Pryor inferred that he still hoped the people of the South would reverse Mr. Davis's action, and would renew the negotiations for peace. Indeed, he declared in terms that he could not believe the senseless obstinacy of Mr. Davis represented the sentiment of the South.   It was apparent to General Pryor that Mr. Lincoln desired him to sound leading men of the South on the subject. Accordingly, on the General's return to Richmond, he did consult with Senator Hunter and other prominent men in the Confederacy, but with one voice they assured him that nothing could be done with Mr. Davis, and that the South had only to wait the imminent and inevitable catastrophe.

The inevitable catastrophe marched on apace.

Agnes wrote from Richmond, March 28 — the last letter I received from the Confederate capital : —

" I do hate to write you bad news just now when you should be so happy with our dear General, but, really and truly, I don't at all like the looks of things here.   Sheridan is at Ashland.   And General Sherman has finished up North Carolina, and is in Virginia !

" I made an excursion through some of the Main Street stores last week — and recognized some of Mrs. Davis's things.   I learned that she had placed a great many articles at the dry-goods stores for sale and had sold her horses.   And now comes the surprising news, that she has left the city with her family.   What does all this mean ?

Some of the girls here have taken their jewellery to the Treasury Department, giving it to help redeem the currency. I am sure they are welcome to all mine!"

On the morning of April 2 we were all up early that we might prepare and send to Dr. Claiborne's Hospital certain things we had suddenly acquired. An old farmer friend of my husband had loaded a wagon with peas, potatoes, dried fruit, hominy, and a little bacon, and had sent it as a welcoming present. We had been told of the prevalence of scurvy in the hospitals, and had boiled a quantity of hominy, and also of dried fruit, to be sent with the potatoes for the relief of the sick.

My husband said to me at our early breakfast: —

" How soundly you can sleep! The cannonading was awful last night. It shook the house."

" Oh, that is only Fort Gregg," I answered. " Those guns fire incessantly. I don't consider them. You've been shut up in a casemate so long you've forgotten the smell of powder."

Our father, who happened to be with us that morning, said: —

" By the bye, Roger, I went to see General Lee, and told him you seemed to be under the impression that if your division moves, you should go along with it. The General said emphatically: 'That would be violation of his parole, Doctor. Your son surely knows he cannot march with the army until he is exchanged.'"

This was a great relief to me, for I had been afraid of a different construction.

After breakfast I repaired to the kitchen to see the pails filled for the hospital, and to send Alick and John on their errand.

Presently a message was brought me that I must join my husband, who had walked out to the fortification behind the garden. I found a low earthwork had been thrown up during the night still nearer our house, and on it he was standing.

I have had, very lately, access to a Federal map of the intrenched lines in the immediate front of Petersburg, drawn by a major of engineers of the United States Army. There I find a double line of breastworks, protected by thirty-four forts sweeping around the city and embracing some six or eight miles of country beyond, on either side. Within the Federal line is a little thread of a line protected by lunettes and only *two* forts (for this map has quite a Chinese feeling), and these two are named by the enemy, Fort Gregg and Fort Baldwin — the latter our Battery 45. To my surprise I find the engineer had his eye on me all winter. Near together are certain dots — two for " Turnbull" (General Lee's headquarters), two for " Green," two for " Laighton," and four for " Pryor," representing the dwelling, office, kitchen, and servants' quarter at Cottage Farm ! I perceive from the map that the engineer knew all about us all the time.

To return to the morning of April 2 — my husband held out his hand and drew me up on the breastwork beside him. Negroes were passing, wheeling their barrows, containing the spades they had just used. Below was a plain, and ambulances were collecting and stopping at intervals. Then a slender gray line stretched across under cover of the first earthwork and the forts. Fort Gregg and Battery 45 were belching away with all their might, answered by guns all along the line. While we gazed on all this the wood opposite seemed alive, and out stepped a division of bluecoats — muskets shining and banners flying in the morning sun. My husband exclaimed: "My God! What a line! They are going to fight here right away. Run home and get the children in the cellar."

When I reached the little encampment behind the house, I found the greatest confusion. Tents were struck and a wagon was loading with them. Captain Glover rode up to me and conjured me to leave immediately. I reminded him of his promise not to allow me to be surprised.

"We are ourselves surprised," he said; "believe me, your life is not safe here a moment." Tapping his breast, he continued, "I bear despatches proving what I say."

I ran into the house and gathered my little children. I bade the servants remain. If things grew warm, they had the cellar, and perhaps their presence would save their own goods and mine, should the day go against us. Uncle Frank immediately repaired to the cellar. "I have only one order," I told the rest, "hide the General's flag." As I left (bareheaded, I could not find my hat), I heard Uncle Frank call from the little portholes of his retreat to his wife, "For Gawd's sake, Jinny, bring me a gode of water."

The morning was close and warm, and as we toiled up the dusty road I regretted the loss of my hat. Presently I met a gentleman driving rapidly from town. It was my neighbor, Mr. Laighton. He had removed his wife and little girls to a place of safety and was returning for me. He proposed, as we were now out of musket range, that I should rest with the children under the shade of a tree, and he would return to the farm to see if he could save something — what did I suggest? I asked that he would bring a change of clothing for the children and my medicine chest.

As we waited for his return some terrified horses dashed up the road, one with blood flowing from his nostrils. When Mr. Laighton finally returned, he brought news that he had seen my husband, that all the cooked provisions were spread out for the passing soldiers, and that more were in preparation; also that he had promised to take care of me, and to leave the General free to dispense these things judiciously. John had put the service of silver into the buggy, and Eliza had packed a trunk, for which he was to return. This proved to be the French trunk in which Eliza sent a change of clothing.

We were all soon in the buggy and on our way to town.

"Where shall I take you?" asked Mr. Laighton. I had no answer ready. I thought I would trust to chance for an invitation. But we found the streets full of refugees like ourselves, and like ourselves, uncertain of shelter. Very few of our friends

had remained in the city after the siege had proven
to be a permanent one.

After a while, as we drove slowly through the
crowded streets, we met Mr. Stuart, my husband's
tailor. He said a good house had been left vacant
by one of his customers, who had authorized him to
rent it.

" I now rent it to General Pryor," said Mr. Stuart,
and he conducted us to the door of a residence near
my old home on Washington Street. When the
door-bell was answered he informed a man whom
he addressed as Robert, that we had become his
master's tenants, and said that Robert and his
mother, now in the house, would not be required
to leave, adding : —

" Take good care of this lady. I will see that
your wages are paid and that you are suitably
rewarded."

The silver service was dumped down in the front
porch, and there we awaited events. About noon
John appeared. He had saved something ! — my
champagne glasses ! He had also brought a basket
of biscuits. I sent him back to the farm, strictly
ordering that the flag should be cared for. John
told me it was safe. He had hidden it under some
fence rails in the cellar. As to the battle, he had no
news, except that " Marse Roger is giving away
everything on the earth. All the presents from the
farmer will go in a little while."

My next envoy from the seat of war was Alick,
who walked into the yard, leading Rosc by a rope,
and at once proceeded to stable her. Go back ?

No, *marm*, not if he knew his name was Alick. His mammy had never borned him to be in no battle! And walking off to give Rose a pail of water, he informed her that "You'n me, Rose, is the only folks I see anywhar 'bout here with any sense."

Neighbors soon discovered us; and to my joy I found that Mrs. Gibson, Mrs. Meade, and Mr. Bishop — one of my father's elders — were in their own houses, very near my temporary shelter.

Our father, I learned afterwards, was with the hospital service of his corps, and had been sent to the rear.

The hospitals under Dr. Claiborne were ordered off early in the day, a significant indication of General Lee's accurate estimate of the probabilities of the hour.   Dr. Claiborne had three thousand sick and wounded men to move.   Among them was Colonel Riddick, from Smithfield, the brother of the spirited girl I had known there.   She had come to Petersburg to nurse her wounded brother, and had left, in a wagon, with the hospital train. Part of this train was captured, and the wagons were ordered to be burned; but Miss Riddick positively refused to leave her seat, and as they could not burn the wagon with her in it, she was suffered to proceed with her brother in her own equipage. Miss Riddick was not a young lady who need fear. "There's a divinity doth hedge" some women. She was courteously treated and passed through the lines to her friends.

In the evening the little boys came in with confidential news.   The day had gone against us;

the city was to be surrendered after the retreat of the army at midnight. Their father would come in with the last.

I remembered with anguish that I had lost my chance to save the important papers of the family. In a trunk in my room I had locked all my one lover's beautiful letters, all the correspondence — so rich I had meant to print it — of his residence in Greece, of his travels in the East and in Egypt; all the letters from statesmen and authors of the years preceding the struggle. There they were. They would be sport for the enemy in a few hours. My eldest son, Theodorick, and Campbell Pryor, my husband's twelve-year-old brother, agreed to return to the farm, draw the trunk out to the rear of the kitchen, break it open, set fire to the contents, and not leave until they were consumed.

In due time the boys returned, having accomplished the burning of the letters, but bearing between them a huge bundle — a sheet full of papers. " Father's sermons," explained Campbell.

When the time came for my tired little brood to go to bed, I found three upper rooms prepared for us. In one of these I put the boys, first placing the large silver tray between two mattresses. A hamper filled with soiled towels and pinafores stood in a corner. Therein I bestowed the six pieces of the service, covering the whole with the soiled linen. A smaller room I reserved for my husband, into which I locked him, putting the key in my pocket — for he had returned in such an excited frame of mind, and in such physical exhaustion, that I was uneasy about him, lest he might, when the army passed, yield to his feelings and go along with it.

Then I took my seat at the window and listened. The firing had all ceased.

A ring at the door-bell startled me. There stood Mayor Townes, come to ask if General Pryor would go out with the flag of truce and surrender the city.

"Oh, he cannot — he cannot," I declared. "How can you ask him to surrender his old home? Besides, he is worn out, and is now sleeping heavily."

About two o'clock, General Lee passed the house with his staff. It is said he looked back and said to his aide: "This is just what I told them at Richmond. The line has been stretched until it snapped." Presently there was a loud explosion — another — another. The bridges were being blown up. Then fires announced the burning of warehouses of tobacco.

And then! As the dawn broke, I saw the Federal pickets entering silently, watchfully. Finding no resistance, they threw their muskets over into the yard and hurried down town to plunder!

I awoke my boys. "Get up, boys! Dress quickly. Now remember, you must be very self-controlled and quiet, and no harm will come to you."

Immediately the door of my room was thrown wide open, and Robert ushered in three armed, German-looking soldiers.

"What do you want?" I asked.

"To search the house," they answered.

"You will find nothing worth your while. There is my shawl! I have just run in from the lines. Here are my children."

"We don't want your clothes," said one; "we want your prisoner."

My husband had heard and knocked at his door. He had not undressed.

"Here I am," he said, coming out and fastening his collar; and, before I could think, they had marched him off.

I was left alone with the boy Robert, who had betrayed him. He stood trembling, not with fear — with excitement.

"Leave this house!" I ordered him.

"What for?" he asked sullenly.

"Because you are no friend of mine. This is now my house. You are not to set foot in it again."

Strange to say, he left.

He had admitted into the house more soldiers than these three. I had brought with me from the farm a little negress, Lizzie, who had been hired by Eliza "to amuse the baby." Lizzie had obeyed the instinct which always leads a child's Southern nurse to the kitchen, and had gone below with my baby. I heard the most tremendous stamping and singing in the basement kitchen, and from the top of the staircase I called to Lizzie, who ran up, frightened, with the child in her arms. A soldier looked up from the bottom.

"What are you doing here?" I asked.

"Getting breakfast," he replied.

"You'll get none here," I told him.

He set his bayonet forward and started up the steps. I slipped back and luckily found a bolt on the door. Quick as thought I bolted him out.

But I was burningly indignant. I saw the street full of troops standing, and a young officer on horseback. I ran out and said to him : —

"Is it your pleasure we should be murdered in our houses? My kitchen is full of soldiers."

"Where, where?" exclaimed the young fellow, dismounting and running in.

I conducted him to the bolted door, unfastened it, and had the satisfaction of seeing him lay about with the flat of his sword to good purpose. He placed a guard around the house. Moreover, his action sustained me in my position, and the old woman in the kitchen greeted me respectfully, apologized for her son, and promised faithful service in the future.

But another and most bitter trial was in store for me. An approaching army corps was hailed with shouts and cheers as it passed down the street. At its head was borne the trophy that had aroused this enthusiasm : our own sacred banner, given by the women of Petersburg to the young colonel at Smithfield, and inscribed with the names of the battles into which he had proudly borne it. It was coming back — a captive! How grateful I felt that my husband had not seen it! "Ole Uncle Frank's at the bottom of that business," said Alick, — and alas! we had reason to suppose the polite old colored gentleman had purchased favor by revealing the hiding-place of our banner. My husband soon returned. He had presented Mr. Lincoln's card, on which the President had written his "parole until exchanged." Thereafter he was arrested and released every time the occupying troops moved and were replaced by new brigades and divisions.

We sat all day in the front room, watching the splendidly equipped host as it marched by on its way to capture Lee. It soon became known that we were there. Within the next few days we had calls from old Washington friends. Among others my husband was visited by Elihu B. Washburne, and Senator Henry Wilson, afterward Vice-President of the United States with General Grant. These paid long visits and talked kindly and earnestly of the South.

Major-General Warren had been relieved of his command and superseded by Sheridan. His old friend, Randolph Harrison, lay ill and wounded near us, and General Warren introduced himself to General Pryor and asked to be conducted to his friend's bedside. From that time he was with us every day, and, indorsed warmly by " Ranny," our old friend, he too was admitted into our friendship.

Mr. Lincoln soon arrived and sent for my husband. But General Pryor excused himself, saying that he was a paroled prisoner, that General Lee was still in the field, and that he could hold no conference with the head of the opposing army.

The splendid troops passed continually. Our hearts sank within us. We had but one hope — that General Lee would join Joseph E. Johnston and find his way to the mountains of Virginia, those ramparts of nature which might afford protection until we could rest and recruit.

2 A

CHAPTER XXIII

RICHMOND SURRENDERS

"RICHMOND, April 5, 1865.

"MY *dear:* — I am not at all sure you will ever receive this letter, but I shall risk it. *First,* I join you in humble thanks to God for the great mercy accorded both of us. Your General lives. My Colonel lives. What words can express our gratitude? What is the loss of home and goods compared with the loss of our own flesh and blood? Alas! Alas! for those who have lost all!

"I am sure you will have heard the grewsome story of Richmond's evacuation. I was at St. Paul's Sunday, April 1, when a note was handed to President Davis. He rose instantly, and walked down the aisle — his face set, so we could read nothing. Dr. Minnegerode gave notice that General Ewell desired the forces to assemble at 3 P.M., and also that there would be no further service that day. I had seen no one speak to the doctor, and I wonder at the acuteness of his perception of the state of affairs. As soon as I reached the hotel I wrote a note to the proprietor, asking for news. He answered that grave tidings had come from Petersburg, and for himself he was by no means sure we could hold Richmond. He requested me to keep quiet and not encourage a tendency to excitement or panic. At first I thought I would read my services in the quiet of my little sky parlor at the Spotswood, but I was literally in a fever of anxiety. I descended to

354

the parlor. Nobody was there except two or three children with their nurses. Later in the afternoon I walked out and met Mr. James Lyons. He said there was no use in further evading the truth. The lines were broken at Petersburg and that town and Richmond would be surrendered late at night — he was going out himself with the mayor and Judge Meredith with a flag of truce and surrender the city. Trains were already fired to carry the archives and bank officials. The President and his Cabinet would probably leave at the same time.

" ' And you, Judge ? '

" ' I shall stand my ground. I have a sick family, and we must take our chances together.'

" ' Then seriously — really and truly — Richmond is to be given up, after all, to the enemy.'

" ' Nothing less ! And we are going to have a rough time, I imagine.'

" I could not be satisfied until I had seen Judge Campbell, upon whom we so much relied for good, calm sense. I found him with his hands full of papers, which he waved deprecatingly as I entered.

" ' Just a minute, Judge ! I am alone at the Spotwood and — '

" ' Stay there, my dear lady ! You will be perfectly safe. I advise all families to remain in their own houses. Keep quiet. I am glad to know the Colonel is safe. He may be with you soon now.'

" With this advice I returned and mightily reassured and comforted the proprietor of the Spotswood. He immediately caused notice to be issued to his guests. I resolved to convey my news to the families I knew best. The Pegrams were in such deep affliction there was no room there for anxious fears about such small matters as the evacuation of cities, but I could see my dear Mrs. Paul, and Mrs. Maben, and say a comforting word at the

Allan home — closed to all the world since poor John fell at Gettysburg. Mrs. Davis was gone and out of harm's way. The Lees were sacred from intrusion. Four members of that household — the General, 'Rooney,' Custis, and Robert — were all at the post of danger. Late in the afternoon three hundred or more prisoners were marched down the street; the negroes began to stand about, quietly observant but courteous, making no demonstration whatever. The day, you remember, was one of those glorious days we have in April, and millions on millions of stars watched at night, looking down on the watchers below. I expected to sit by my window all night as you always do in a troubled time, but sleep overtook me. I had slept, but not undressed, when a loud explosion shook the house — then another. There were crashing sounds of falling glass from the concussion. I found the sun had risen. All was commotion in the streets, and agitation in the hotel. The city government had dragged hogsheads of liquor from the shops, knocked in the heads, and poured the spirits into the gutters. They ran with brandy, whiskey, and rum, and men, women, and boys rushed out with buckets, pails, pitchers, and in the lower streets, hats and boots, to be filled. Before eight o'clock many public buildings were in flames, and a great conflagration was evidently imminent. The flames swept up Main Street, where the stores were quickly burned, and then roared down the side streets almost to Franklin.

" The doors of all the government bakeries were thrown open and food was given to all who asked it. Women and children walked in and helped themselves. At ten o'clock the enemy arrived, — ten thousand negro troops, going on and on, cheered by the negroes on the streets.

" So the morning passed — a morning of horror, of terror! Drunken men shouted and reeled through the

streets, a black cloud from the burning city hung like a
pall over us, a black sea of faces filled the street below,
shells burst continuously in the ashes of the burning
armory. About four in the afternoon a salute of thirty-
four guns was fired. A company of mounted dragoons
advanced up the street, escorting an open carriage drawn
by four horses in which sat Mr. Lincoln and a naval
officer, followed by an escort of cavalry. They drove
straight to Mr. Davis's house, cheered all the way by
negroes, and returned the way they came. I had a good
look at Mr. Lincoln. He seemed tired and old — and
I must say, with due respect to the President of the United
States, I thought him the ugliest man I had ever seen.
He was fairly elected the first time, I acknowledge, — but
was he the last? A good many of the 'free and equal'
were not allowed a vote then.

"The next day I persuaded one of the lads in the hotel
to take a walk with me early in the morning, and I
passed General Lee's house. A Yankee guard was pacing
to and fro before it — at which I felt an impulse of indignation, — but presently the door opened, the guard took
his seat on the steps and proceeded to investigate the
contents of a very neatly furnished tray, which Mrs. Lee
in the kindness of her heart had sent out to him.

"I am obliged to acknowledge that there is really no hope
now of our ultimate success. Everybody says so. My heart
is too full for words. General Johnson says we may comfort
ourselves by the fact that war may decide a *policy*, but never
a *principle*. I imagine our *principle* is all that remains to us
of hope or comfort.

" Devotedly,
"AGNES."

From my friend Admiral Porter I learned that he
landed with President Lincoln, and that through

some *contretemps* no equipage was in waiting to conduct them through the streets of Richmond. They set out to walk, escorted by twelve of the boat's crew with bayonets fixed on their rifles. The day was warm, and the streets dusty, "owing to the immense gathering of the crowd, kicking up the dirt." Mr. Lincoln took off his hat and fanned his face, from which the perspiration was pouring, and looked as if he would give his presidency for a glass of water.

The admiral, *par parenthèse*, told many negro anecdotes in negro dialect, but, like all Northern imitators of that inimitable lingo, he "slipped up" on many words. The negro does not say "Massa" — his word is "Marster"; he does not say "*Bress de Lawd*," — "Thank Gawd A'mighty" being his pious preference.

The triumphing party was overtaken by an equipage and a military escort, and proceeded, according to the admiral, "to the mansion of Mr. Davis.[1] It was quite a small affair compared with the White House, and modest in all its appointments, showing that while President Davis was engaged heart and soul in endeavoring to effect the division of the states, he was not, at least, surrounding himself with regal style, but was living in a modest, comfortable way, like any other citizen. Amid all his surroundings the refined taste of his wife was apparent, and marked everything about the apartments." Admiral Porter thought that the Confederate government

---

[1] "Incidents and Anecdotes of the Civil War," Porter, p. 302.

had departed in an ignoble manner, " that it should have remained at the capital and surrendered in a dignified way, making terms for the citizens of the place, guarding their rights, and acknowledging they had lost the game.   There was nothing to be ashamed of in such a surrender to a vastly superior force; their armies had fought as people never fought before.   They had 'robbed the cradle and the grave' to sustain themselves, and all that was wanted to make them glorious was the submission of their leaders and troops in a dignified way," etc.

This was also the feeling of many of our own best men — of General Lee and scores of his officers, of Judge Campbell, of the private citizens of Richmond.   Mr. Davis differed from these men.   General Lee's opinion was known to his officers.   General Gordon once said to him : —

" Have you expressed an opinion, as to the propriety of making terms, to the President or to Congress ? " [1]

His reply was : " General Gordon, I am a soldier. It is my duty to obey orders. . . .   It is enough to turn a man's hair gray to spend one day in that Congress.   The members are patriotic and earnest, but they will neither take the responsibility of acting nor will they clothe me with authority to act.   As for Mr. Davis, he is unwilling to do anything short of independence, and feels that it is useless to try to treat on that basis."   This conversation immediately

[1] " Camp-fire and Battle-field," pp. 486, 487.

preceded the terrible battle at Petersburg, and the
consequent loss of that city and Richmond.   Much
could have been saved in blood and in treasure had
the final battles never taken place.   " Whom the
gods destroy they first infatuate."

CHAPTER XXIV

SHERIDAN'S OCCUPATION OF PETERSBURG

SUCH alarming rumors reached us from the neighboring counties, of marauding parties plundering private houses and frightening defenceless women, that my husband obtained an extension of his parole, and permission to visit his sisters in Nottoway County. He had not heard from his father since the fight at Cottage Farm. Leaving me in the care of my neighbor, good Mr. Bishop, he set forth.

The first stirring event of our new position was the arrival of prisoners, marched through the streets under a strong guard. They were a forlorn body of ragged, hatless, barefoot men. They had found poles or sticks somewhere, and upon them they waved their hats and handkerchiefs—the poor, brave fellows! We women stood at the doors of our houses with smiles and encouraging words. One of the soldiers darted from the ranks, rushed to me, *embraced me* as if I were a sister, and slipped his watch into my hands! It was a novel experience; but I think if he had appeared as a prisoner in the garb of Beelzebub, horns, hoofs, and all, I should not have flinched. Within the watch I found his name — a connection of our family and a valued friend. He had recognized me, but I could not recognize the elegant young colonel in his imperso- nation of a ragged barefoot boy.

My little sons soon found the destination of the captives, also that citizens were getting permits from headquarters to take them home.

"Then you must go and ask General Hartsuff for a permit," I said. Upon inquiry it appeared that this could not be done by proxy. Some adult member of the family must apply in person.

So I took my young escorts with me, and we went to "Centre Hill," the fine Bolling House, where the General had made his headquarters. I presented my plea. How many did I want? I thought I could take care of eight. Their names? I could give only one, the owner of the watch. The General kindly conceded that I might select my men, adding, "Would to God I could release them all!"

The first impression I had of the temporary prison was of stifling heat in which no one could live. The place smelt violently! My friend helped me choose my men, and I was required to present myself with them, armed with my order, to have my name and theirs entered in an army register, with an order that they report every day until the command moved on. As I was leaving the warehouse a fair-haired boy said to me, "Oh, take me along too!"

"Take my arm," I said; and not until I reached the street did I realize the enormity of my mistake. I had stolen a prisoner!

I knew well I could be severely punished. My
boy soon told me his name. He was Frank
Brooke, nephew of our dear Judge Randolph
Tucker.

But here was a dilemma. All night I revolved
it in my mind. I had nine men — eight were to
report next morning. Very early Alick knocked
at my door.

" What is it now, Alick ? "

" One of dem prisoners run away las' night ! I
hear de do' open and jump up to see what's de
matter. He say, ' Keep still, boy ! Hit's all
right ! ' "

" So it is, Alick," I said, " it's perfectly delightful."

I took a piece of my husband's silver service
down to the Northern sutler, and pawned it for
two hundred dollars. With this money I purchased shoes, handkerchiefs, and hats for my men,
and kept them in comfort for a week or more.
They were then " moved on " to other and distant
quarters, — and all very soon liberated.

One morning early I was summoned from my
room by Alick, who informed me that four gentlemen had called. Descending to the parlor, I found
four officers in Federal uniform. As soon as I
entered, one of them asked brusquely : —

" How many rooms are in this house ? "

" I think there are eight or ten."

" General Sheridan wants the house for his
adjutant's office."

I was aware that General Sheridan had arrived

the day before, and had taken possession of Mr. Hamilton's elegant mansion on the next street, in the rear of my little dwelling.

I at once perceived that the General, although in a house of twenty or more rooms, had not desired the noise and inconvenience of an adjutant's office under his own roof. I answered coldly : —

" I cannot oblige General Sheridan. My house is small. I need it for my own family."

One of the officers rose, crossed the room, and, standing before me, said sternly : —

" Madam, you seem to be unaware that when General Sheridan sees a house that suits him, he knows how to make the terms for it."

" Ah, well," I replied, " I had forgotten that fact for the moment. Do I understand my family must go in the street ? How much time can you give me to remove them ? "

The officers withdrew into the hall and conferred together. Presently one of them returned, and informed me courteously that they had concluded not to annoy me. He was aware he was addressing Mrs. General Pryor. His own name was Captain Lee, and he had been happy to spare me inconvenience.

The next morning I was awakened soon after dawn by a tremendous hubbub below me, and sending my little maid, Lizzie, to ascertain the cause, she beckoned to me to come to the head of the stairs. I threw on my gown, thrust my feet into my carpet slippers, and peeped over the banister. Captain Lee was standing at the foot of the stair, writing a note on the top of the newel post. Looking up, he saw me, and said : " I was writing to you, Madam. General Sheridan has ordered us to take your house. It is a military necessity. I pray you will try to be patient, and I will do all I can to save you annoyance."

" How soon must I leave ? "

" Not at all ! We can allow you two rooms — the one you already occupy and the one below it."

I appreciated the concession of the latter room, and busied myself to make of it dining room and sitting room.

I brought beds from a rear room to my own chamber, for the lodging of my family. Alick was positively stricken at the new turn things had taken; but I represented to him and to the boys the grave necessity, in their father's absence, of discreet and always courteous behavior.

To add to my embarrassment, John brought in several hundred books he had picked up on the farm. They were dumped down in a pile in the corner of my reception room.

The weather was intensely hot. It was impossible to sit with closed doors. I locked the doors of my bedroom during the day, and all the family, except myself, lived in the yard under my eyes, unless the rain drove them within.

The first night of our captivity I had sent my baby with her small nurse to bed. Hearing a heavy step overhead, I ran up to my room. Standing in an easy attitude, leaning on the mantel, was a large negro man. He was smoking a cigar and talking to Lizzie.

" What is your business here ? " I asked.

" Only my pleasure — to pass away a little time."

" Look at me ! "

The negro raised his eyes with an insolent smile. Slowly and with emphasis I said : —

" Do you leave this room instantly ! And mark well my words. If ever you enter it again, I shall KILL you ! "

He left, and alas, alas ! my poor little Lizzie, whom I had hired from her mother, left also ; and not by me or by her friends was she ever seen again !

Only those who have lived in an adjutant's office can know the ceaseless noise, turmoil, tramping to and fro, loud talking night and day. There was *no* night. The gas (which they left me to pay for) burned brightly all night. Officers were coming in for orders day and night. I never knew to what use the upper rooms were put; I only know they were rarely silent. All the business of a great army was transacted here, that the General's entertaining, his elegant life, his sleep, might be undisturbed.

The sentry was drawn so closely around my doors that I could never enter the yard or garden without passing them. Finally, upon going out to the little vine-clad summer-house to give my baby air — I cannot say fresh air — one of the sentinels shook my equilibrium by informing me as I passed : —

" We've caught Jeff Davis."

When I returned, my eyes cast down to avoid him, he stepped close to me and hissed in my ear, " He shall be *hanged*."

Mr. Davis had not then been arrested, but this I did not know. Leaving my baby with her brothers, I walked straight into the veranda of Mr. Hamilton's house, asked for General Sheridan, was ushered into a room where a number of officers were sitting around a table, and announced myself.

"I am Mrs. Pryor, whose house you have taken for an adjutant's office. Sentinels have been placed around my house who insult me when I cross the threshold."

General Sheridan rose: "What can we do for you, Madam? What do you demand?"

"That the sentry around my house be removed to the street enclosure."

I was invited to take a seat, but I preferred standing while an order was made out. I have often smiled to think what I must have looked like to those officers. My gown was of chocolate-colored percale, with a white spot. Enormous hoops were then in fashion. I had long since been abandoned by mine. I fancy I resembled nothing so much as the wooden Mrs. Noah who presides over the animals in the children's "Noah's Arks." I took the order given me, bowed my thanks, and walked through a line of soldiers home. After this I had the larger liberty my children needed.

It was my custom, in these days of my captivity, to descend early, that I might guard my books, to my little reception room. A dining room it did not become for a long time afterward. I had nothing whatever to eat except the biscuits brought me by Mr. Bishop, and a daily tray sent at noon by my

angel friend, Mrs. Meade. She had some Northern
men boarding with her and could command such fare
as the sutler was willing to sell, for the farmers were
as destitute of fresh food as ourselves.

We had been excellent customers of a cigar shop
in old times, and the proprietor now opened his
establishment, and intrusted my boys and Campbell
with a "walking agency." They sold cigars at
good profit to the officers and soldiers around us;
and we made acquaintance once more with United
States pennies and dimes.

Sitting all day in my little reception room, I was
cheered by visits from my friends, and occasionally
the tenants of the house would ask for a glass of
water from the sideboard. Captain Lee came often.
He confided to me his chagrin at the manners of
the Petersburg ladies. He had picked up a veil for
a pretty girl, and she had turned away her head
when her hand was extended to receive it. The
Captain was deeply hurt: he was "a Northern man,
yes, but" he was "a gentleman."

One day Captain Lee informed me that he had
good news for me. "We have marching orders!
We go to-night! I know you are pleased! We
have given you so much trouble!"

"Not more, I suppose, than was necessary!"

"Well, I must say, you have been very patient.
General Sheridan is in the office and wishes to make
his respects to you."

The General entered and thanked me for the manner in which I had endured all the inconvenience to
which he had subjected me. He seemed, for some

reason, to wish me to think well of his course toward us, and began to explain it. He alluded to the policy that he had adopted.

"It was the very best thing to do," he declared. "The only way to stamp out this rebellion was to handle it without gloves."

If he fancied I would either argue or agree with him, he mistook me. I was silent. There was an embarrassing pause, and he began to berate our government for bad management. "Ladies should be better cared for," he said.

"Why, I assure you there was no necessity for your starving! I have unearthed, within forty miles of this place, enough provisions to keep you in perfect comfort."

Looking down, he espied the brown eyes of my baby steadfastly fastened on his face.

"I think I must borrow this little lady," he said. "It is not often General Sheridan has anything in his arms as sweet as this."

He still had her in his arms as he turned to leave the room, and she gladly went with him. Presently she was brought back with a parcel in her own arms — figs, bananas, cakes, and nuts.

Captain Lee came in late to bid me good-by, and to reiterate his thanks.

"You really have been so very nice! Now I am going to beg you will allow me to make some return."

I hastened to accept his offer. I told him that my General's pet mare, Lady Jane, was in his command. She had been missing ever since the battles around Richmond. John was sure he had seen her.

2 B

By some chance she had fallen into the hands of the troops now in Petersburg. *Could* it be possible for me to reclaim her?

The Captain looked grieved.

" No," he said ; " I had no thought of anything of that kind. But a great many ladies have asked for what I am going to give you. I have brought you General Sheridan's autograph."

He instantly interpreted my disappointment. Before I could recover he added, " But it appears you don't wish it," and threw it on the table.

" I can at least, Captain, be grateful that you tried to please me."

That night the adjutant's office was closed. Next morning my husband returned. General Warren came in to see him. General Sheridan stood on our porch to receive the homage of his men, bowing to their cheers. General Warren looked on from our window. Presently the troops he had commanded when he was superseded by Sheridan passed the house. They saw their old commander, and the shouts, " Hurrah for General Warren," must have been harsh sounds for General Sheridan.

I was alone one afternoon in my accustomed seat, when a tall, lantern-jawed soldier with a musket on his shoulder marched in.

" I want some whiskey ! " he informed me.

" You'll not get it here ! "

" Wall, I guess you'll have to scare it up. I'll search the house.'

" Search away ! I'll call the provost guard to help you," I said.

He turned and marched out.   At the door he
sent me a parting shot : —

" Wall! you've got a damned tongue ef you
ain't got no whiskey ! "

My husband has always considered this a very
good story.   I forestall him by telling it myself!

I grew very fond of General Warren.   He spent
many hours with us; tactful, considerate, and kind,
he never grieved or offended us.

One evening he silently took his seat.   Presently
he said : —

" I have news which will be painful to you.   It
hurts me to tell you, but I think you had rather
hear it from me than from a stranger — General
Lee has surrendered."

It was an awful blow to us.   All was over.   All
the suffering, bloodshed, death — all for nothing !

General Johnston's army was surrendered to
General Sherman in North Carolina on April 26.
The banner which had led the armies of the South
through fire and blood to victory, to defeat, in times
of starvation, cold, and friendlessness ; the banner
that Helen's lover had waved aloft on a forlorn hope
until it fell from his lifeless hands ; the banner found
under the dying boy at Gettysburg, who had smil-
ingly refused assistance lest it be discovered, — the
banner of a thousand histories was furled forever,
with none so poor to do it reverence.

CHAPTER XXV

WOE TO THE VANQUISHED!

IMMEDIATELY after General Lee's surrender, the United States Crcuit Court held a session at Norfolk, Virginia, and made haste to indict for treason Robert E. Lee, John C. Breckenridge, Roger A. Pryor, and others. These men thereafter were not to feel any sense of personal security. A cloud of doubt and possible disaster still hung over them. Under this cloud they were to commence their lives anew.

Every one who has suffered an overwhelming misfortune must be conscious of a strange deadening of feeling — more intolerable even than pain. It may be a merciful provision of nature. Insensibility at a crucial moment may be nature's anæsthesia. Dr. Livingstone, the African explorer, relates that he was conscious of this insensibility when in the paws of a lion. He had a theory that the instinct of all animals to shake their victim, as the cat does a mouse, may be given in mercy to the vanquished. I was so completely stunned by the thought that all the suffering, all the spilt blood, all the poverty, all the desolation of the South was *for naught;* that her very fidelity, heroism, and fortitude, qualities so noble in themselves, had wrought her undoing, that I seemed to become dead to everything around me. My husband was compelled to leave me, to seek employment in Richmond. My neighbors, like myself, were stunned into silence. " Here I and sorrow sit " might have been said truly of any one of us.

When the passing troops left us with only General Hartsuff's guard, the small earnings of my little boys ceased. John and his fellow-servants came into town, and reported to me.

" I can no longer maintain you or give you wages," I said to Eliza Page and her sisters.

" We will serve you for the good you have already done us," they said, but of course I could not allow this to any extent. Eliza returned to her husband and their little home.

With John I had more trouble. It was hard to make him understand that I could not afford his services on any terms.

" I will never leave you," was his reply to everything I urged.

" You *must*, John! You must go home to your father in Norfolk. He will advise you."

" The old man is in the oyster business," said John. " What do I care about oysters? All I care for is Marse Roger and these boys."

I knew that my poor John had an infirmity. Once when I had sent him with Alick from Cottage Farm on an errand he had returned very late. I could see the pair walking down the road alone, followed at some distance by the horse and wagon. They seemed to be trying to compass both sides of

the road at once.   Alick was the first to report to
me, with these words : —

"I — I — ain' drunk, — but *Jawn!*   Jawn, he
ve'y drunk!"

This painful scene had been reënacted often enough
to make me anxious.

"You really must go to your father, John," I
insisted.   "How much money have you?"   He
had five dollars.   I also had five, which I gave him.

"Now don't let me see you again," I said.
"Write to me from Norfolk."

He left, protesting, but next morning he was
gone.   I heard from him soon and from his father.
The old gentleman expressed gratitude and also
some anxiety about John's "army habits."

And so no more of the only slave I ever owned!

Agnes wrote from Richmond early in May :—

"My Dearest: What could I do without you?   Now
don't flatter yourself that I need now, or ever did need, those
beautiful moral reflections in well-chosen language by means
of which you have striven to educate me.   But you are an
unmitigated blessing when my 'feelings are too many for
me' — when, in short, I boil over.

"Now when a kettle boils over it puts out the fire, and
then we go tea-less to bed.   How nice it would be for the
kettle if some convenient utensil were at hand to receive its
excited bubbles.

"I am aggrieved and indignant at the sermons people are
preaching to us.   And I have caught a young brother in a
flagrant theft.   All Richmond is in a state of beautiful
admiration at a sermon it listened to last week on the uses
of our great misfortune.   War was declared to be a blessing.

'The high passion of patriotism prevents the access of baser passions. Men's hearts beat together, and woman is roused from the frivolousness and feebleness into which her nature is apt to sink. Death, insult, carnage, violated homes, and broken hearts are all awful. But it is worse than a thousand deaths when a people has adopted the creed that the wealth of nations consists — not in generous hearts, in primitive simplicity, in preference of duty to life; not in MEN, but in silk, cotton, and something that they call " capital." If the price to be paid for peace is this — that wealth accumulates and men decay, better far that every street in every town of our once noble country should run blood.'

" Now all this is very fine, but very one-sided. And my brother didn't believe a word of it. He has been away in England and has seen none of the horrors of war; but he has seen something else — a very charming lecture printed in London some time before the war.[1]

" Strange are the ways of Providence. Precisely that I might convict him did this address fall into my hands in Washington. It struck me forcibly at the time. Little did I think I should hear it in Richmond after a terrible civil war of our own.

" I feel impatient at this attempt to extort good for ourselves out of the overwhelming disaster which brought such ruin to others; to congratulate ourselves for what is purchased with their blood. Surely, if for no other reason, for the sake of the blood that has been spilt, we should not hasten to acquiesce in the present state of things. If I catch my Colonel piously affirming too much resignation, too prompt a forgetfulness of the past, I'll — well, he knows what I am capable of saying!

" But, now that I have safely boiled over, I will tell you my news. We cannot remain here. We are literally stripped to the ' primitive ' state my reverend brother thinks

---

[1] Lecture to members of the Mechanics' Institution, February, 1853.

so good for us.   We are wofully in need of ' silk, cotton, and something they call capital,' and we'll never get it here. And so my Colonel and I are going to New York.   He has secured a place in some publishing house or other.   I only wish it were a dry-goods store !

"Of course our social life is all over.   I have taken my resolution.   There are fine ladies in New York whom I used to entertain in Washington.   Just so far as they approach me, will I approach them !   A card for a card, a visit for a visit.   But I imagine I shall not be recognized. I am content.   There will be plenty to read in that publishing house.   I shall not repine.   All the setting, the *entourage*, of a lady is taken from me, but the lady herself has herself pretty well in hand, and is quite content if she may always be

"Your devoted
"AGNES."

The time now came when I must draw rations for my family.   I could not do this by proxy.   I was required to present my request in person.

As I walked through the streets in early morn-ing, I thought I had never known a lovelier day. How could Nature spread her canopy of blossoming magnolia and locust as if nothing had happened ? How could the vine over the doorway of my old home load itself with snowy roses, how could the birds sing, how could the sun shine as if such things as these could ever again gladden our broken hearts ?

My dear little sons understood they were to escort me everywhere, so we presented ourselves together at the desk of the government official and announced our errand.

"Have you taken the oath of allegiance, Madam?" inquired that gentleman.

"No, Sir." I was quite prepared to take the oath. The young officer looked at me seriously for a moment, and said, as he wrote out the order : —

"Neither will I require it of you, Madam !"

I was in better spirits after this pleasant incident, and, calling to Alick, I bade him arm himself with the largest basket he could find and take my order to the commissary.

"We are going to have all sorts of good things," I told him, "fresh meat, fruit, vegetables, and everything."

When the boy returned he presented a drooping figure and a woebegone face. My first unworthy suspicion suggested his possible confiscation of my stores for drink, but he soon explained.

"I buried that ole stinkin' fish! I wouldn't bring it in your presence. An' here's the meal they give me."

Hairy caterpillars were jumping through the meal! I turned to my table and wrote : —

"Is the commanding general aware of the nature of the ration issued this day to the destitute women of Petersburg?" (signing myself)

"MRS. ROGER A. PRYOR."

This I gave to Alick, with instructions to present it, with the meal, to General Hartsuff.

Alick returned with no answer; but in a few minutes a tall orderly stood before me, touched his cap,
and handed me a note.

"Major-General Hartsuff is sorry he cannot make *right*
all that seems so wrong. He sends the enclosed. Some
day General Pryor will repay

"GEORGE L. HARTSUFF,
"*Major-General Commanding.*"

The note contained an official slip of paper : —

"The Quartermaster and Commissary of the Army of
the Potomac are hereby ordered to furnish Mrs. Roger A.
Pryor with all she may demand or require, charging the
same to the private account of

"GEORGE L. HARTSUFF,
"*Major-General Commanding.*"

Without the briefest deliberation I wrote and
returned the following reply : —

"Mrs. Roger A. Pryor is not insensible to the generous
offer of Major-General Hartsuff, but *he ought to have known*
that the ration allowed the destitute women of Petersburg
must be enough for

"MRS. ROGER A. PRYOR."

As I sat alone, revolving various schemes for our
sustenance, — the selling of the precious testimonial
service (given by the Democracy of Virginia after
my husband's noble fight against "Know-noth-
ingism"), the possibility of finding occupation for

myself, — the jingling of chain harness at the door arrested my attention. There stood a handsome equipage, from which a very fine lady indeed was alighting. She bustled in with her lace-edged handkerchief to her eyes, and announced herself as Mrs. Hartsuff. She was superbly gowned in violet silk and lace, with a tiny *fanchon* bonnet tied beneath an enormous cushion of hair behind, the first of the fashionable *chignons* I had seen — an arrangement called a "waterfall," an exaggeration of the plethoric, distended "bun" of the Englishwoman of a few years ago.

"Oh, my dear lady," she began, "we are in such distress at headquarters! George is in despair! You won't let him help you! Whatever is he to do?"

"I really am grateful to the General," I assured her; "but you see there is no reason he should do more for me than for others."

"Oh, but there *is* reason. You have suffered more than the rest. You have been driven from your home! Your house has been sacked. George knows all about you. I have brought a basket for you — tea, coffee, sugar, crackers."

"I cannot accept it, I am so sorry."

"But what are you going to do? Are you going to starve?"

"Very likely," I said, "but somehow I shall not very much mind!"

"Oh, this is too utterly, utterly dreadful!" said the lady as she left the room.

The next day the ration was changed. Fresh

beef, canned vegetables, bread, and coffee were issued to all the women of Petersburg. Mrs. Hartsuff came daily to see me. "Not that George has gotten over it!" she declared. "His feelings are constantly hurt here. And as to myself, that old black Irene I found in the kitchen at Centre Hill just walks over me!"

"Why don't you dismiss her?"

"*Dismiss Irene?* I should like to see anybody dismiss Irene! Besides, she cooks divinely. But I can't enter her kitchen! 'Dear me,' I said one day, '*what* a dirty kitchen!' 'Ladies don't nuvver come in kitchens,' she told me. Evidently I am not a lady! And I once asked her please to be careful of the gold studs the General was apt to leave in his cuffs. 'Gold studs!' she repeated with a sniff, 'my master wore diamond studs, an' I never see cuffs loose from shirts before in all my born days. 'Cose the wind'll blow 'em away! I can't be 'sponsible for no shirt that's in three or four pieces.'"

All the good citizens of Petersburg who had been driven away by the shelling now began to return, and among them came the owners of the house I was occupying. I was told that I could, on no account, be safe at Cottage Farm without a guard. For this, too, I must make personal request. So my little body-guard and I wended our way to interview General Hartsuff.

We found him in the noble mansion of the Bollings. At the entrance two fine greyhounds in marble had for many years guarded the incoming and outgoing of the Bolling family. In the rear there was a long veranda with lofty pillars, and beyond, extensive grounds set with well-grown evergreens, and with that princely tree, the *Magnolia grandiflora*, now in bloom. White marble statues and marble seats were scattered through the grounds. A rustic staircase led down to a conservatory, built low for the better care of the plants. The mansion stood on an eminence sloping sharply in front, and a legend-haunted subterranean passage led from the dwelling to the street, the entrance to which was covered by shrubs and vines.

As I stood in the veranda waiting for audience, a young officer called my attention to the beauty of the grounds and the magnificence of the flowering plants in tubs on the veranda. " I should like," he said, " to fight it out on this line all summer."

I thought of the family driven from their own, and was wicked enough to tell him : —

" That would be most unfortunate for you. This place is very sickly in summer — deadly, in fact. Typhoid fever is fatal in this section."

But I was summoned to the presence of the great man. As I entered, he continued writing at a table, without greeting me or looking up from his paper.

" General," I commenced, " I have come to ask if I may have a guard. I am about to return to my home — Cottage Farm."

No answer, except the rapid scratching of his pen as it travelled over his sheet.

" General Hartsuff, are you still angry with me because I did not feel I could accept your kind offer ?

I couldn't take it! I couldn't trust myself with it!
I should have given a ball and ruined you."

He laughed outright at this and threw down his
pen.

"It is impossible for you to go to Cottage
Farm," he said; "there are fifty or more negroes
on the place. You cannot live there."

"I must! it is my only shelter."

"Well, then, I'll allow you a guard, and Mrs.
Hartsuff had better take you out herself, that is,
if you can condescend to accept as much."

I was not aware that Mrs. Hartsuff had entered
and stood behind me.

"And I think, George," she said, "you ought to
give Mrs. Pryor a horse and cart in place of her
own that were stolen."

"All right, all right," he said hastily. "Madam,
you will find the guard at your door when you arrive.
You go this evening? All right — good morning."

Mrs. Hartsuff duly appeared in the late afternoon with an ambulance and four horses, and we
departed in fine style. She was very cheery and
agreeable, and made me promise to let her come
often to see me. As we were galloping along in
state, we passed a line of weary-looking, dusty
Confederate soldiers, limping along, on their way
to their homes. They stood aside to let us pass.
I was cut to the heart at the spectacle. Here was
I, accepting the handsome equipage of the invading
commander — I, who had done nothing, going
on to my comfortable home; while they, poor fellows, who had borne long years of battle and star-

vation, were mournfully returning on foot, to find, perhaps, no home to shelter them. "Never again," I said to myself, "shall this happen! If I cannot help, I can at least suffer with them."

But when I reached Cottage Farm I found a home that no soldier, however forlorn, could have envied me. A scene of desolation met my eyes. The earth was ploughed and trampled, the grass and flowers were gone, the carcasses of six dead cows lay in the yard, and filth unspeakable had gathered in the corners of the house. The evening air was heavy with the sickening odor of decaying flesh. As the front door opened, millions of flies swarmed forth.

"If this were I," said Mrs. Hartsuff, as she gathered her skirts as closely around her as her hoops would permit, "I should fall across this threshold and die."

"I shall not fall," I said proudly; "I shall stand in my lot."

Within was dirt and desolation. Pieces of fat pork lay on the floors, molasses trickled from the library shelves, where bottles lay uncorked. Filthy, malodorous tin cans were scattered on the floors. Nothing, not even a tin dipper to drink out of the well, was left in the house, except one chair out of which the bottom had been cut, and one bedstead fastened together with bayonets. Picture frames were piled against the wall. I eagerly examined them. Every one was empty. One family portrait of an old lady was hanging on the wall with a sabre-cut across her face.

" Now, what in the world are you going to do? "
asked Mrs. Hartsuff.

" The best I can," I said.

But old Aunt Jinny had espied me, and, with a
courtesy to Mrs. Hartsuff, had seized my little girl.

" This is a hard home-coming for you, my po'
lamb! But never mind! Jinny has got plenty
of clean bedclothes and things. Yes, marm (to
Mrs. Hartsuff), I can take care of 'em! The
colored people? Oh, the colored people will give
no trouble. They are very peaceable."

She gathered us into her kitchen while she swept
a room for us and spread quilts upon the floor.
Later in the evening an ambulance from Mrs.
Hartsuff drove up. She had sent me a tin box of
bread-and-butter sandwiches, some tea, an army cot,
and army bedding.

The guard, a great, tall fellow, came to me for
orders. I felt nervous at his presence and wished
I had not brought him. I directed him to watch
all night at the road side of the house, while I
would sit up and keep watch in the opposite direction. The children soon slept upon the floor.

As the night wore on, I grew extremely anxious
about the strange negroes. Aunt Jinny thought
there were not more than fifty. They had filled
every outhouse except the kitchen. Suppose they
should overpower the guard and murder us all.

Everything was quiet. I had not the least disposition to sleep — thinking, thinking, of all the
old woman had told me of the sacking of the house,
of the digging of the cellar in search of treasure, of

the torch that had twice been applied to the house, and twice withdrawn because some officer wanted the shaded dwelling for a temporary lodging. Presently I was startled by a shrill scream from the kitchen, a door opened suddenly and shut, and a voice cried, "Thank Gawd! Thank Gawd A'mighty." Then all was still.

Was this a signal? I held my breath and listened, then softly rose, closed the shutters and fastened them, crept to the door, and bolted it inside. I might defend my children till the guard could come.

Evidently he had not heard! He was probably sleeping the sleep of an untroubled conscience on the bench in the front porch. And with untroubled consciences my children were sleeping. It was so dark in the room I could not see their faces, but I could touch them, and push the wet locks from their brows, as they lay in the close and heated atmosphere.

I resumed my watch at the window, pressing my face close to the slats of the shutters. A pale half-moon hung low in the sky, turning its averted face from a suffering world. At a little distance I could see the freshly made soldier's grave which Alick had discovered and reported. A heavy rain had fallen in the first hours of the night, and a stiff arm and hand now protruded from the shallow grave. To-morrow I would reverently cover the appealing arm, be it clad in blue or in gray, and would mark the spot. Now, as I sat with my fascinated gaze upon it, I thought of the tens of thousands, of the hun-

2 c

dreds of thousands, of upturned faces beneath the
green sod of old Virginia.   Strong in early manhood, brave, high-spirited men of genius, men
whom their country had educated for her own
defence in time of peril, — they had died because
that country could devise in her wisdom no better
means of settling a family quarrel than the wholesale slaughter of her sons by the sword.   And now ?
" Not till the heavens be no more shall they awake
nor be raised out of their sleep."

And then, as I sorrowed for their early death in
loneliness and anguish, I remembered the white-
robed souls beneath the altar of God, — the souls
that had " come out of great tribulation," — and
because they had thus suffered " they shall hunger
no more, neither thirst any more ; . . . and God
shall wipe away all tears from their eyes."

And then, as the pale, distressful moon sank
behind the trees, and the red dawn streamed up
from the east, the angel of Hope, who had " spread
her white wings and sped her away " for a little
season, returned.   And Hope held by the hand an
angel stronger than she, who bore to me a message :
" In the world ye have tribulation : but be of good
cheer ; I have overcome the world."

The sun was rising when I saw my good old
friend emerge from her kitchen, and I opened the
shutters to greet her.   She had brought me a cup
of delicious coffee, and was much distressed because
I had not slept.   Had I heard anything ?

" Course I know you was bleeged to hear," said
Aunt Jinny, as she bustled over the children.   " That

was Sis' Winny!   She got happy in the middle of the
night, an' Gawd knows what she would have done,
if Frank hadn't ketched hold of her and pulled her
back in the kitchen!   Frank an' me is pretty nigh
outdone an' discouraged 'bout Sis' Winny.   She
prays constant all day ; but Gawd A'mighty don't
count on bein' bothered all night.   Ain' He 'ranged
for us all to sleep, an' let Him have a little peace?
Sis' Winny must keep her happiness to herself, when
folks is trying to git some res'."

The guard now came to my window to say he
"guessed" he'd "have to put on some more harness.   Them blamed niggers rcfused to leave.
They might change their minds when they saw the
pistols."

"Oh, you wouldn't shoot, would you?" I said,
in great distress.   "Call them all to the back door
and let me speak with them."   I found myself in
the presence of some seventy-five negroes, men,
women, and children, all with upturned faces, keenly
interested in what I should say to them.

I talked to them kindly, and told them I was
sorry to see so many of them without homes.   One
of them, an intelligent-looking man, interrupted me.

"We are not without homes," he said.   "I planted
and worked on this place for years before the war.
It is right I should have some choice in the land
the government promises us, and I have come here
because I shall ask for the land I have worked."

"You are mistaken, I am sure," I said.   "This
farm belongs to my brother, not to me.   I am here
through his kindness, and I am perfectly willing

you should remain through mine until you find other shelter, provided you consider my husband master here, give no trouble, and help me clean up this place. All who are not willing to do this must leave. You must distinctly understand this is private property which will be protected by the government."

"That's so!" said the guard, emphatically. Thereupon an old, gray-haired man stepped forth and said : —

"My name's Abram! I'se toted Marse Roger on my back to school many a time. Me an' my family will stay an' clean up, an' thank you, Mistis! Come now! You all hear what the Yankee gentleman say! Git to work now on them dead cows — hurry up!"

I sent Abram to the quartermaster, and borrowed a team to haul away the filth and the dead animals. My faithful old friend in the kitchen lent me chairs and a table, and before night we were comparatively clean, having had a score or more scrubbers, and as many out-of-door laborers at work. My husband returned to us, and we commenced our new life of hopeless destitution. Not before October could I get my consent to eat a morsel in the house. I took my meals under the trees, unless driven by the rains to the shelter of the porch. The old woman who had been so unreasonably happy — "Sis' Winny" — proved to be a mere atom of a creature, withered, and bent almost double with age and infirmities, whom Aunt Jinny had taken in out of sheer compassion. If she could find something for which to thank God, surely none need despair.

To my great joy, my dear General had not remained in Richmond. There was no hope there for immediate occupation. His profession of law, for which he had been educated, promised nothing, for the very good reason that he had forgotten all he ever knew in his later profession of editor and politician. The latter field was closed to him forever. There was nothing for a rebel to earn in editing a newspaper.

CHAPTER XXVI

STARTING LIFE ANEW

WE suffered terribly during the ensuing months for want of something in which we might occupy ourselves. We sat silently, looking out on a landscape marked here and there by chimneys standing sentinel over the blackened heaps where our neighbors had made happy homes. A few books had been saved, only those for which we had little use. A soldier walked in one day with a handsome volume which Jefferson Davis, after inscribing his name in it, had presented to the General. The soldier calmly requested the former owner to be kind enough to add to the value of the volume by writing beneath the inscription his own autograph, and, his request granted, walked off with it under his arm. "He has been at some trouble," said my husband, "and he had as well be happy if I cannot!"

As the various brigades moved away from our neighborhood a few plain articles of furniture that had been taken from the house were restored to us, but nothing handsome or valuable, no books, pictures, *bric-à-brac*, or house-furnishings of any kind — just a few chairs and tables. I had furnished an itemized list of all the articles we had lost, with only this result.

We had news after a while of our blooded mare, Lady Jane. A letter enclosing her photograph came from a New England officer : —

" To Mr. Pryor,

" Dear Sir : A very fine mare belonging to you came into my camp near Richmond and is now with me. It would add much to her value if I could get her pedigree. Kindly send it at your earliest convenience, and oblige

" Yours truly,

_____ _____

" P.S. The mare is in good health, as you will doubtless be glad to know."

Disposed as my General was to be amiable, this was a little too much ! The pedigree was not sent.

A great number of tourists soon began to pass our house on their way to visit the localities near us, now become historic. They wished to stand on the site of General Lee's headquarters, to pluck a blade of grass from the hollow of the crater, to visit the abattis, lunettes, and fortifications of both lines, especially Fort Steadman, Fort Gregg, and Battery 45, where the lines were broken the last of March and on April 2.

These tourists, men and women, would pause at the well, some on horseback, others in the dilapidated landaus or buggies for hire in Petersburg. Uncle Frank, with his flow of courteous language and his attractive manners, would usually meet and discourse to them, earning many a *douceur* by drawing from the well the cold water for which it was famous. Abram's family was abroad in the fields, where the old man had planted corn in June — too late to hope for other harvest than the fodder to feed the horse the quartermaster had given him at my earnest request. Under the impression that we were still working our negroes, some of the tourists would dismount and harangue Abram at length upon his " rights." The old man would listen respectfully, shaking his gray head dubiously as they rode off. " Recollect, boy," said one of these travellers to Alick, " the white woman in that house is now *your* slave!" Alick was standing beneath my window, amusing himself by tying up a rosebush. He looked up, simply advising me, — " Let 'em go 'long," — and resumed his work in training the rosebush.

Sometimes the tourists would ask permission to call on us, claiming some common acquaintance. My husband was inclined to resent this. Their sympathetic attitude was offensive to him. Like the Douglas he had endured much, but —

> " Last and worst, to spirit proud
> To bear the pity of the crowd : " —

this was more than he could endure.

We were perfectly aware that they wished to see *us*, and not to gain, as they affected, information about the historic localities on the farm. Still less did they desire ignobly to triumph over us. A boy, when he tears off the wings of a fly, is much interested in observing its actions, not that he is cruel — far from it! He is only curious to see how the creature will behave under very disadvantageous circumstances.

One day a clergyman called, with a card of introduction from Mrs. Hartsuff, who had, I imagine, small discernment as regards clergymen. This one was a smug little man, — sleek, unctuous, and trim, with Pecksniffian self-esteem oozing out of every pore of his face.

"Well, Madam," he commenced, "I trust I find you lying meekly under the chastening rod of the Lord. I trust you can say 'it is good I was afflicted.'"

Having no suitable answer just ready, I received his pious exhortation in silence. One can always safely do this with a clergyman.

"There are seasons," continued the good man, "when chastisement must be meted out to the transgressor; but if borne in the right spirit, the rod may blossom with blessings in the end."

A little more of the same nature wrung from me the query, "Are there none on the other side who need the rod?"

"Oh — well, now — my dear lady! You must consider! You were in the wrong in this unhappy contest, or, I should say, this most righteous war."

"*Væ victis!*" I exclaimed. "Our homes were invaded. We are on our own soil!"

My reverend brother grew red in the face. Rising and bowing himself out, he sent me a Parthian arrow: —

> "No thief e'er felt the halter draw
> With good opinion of the law."

On the afternoon of a sultry day, a black cloud suddenly darkened the sky, thundered, lightened, and poured down a pelting storm of hailstones and rain. A party of young people galloped up to the gate, hastily dismounted, and ran for the shelter of our porch. There were half a dozen or more young girls and men. The small roof affording them scant shelter, I invited them into the parlor, where they stood dripping and shivering until a fire was kindled. A sudden cold wind came on with the hail. It had been a long time since I had seen happy, cheerful young girls in their riding-habits, and I fell in love with them at once, putting them at ease, chafing their hands, and drying their little coats. I never saw young folk so much embarrassed. They were Northern tourists, and felt the full force of our relative positions. When hot tea was brought in, they were overwhelmed. I was loath to give them up — these pretty girls. When they bade me good-by and thanked me for my nice tea and fire, the black eyes of one little beauty snapped with an unmistakable expression — "for your coals of fire!"

Such incidents as these were our only events. Our friends in town were in too much poverty and sorrow to visit us. A deadly silence and apathy had succeeded the storm. It was a long time before the community waked up from this apathy — not, indeed, until the cool, invigorating weather of autumn. The blood-soaked soil and the dead animals emitted sickening odors until the frosts came to chain them up.

A bachelor friend occasionally visited us and

invited the little boys to accompany him upon relic-hunting expeditions to the narrow plain which had divided the opposing lines on that fateful April morning, just three months before. Ropes were fastened around extinct shells, and they were hauled in, to stand sentinel at the door. The shells were short cylinders, with one pointed end like a candle before it is lighted. Numbers of minie balls were dug out of the sand.

One day Mr. Kemp brought in a great curiosity — two bullets welded together, having been shot from opposing rifles.

Twenty years afterward I showed this twin-bullet to General Grant, not long before his last illness. With Mrs. Grant, he had called at my home in Brooklyn to inquire if I had good news of General Pryor, who was in England, having been sent by Irish Americans to see what could be done for O'Donnell, the Irish prisoner. General Grant was much interested in this case. He found me at my late breakfast of tea, toast, and a dozen oysters, which were divided among the three of us. After breakfast I brought out the bullet. He laid it on the palm of his hand and looked at it long and earnestly.

"See, General," I said, "the bullets are welded together so as to form a perfect horseshoe — a charm to keep away witches and evil spirits."

But the General was not interested in amulets, charms, or evil spirits. After regarding it silently for a moment, he remarked : —

"Those are minie balls, shot from rifles of equal caliber. And they met precisely equidistant to a hair.   This is very interesting, but it is not the only one in the world.   I have seen one other, picked up at Vicksburg.   Where was this found and when?" he asked, as he handed the relic back to me.   "At Petersburg, possibly."

"Yes," I answered, "but not when you were shelling the city.   It was picked up on our farm after the last fight."

Met Bullets found near Fort Gregg, 1865.

He looked at me with a humorous twinkle in his eye. "Now look here," he said, "don't you go about telling people I shelled Petersburg."

A short time before his death, just before he was taken to Mount McGregor, he dictated a note to me, sending his kind regards to my General, and saying he remembered with pleasure his talk with me over a cup of tea.

But we must return (and I am sure I am pardoned for this disgression) to the weary life of enforced idleness at the cottage.

I had no garments to mend or to make, no household to manage.   The sultry days were begun and rounded by hours of listless endurance, followed by troubled sleep. A bag of army " hard-tack " stood in a corner, so the children were never hungry. Presently they, too, sat around us, too listless to play or talk. A great army of large, light brown Norway rats now overran the farm. They would walk to the corner before our eyes and help themselves to the army ration. We never moved a finger to drive them away. After a while Alick appeared with an enormous black-and-white cat.

" Dis is jest a leetle mo'n I can stand," said Alick. " De Yankees has stole ev'rything, and dug up de whole face o' the yearth — and de Jews comes all de time and pizens de well, droppin' down chains an' grapplin'-irons to see ef we all has hid silver — but I ain' obleedged to stan' sassyness fum dese outlandish rats."

Alick had to surrender. The very first night after the arrival of his valiant cat there was a scuffle in the room where the crackers were kept, a chair was overturned, and a flying cat burst through the hall, pursued by three or four huge rats. The cat took refuge in a tree, and, stealthily descending at an opportune moment, stole away and left the field to the enemy.

Of course there could be but one result from this life. Malaria had hung over us for weeks, and now one after another of the children lay down upon the " pallets " on the floor, ill with fever. Then I succumbed and was violently ill. Our only nurse was my dear General; and not in all the years when he never shirked duty, or lost a march,

or rode on his own horse when his men had a toil-
some march or if one of them failed by the way,
and never lost one of the battles into which he
personally led them, — not in all those trying times
was he nobler, grander, than in his long and lonely
vigils beside his sick family.   And most nobly did
the aged negress in the kitchen stand by us.   My
one fevered vision was of an ebony angel!

After we recovered, my dear husband was ill —
ague and fever had fastened on him.   When he,
too, grew better, he would sit for days in hopeless
despair, looking out on the desolate landscape.

General Hartsuff and his wife often visited us.
They were terribly afraid of fever, and would send
in messages from the gate while we were all so ill.
But after we had recovered, General Hartsuff came
himself — and finally sent Captain Gregory, the
commissary-general, to see me, and to reason
seriously with me about the necessity of sending
General Pryor away.   He had never been pardoned.
There were men in power who constantly hinted at
punishment and retribution.   General Pryor would
die here.   He should go to New York, go by sea,
shake off the chills that shook him so relentlessly
every third day, meet friends (many Southerners
were in New York), and something might result
for his benefit.

This idea grew in our minds as feasible, if only
we had the money.   It had never occurred to me
to make a second attempt (one had failed) to sell
my watch.   I now took it to a banker in Petersburg, added to it a cherished antique cameo set in

diamonds which had never left my finger since it
was given me, like Shylock's turquoise from his
Leah, when my husband "was a bachelor."
Leaving these in pledge, I received three hundred
dollars. I bought some quinine forthwith, ordered
a suit of clothes to replace the threadbare Confederate gray, and sent Roger A. Pryor, the sometime
" rebel," to New York, upon an experiment of which
the most sanguine imagination could not have fore-
seen the successful result.

A difficult task lay before him. Ruined in fortune, his occupation gone, his friends dead or impoverished, his health impaired, his heart broken,
he had yet to win support for a wife and seven
children, and that in a hostile community. Only
two things were left to him — the ability to work
and the willingness to work. With what courage
he commenced the study of his profession, what
difficulties he surmounted, what rebuffs he bore
with fortitude, I can give here no adequate idea.
He labored incessantly, often breaking down and
fainting, at his task. In one of his early letters he
says, " Sometimes I sink in despair ; but then I rally
and press on. Don't you think heaven will prosper
me for *your* sake? The obstacles to the success of
' a rebel' in this city are almost insurmountable."

He accepted a position on the *Daily News* which
yielded him twenty-five dollars a week. Meanwhile he must learn New York law.

There has been too much sorrow already in this
story. Why tell of all the anguish, all the suffering
of the next years? During the long, lonely winter

of 1865 my husband nobly strove to sustain my hopes, and for his sake I would not allow my heart to break.

One morning in January old Abram stood before me with a troubled face.

" What we all goin' to do now for wood, Mistis ? "

" What you have done all along, I suppose."

" No'm. Dat's onpossible. We done burn up Fort Gregg an' Battery 45. Der ain' no mo' fortifications on de place as I knows of."

" Fortifications ! " I exclaimed. " Why, Abram ! you surely haven't been burning the fortifications ? "

" Hit's des like I tell you, Mistis. De las' stick's on yo' wood-pile now."

" Well, Abram," I said gravely, " if we have destroyed our fortifications — burned our bridges — the time has come to change our base. We will move into town."

And so we did — and my old friend the wolf was kept from the door to the tune of a piano, where I daily gave lessons to my neighbors' children.

Eighteen months after he left me I had the following letter from him : —

" Don't imagine I have the least idea of abandoning my experiment here. I mean 'to fight it out on this line,' to the end of the struggle. My practice increases slowly, but is based, I believe, on a conviction of my competency. Thank God, what I have accomplished, though small, has been achieved by my own unaided exertions and without the least obligation to a human being. I have no patron. I have never solicited business. My only arts are study and devotion to duty. These expedients may be slow of operation but they are sure, and they leave my dignity and self-respect uncompromised. I am not conscious of having received a favor since my residence in New York: and when the victory is achieved, I shall have inexpressible satisfaction in saying, with Coriolanus — ' *alone* I did it !' When I speak of ' favors,' I mean in the way of my profession. Of some personal kindness I have been the grateful recipient, — though not in many instances."

Within two years I followed him with our children, and if I cannot say with Mr. Burke, " my adopted and my *dearer*" home, yet so warm and abounding was the welcome accorded us that we are attached to it by the strongest ties of gratitude and affection.

The last time I visited Petersburg I drove out to her battle-fields. Nature had hidden the scars with beauty. The seeds of the daisy had been scattered wherever the Federal forces had been encamped, and they had whitened the fields and covered the graves by the wayside. Nature had not forgotten these lonely unmarked graves, nor will she ever forget, until time shall be no more.

It is not easy to write about the dreadful war between the North and the South. We press our breasts against a thorn when we recall the anguish of those days of death and disaster. It is often said that it is still too early to write the story of our Civil War. It will soon be too late. Some of us still live who saw those days. We should not shrink from recording what we know to be true. Thus only will a full history of American courage and

2 D

fidelity be preserved, — for all were Americans. The glory of one is the glory of all — in 1861 when brothers were in conflict, as well as in 1898 when they stood shoulder to shoulder and heart to heart against a foreign foe. Circumstances do not rule the heart, and "where the heart is right, there is true patriotism."

The Mother of Washington and Her Times

By MRS. ROGER A. PRYOR

With Many Illustrations

Cloth   Crown 8vo $2.50 *net*

THE MACMILLAN COMPANY

66 FIFTH AVENUE, NEW YORK